Contents

Introduction

The old Wabash is still the Wabash...

Soon after I completed the book entitled WABASH in 1984, I realized that even though the book was 320 pages and contained 550 photographs, there were more facets of the Wabash that could be covered.

As time went on, I learned of more Wabash material available that wasn't in the first book, and subsequently kept gathering material associated with the railroad. Many friends were kind enough to help me locate additional photographs and literature, and the material that didn't get into the first book was assigned to this one.

This book is intended for railfans and historians as a quick reference, and is divided into a variety of sections to accommodate that goal. Various important aspects of the railroad are covered. These include history, passenger service, steam and diesel locomotive classes, miscellaneous which features freight cars and cabooses, cranes and ships, plus a good selection of the more important Wabash paint folio descriptions from the locomotive, car and maintenance-of-way departments.

ABUNDANT MATERIAL

There is little overlap between this book and the first, which goes to prove that even though the Wabash was only a bridge railroad of 2,500 miles, it was well attended by railfan photographers, and there were enough company documents remaining after the merger in 1964 with the Norfolk and Western to be of interest to fans and others in later years.

It's surprising how vivid the memory of the Wabash is in the minds of many fans. While it was almost 30 years ago that it merged with the Norfolk & Western, to many it is only a few memories back in time. But good memories of good railroads are apt to do that to a person, making them believe the past was only a few years away.

I recall the fond memories I had of the Wabash as a youth growing up in Tolono, Illinois. I watched every Wabash train I could very intently, trying to pick out the class of diesels that were pulling the trains (steam had disappeared by the time my interest in trains developed).

Many Wabash trains stopped in Tolono for switching duties with the main line trains of the Illinois Central which crossed the Wabash there. I enjoyed watching the switching moves, and often dreamed of riding one of those Wabash diesels to far away places such as St. Louis or Detroit.

A CAB RIDE

I did get to ride in an F unit one Saturday morning. My father was the local Standard Oil agent and had the pleasant duty of fueling both IC and Wabash diesel passenger train specials that came to town for University of Illinois fall football games.

Sometimes as many as six trains jammed the trackage at Tolono. Passengers would ride school buses to the university for the game, and return mid-afternoon after the game for the train ride home.

Wabash 4-6-4 P1 #706 is on the turntable at Delray, Michigan in June of 1947, the year this locomotive came from the Decatur shops. The engine was scrapped in 1956. *Collection of Don Heimburger*

Once the engineer invited my dad and I to ride the cab as the switching was done for the return trip home. To this day, it's a high point for me, as seeing those long Wabash specials gliding into that small Midwestern town for a few hours. The fun and excitement of having more than 100 passenger cars and a dozen diesels to view for a few hours was a railfan's dream!

STILL THE WABASH

I always regretted seeing the Wabash identity fade into another railroad's name. And I've always felt that the old Wabash line was *still* the Wabash; I still call that trackage Wabash trackage. I don't think I could believe in my heart that it still is anything but the Wabash. It'll always be the blue, white and gray colors for me.

* * * * * * * * * *

No book is complete without acknowledgement of those who graciously helped in some way bring the book to life. I wish to thank William Raia, Don Gruber, M.D. McCarter, Charles Felstead, Louis Marre, J.M. Gruber, Richard Ganger, Luvergne Isaac, Bruce Meyer, Owen Leander, Ted Lemen, Arndt Gerritan, Mark Vaughn, Kevin Kohls, R.R. Wallin, FJC Products, American Car & Foundry and the Allen County Historical Society for their help.

Donald J. Heimburger

Wabash #2507 awaits orders at Brooklyn, Illinois in 1949. *Collection of Don Gruber*

Wabash steeped in history
'Follow the Flag' railroad served Midwest with 2,500 miles of track

Through the years the Wabash has been many things to many people. It has been a proud railroad serving the heartland of America, it has been through enough reorganizations to make most stockholders wary, it has operated some of the finest passenger trains in the country and provided dependable freight service to hundreds of communities and shippers along the line.

Eighty-five years before it was merged into a larger railroad system in 1964, its tracks didn't cross the wide Mississippi.

In 1879, the Wabash Railway Company, operating east of the Mississippi, and the St. Louis, Kansas City and Northern, operating west of the Mississippi, were merged into the Wabash, St. Louis and Pacific Railway Company. In 1889, both the lines east and west of the Mississippi River were reorganized, this time as the Wabash Railroad Company.

Financial problems of the next two decades made that period one of great difficulty, but in 1889 came a turn for the better, so that in the succeeding decade the Wabash found it possible to proceed with the construction of new trackage and the expansion of facilities to serve the city of Chicago during its World's Columbian Exposition of 1893 and the city of St. Louis during its Louisiana Purchase Exposition in 1904.

ONE OF LEADING RAILROADS

In the 15 years of its operation following the formation of the company in 1889, the Wabash took its place as one of the nation's leading enterprises, contributing to the well-being of the public in the territories reached by its rails.

In 1915, after foreclosure and reorganization, the Wabash *Railroad* Company of 1889, a company which had done much during its corporate life to establish the importance of American railroads in

the life of the nation, was sold to a new Wabash *Railway* Company, incorporated under the laws Indiana.

The worldwide depression of the early '3 struck the Wabash and other United Stat railroads severely. With industry paralyzed, tl price of farm products at a new low, personal ar corporate incomes slashed, and with market pric for commodities and securities nearing tl vanishing point, the Wabash was forced in receivership.

The receivers were confronted with a difficu task. The welfare of entire communities along tl more than 2,500 miles of territory served by tl Wabash, the continued operation of many i dustries contiguous to its rails, and the livelihoc of the families of thousands of men and wome employed by the railroad depended upon the jud ment and wisdom of the receivers.

Due in large measure to the efficient handlir of the receivership and the reorganization pr ceedings, the Wabash was one of the very fir railroads to come back from the effects of tl depression. By 1940, when war clouds again a| peared on the horizon, the Wabash had even mo solidly established its reputation as one of the mo important rail traffic arteries in the nation.

NAME CHANGED

In January, 1942 the name of the railroad wa again changed to the Wabash Railroad Compan

Through the period of World War II the Wabas performed outstanding service in transportir men, material and supplies at an accelerated pac to serve the needs of the nations involved in th war.

During the war years it was not possible t secure either materials or labor for making add tions or improvements to Wabash property. Pos war, however, the Wabash invested more tha $100 million in new facilities to serve the shippin and traveling public. In addition to modernizin

The Wabash and Pennsylvania railroads jointly operated the *Detroit Arrow*, one of the fastest passenger trains in the country, making the 295-mile Chicago to Detroit run via Fort Wayne, Indiana in five hours. The *Detroit Arrow* appears phantom-like in this May, 1938 scene. *Mrs. Francis Mather collection*

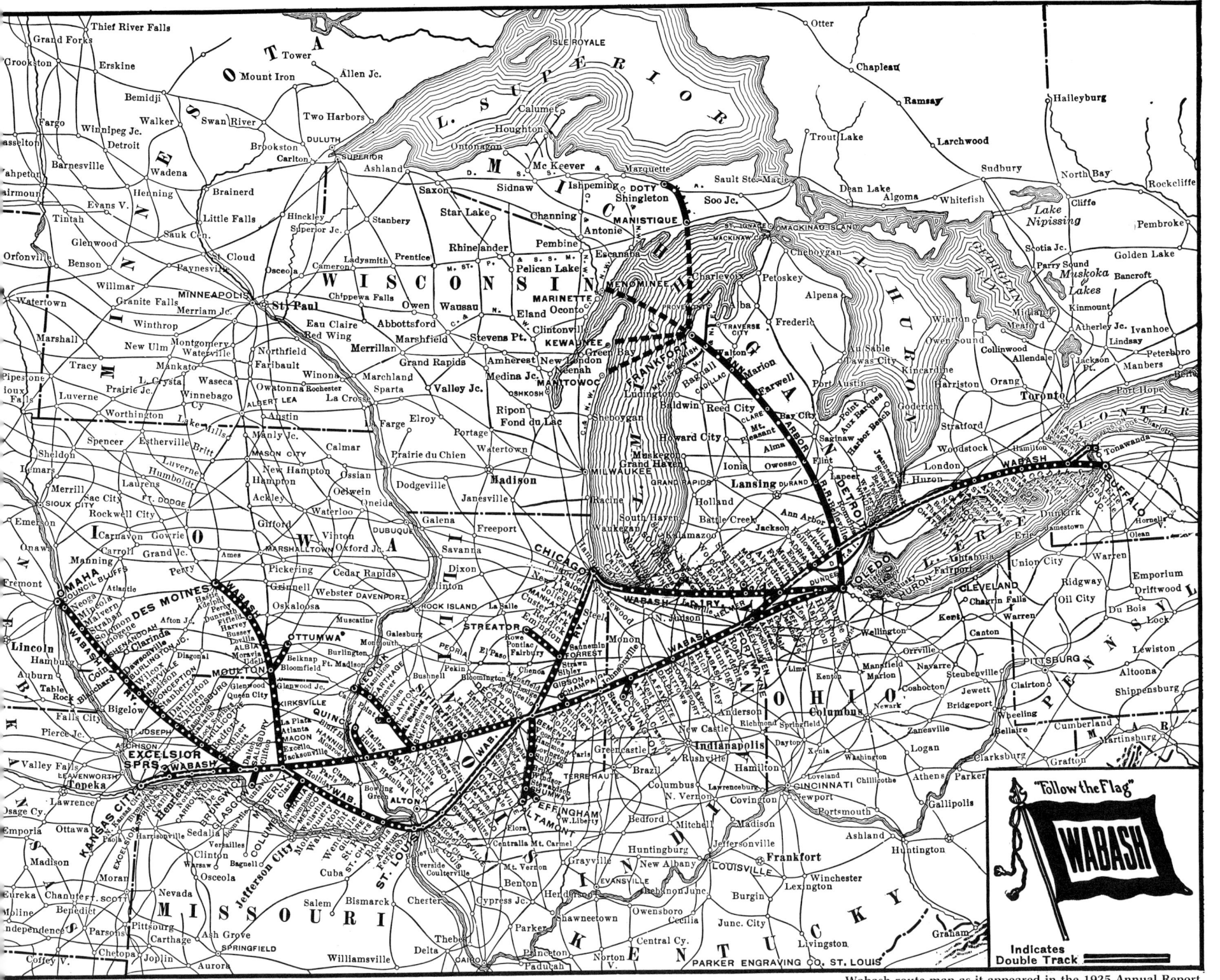

Wabash route map as it appeared in the 1925 Annual Report.

its freight yards, communication facilities and signaling devices, the Wabash improved its passenger train equipment. First was the inauguration of a totally new streamlined service between St. Louis and the West coast.

On June 2, 1946, in conjunction with the Union Pacific and Southern Pacific railroads, the new train *City of St. Louis* began operation. In addition to drastically reducing the overall running time between St. Louis and the West coast, the new train offered the public through service in both coach and Pullman sleeping cars to Los Angeles, San Francisco, Portland or Seattle.

On November 26, 1947 another new streamliner, operating between St. Louis and Kansas City, was placed in service. Called the *City of Kansas City,* the train met with instantaneous success and was highly acclaimed by the many new passengers attracted to Wabash rails.

BLUE BIRD INTRODUCED

Inauguration of another Wabash streamliner on February 26, 1950 was an epoch-making event. It marked the first time in history that dome cars were operated between St. Louis and Chicago. The new Wabash *Blue Bird,* containing four dome cars in its six-car consist, was put into service and offered Wabash passengers a new view of Wabash territory.

A handsome Class J #692 built by Richmond in 1912 poses for its portrait. The locomotive work on the Wabash for 40 years. *Paul Eilenberger*

The Wabash was 100% dieselized by 1953. One steam engine was operated for a short run on the Keokuk branch because the bridge at Meredosia, Illinois could not support the weight of diesel engines until extensive changes had been completed. The steam locomotive made its last trip on January 28, 1955 and thus by a strange turn of fat the reign of steam power on the Wabash ende where it had begun 117 years ago. The engine, No 573, a 2-6-0 Mogul Class F-4, built by Rhode Islan Locomotive Works in 1899, was donated to the Na tional Museum of Transport in St. Louis Count in August, 1955.

A six-car passenger train glides effortlessly down the main on July 7, 1947. *Paul Slager, collection of William Raia*

J-1 #665 backs down to connect with her train on August 22, 1948 in Chicago. *Collection of Don Heimburger*

In July, 1954 the Wabash entered the trailer-on-flat car field. This new piggyback service was first operated between Chicago and New York and was shortly thereafter expanded from Chicago to St. Louis, then from St. Louis to Detroit and from Chicago to Detroit.

In the 1960s the Wabash operated four large divisions, as well as five terminal divisions. The divisions included the Moberly Division, Decatur Division and the St. Thomas Division. Terminal divisions included the Kansas City Terminal, the St. Louis Terminal, Detroit Terminal, Chicago Terminal and Buffalo Terminal.

MERGED WITH N&W

On October 16, 1964 the Wabash merged with the Norfolk & Western Railway system. The Wabash, a 2,500-mile bridge railroad that ran from Buffalo on the east to Omaha on the west and to such cities as Chicago, St. Louis, Toledo, Detroit, Kansas City and Des Moines, has faded quietly from the land. But the memories and fondness of the Wabash—by railfans, historians and people who used to work for and ride the Wabash, has not diminished. The "Follow the Flag" line still lives. **WAB**

H10-44 #381 taken at Decatur, Illinois in 1961.
Collection of Louis Marre

The largest of the Wabash steam locomotives—the 2900 Class, the 4-8-4s, were built in 1930 and 1931. *I.W. Gaus, collection of C.T. Felstead*

Wabash Standard Plans
(1920s, 1930s, 1940s)

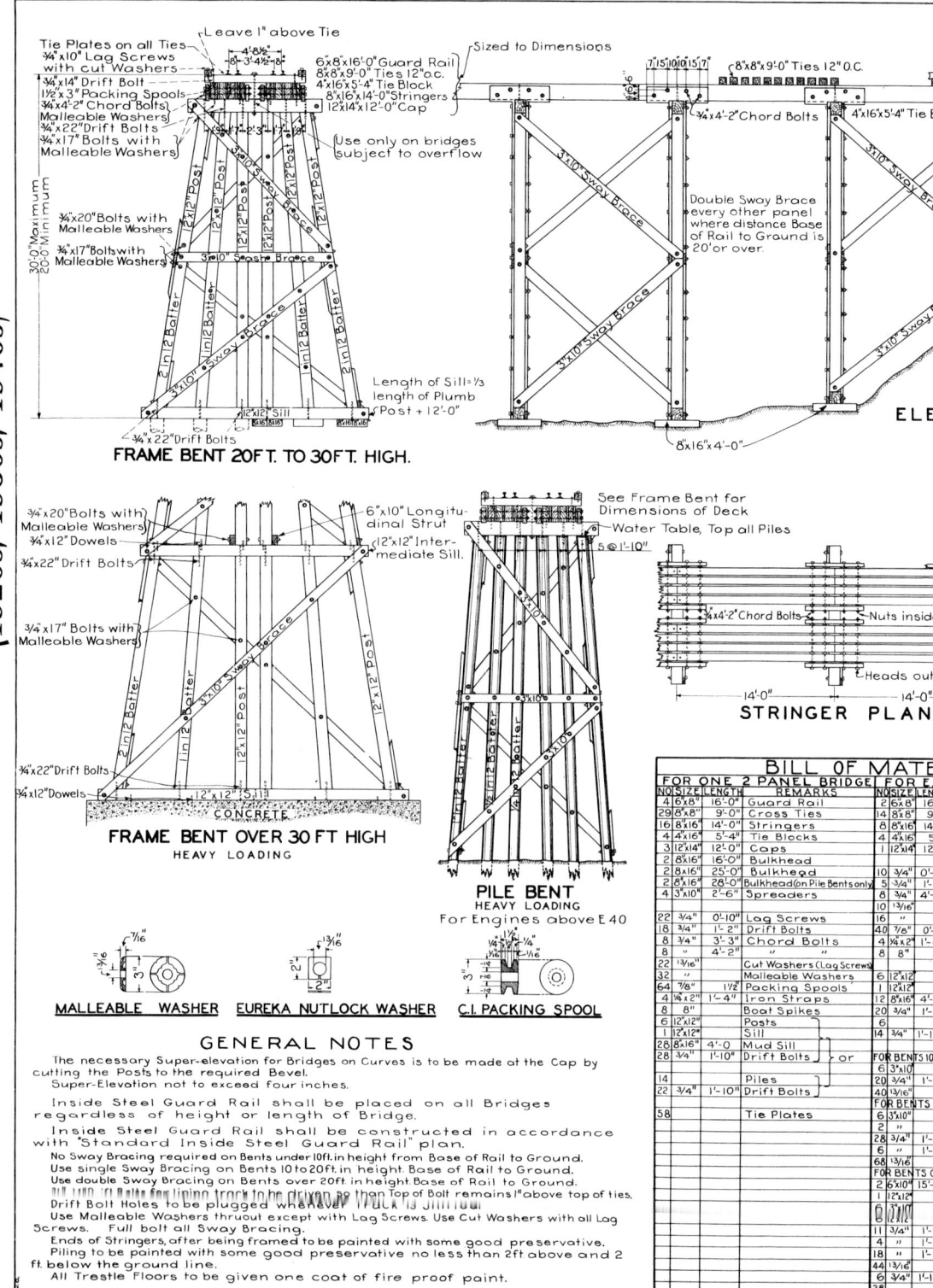

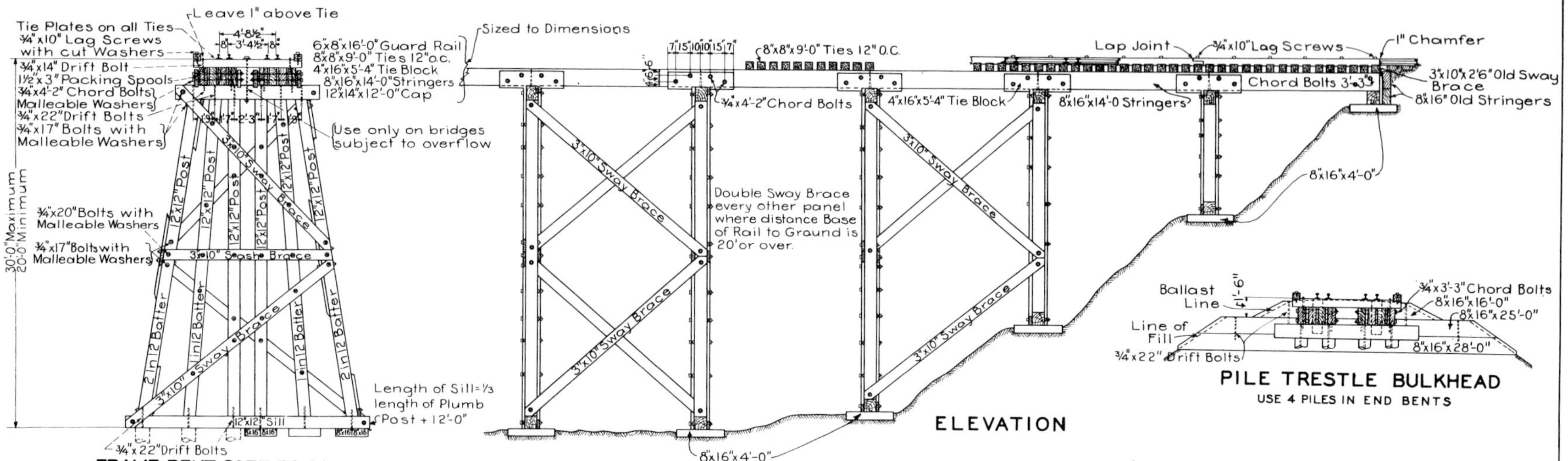

FRAME BENT 20 FT. TO 30 FT. HIGH.

Tie Plates on all Ties
¾"x10" Lag Screws with cut Washers
¾"x14" Drift Bolt
1½"x3" Packing Spools
¾"x4'-2" Chord Bolts Malleable Washers
¾"x22" Drift Bolts
¾"x17" Bolts with Malleable Washers

Leave 1" above Tie

6x8"x16'-0" Guard Rail
8"x8"x9'-0" Ties 12" o.c.
4"x16"x5'-4" Tie Block
8"x16"x14'-0" Stringers
12"x14"x12'-0" Cap

Use only on bridges subject to overflow

¾"x20" Bolts with Malleable Washers

¾"x17" Bolt with Malleable Washers

3"x10" Sash Brace

Length of Sill = ⅓ length of Plumb Post + 12'-0"

¾"x22" Drift Bolts

FRAME BENT OVER 30 FT HIGH — HEAVY LOADING

¾"x20" Bolts with Malleable Washers
¾"x12" Dowels
¾"x22" Drift Bolts
¾"x17" Bolts with Malleable Washers
¾"x22" Drift Bolts
¾"x12" Dowels

6"x10" Longitudinal Strut
12"x12" Intermediate Sill

PILE BENT — HEAVY LOADING — For Engines above E 40

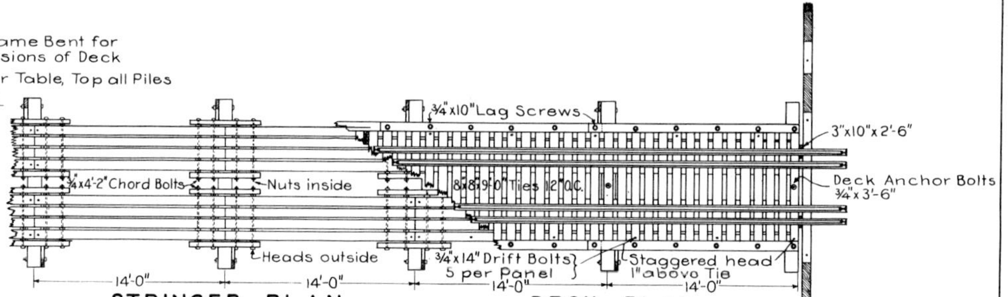

See Frame Bent for Dimensions of Deck
Water Table, Top all Piles

ELEVATION

Sized to Dimensions
7 15 10 10 15 7
8"x8"x9'-0" Ties 12" O.C.
¾"x4'-2" Chord Bolts
4"x16"x5'-4" Tie Block
8"x16"x14'-0" Stringers

Lap Joint
¾"x10" Lag Screws
Chord Bolts 3'-3"
1" Chamfer
3"x10"x2'-6" Old Sway Brace
8"x16" Old Stringers
8"x16"x4'-0"

Double Sway Brace every other panel where distance Base of Rail to Ground is 20' or over.

PILE TRESTLE BULKHEAD — USE 4 PILES IN END BENTS

Ballast Line
Line of Fill
¾"x3'-3" Chord Bolts
8"x16"x16'-0"
8"x16"x25'-0"
¾"x22" Drift Bolts
8"x16"x28'-0"

STRINGER PLAN

¾"x4'-2" Chord Bolts — Nuts inside
¾"x10" Lag Screws
8"x8"x9'-0" Ties 12" O.C.
Heads outside
14'-0"

DECK PLAN

3"x10"x2'-6"
Deck Anchor Bolts ¾"x3'-6"
¾"x14" Drift Bolts 5 per Panel
Staggered head 1" above Tie
14'-0"

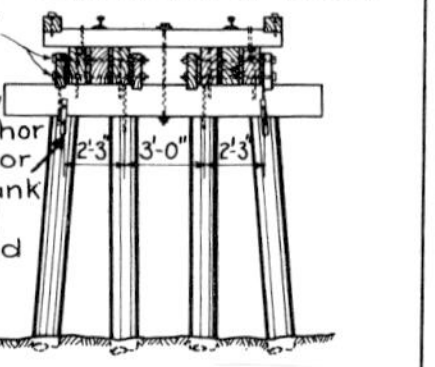

PILE BENT — LIGHT LOADING — For Engines up to and including E 40 Class

¾"x3'-4" Chord Bolts Malleable Washers
NOTE:- Where no Sway Bracing is used, anchor caps to outside Post or Piling with ¼"x2"x16" Tank Iron Straps, punched for 8" Boat Spikes and fastened therewith.

See Frame Bent for Dimension of Deck.

MALLEABLE WASHER **EUREKA NUTLOCK WASHER** **C.I. PACKING SPOOL**

GENERAL NOTES

The necessary Super-elevation for Bridges on Curves is to be made at the Cap by cutting the Posts to the required Bevel.

Super-Elevation not to exceed four inches.

Inside Steel Guard Rail shall be placed on all Bridges regardless of height or length of Bridge.

Inside Steel Guard Rail shall be constructed in accordance with "Standard Inside Steel Guard Rail" plan.

No Sway Bracing required on Bents under 10ft. in height from Base of Rail to Ground.

Use single Sway Bracing on Bents 10 to 20ft. in height. Base of Rail to Ground.

Use double Sway Bracing on Bents over 20ft. in height. Base of Rail to Ground.

Drift Bolt Holes to be plugged whenever track is shifted.

Use Malleable Washers throughout except with Lag Screws. Use Cut Washers with all Lag Screws. Full bolt all Sway Bracing.

Ends of Stringers, after being framed to be painted with some good preservative.

Piling to be painted with some good preservative no less than 2ft. above and 2 ft. below the ground line.

All Trestle Floors to be given one coat of fire proof paint.

BILL OF MATERIAL

FOR ONE 2 PANEL BRIDGE				FOR EACH ADDITIONAL PANEL			
NO	SIZE	LENGTH	REMARKS	NO	SIZE	LENGTH	REMARKS
4	6"x8"	16'-0"	Guard Rail	2	6"x8"	16'-0"	Guard Rails
29	8"x8"	9'-0"	Cross Ties	14	8"x8"	9'-0"	Cross Ties
16	8"x16"	14'-0"	Stringers	8	8"x16"	14'-0"	Stringers
4	4"x16"	5'-4"	Tie Blocks	4	4"x16"	5'-4"	Tie Blocks
3	12"x14"	12'-0"	Caps	1	12"x14"	12'-0"	Caps
2	8"x16"	16'-0"	Bulkhead				
2	8"x16"	25'-0"	Bulkhead	10	¾"	0'-10"	Lag Screws
2	8"x16"	28'-0"	Bulkhead(on Pile Bents only)	5	¾"	1'-2"	Drift Bolts
4	3"x10"	2'-6"	Spreaders	8	¾"	4'-2"	Chord Bolts
				10	13/16"		Cut Washers
22	¾"	0'-10"	Lag Screws	16	"		Malleable Washers
18	¾"	1'-2"	Drift Bolts	40	7/8"	0'-1½"	Packing Spools
8	¾"	3'-3"	Chord Bolts	4	¼"x2"	1'-4"	Iron Straps, for Bents under 10' high
8	"	4'-2"		8	8"		Boat Spikes " " " "
22	13/16"		Cut Washers (Lag Screws)				
32	"		Malleable Washers	6	12"x12"		Posts
64	7/8"	1'½"	Packing Spools	1	12"x12"		Sill
4	¼"x2"	1'-4"	Iron Straps	4	8"x16"	4'-0"	Mud Sills
8	8"		Boat Spikes	20	¾"	1'-10"	Drift Bolts } or
6	12"x12"		Posts	6			Piles
1	12"x12"		Sill	14	¾"	1'-10"	Drift Bolts
28	8"x16"	4'-0"	Mud Sill				FOR BENTS 10 to 20' HIGH (in addition for Bents 10' High)
28	¾"	1'-10"	Drift Bolts } or	6	3"x10"		Sway Braces
				20	¾"	1'-5"	Bolts
14			Piles	40	13/16"		Malleable Washers
22	¾"	1'-10"	Drift Bolts				FOR BENTS 20 to 30' HIGH (in addition for Bents
58			Tie Plates	6	3"x10"		Sway Braces
				2	"		Sash "
				28	¾"	1'-5"	Bolts
				6	"	1'-8"	"
				68	13/16"		Malleable Washers
							FOR BENTS OVER 30' HIGH (in addition for Bents 20 to 30' H.
				2	6"x10"	15'-0"	Longitudinal Struts
				1	12"x12"		Intermediate Sill
				8	3"x10"		Sway Braces
				11	¾"	1'-0"	Dowels
				4	"	1'-8"	Bolts
				18	"	1'-5"	"
				44	13/16"		Malleable Washers
				6	¾"	1'-10"	Drift Bolts
				28			Tie Plates

Approved:
A.O. Cunningham
Chief Engineer

Approved:
H.G. Etter
Asst. Federal Manager

Approved:
J.E. Taussig
Federal Manager

WABASH RAILWAY STANDARD FRAME AND PILE TRESTLE

OFFICE OF THE CHIEF ENGINEER
ADOPTED JUNE 24, 1919.
Revised-Jan. 22, 1923.
PLAN 3035

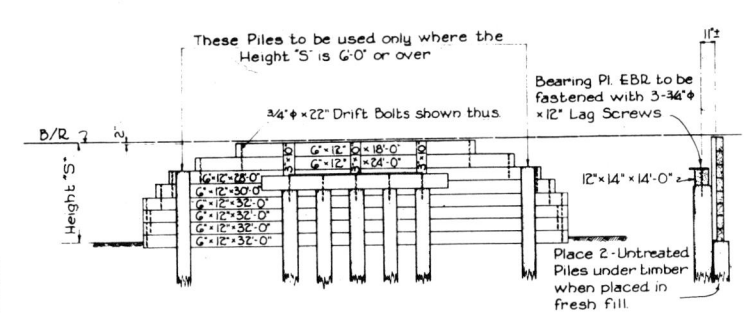

These Piles to be used only where the Height "S" is 6'-0" or over

3/4"φ × 22" Drift Bolts shown thus.

Bearing Pl. EBR to be fastened with 3-3/4"φ × 12" Lag Screws

B/R

Height "S"

6"×12"×28'-0"
6"×12"×30'-0"
6"×12"×32'-0"
6"×12"×32'-0"
6"×12"×32'-0"

12"×14"×14'-0"

11'±

Place 2-Untreated Piles under timber when placed in fresh fill.

DETAILS OF END BENT

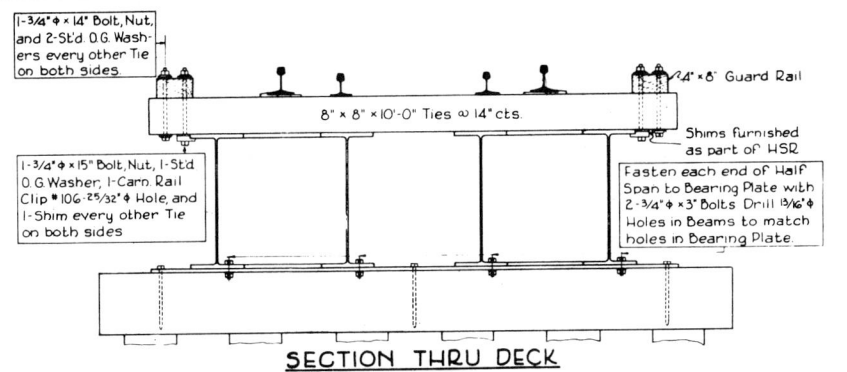

1-3/4"φ × 14" Bolt, Nut, and 2-St'd. O.G. Washers every other Tie on both sides

8" × 8" ×10'-0" Ties @ 14" cts.

2/4"×8" Guard Rail

1-3/4"φ × 15" Bolt, Nut, 1-St'd O.G. Washer, 1-Carn. Rail Clip #106-25/32"φ Hole, and 1-Shim every other Tie on both sides

Shims furnished as part of HSR

Fasten each end of Half Span to Bearing Plate with 2-3/4"φ×3" Bolts. Drill 13/16"φ Holes in Beams to match holes in Bearing Plate.

SECTION THRU DECK

MATERIAL REQUIRED FOR END BENTS

NUMBER OF PILES		5 PILE				6 PILE				7 PILE			
HEIGHT, BASE OF RAIL TO GROUND "S"		4'	5'	6'	8'	4'	5'	6'	8'	10'	4'	5'	6'	8'	10'
Bulkhead Timber 6"×12"×18'-0"		1	1	1	1	1	1	1	1	1	1	1	1	1	1
" × 24'-0"		1	1	1	1	1	1	1	1	1	1	1	1	1	1
" × 28'-0"		1	1	1	1	1	1	1	1	1	1	1	1	1	1
" × 30'-0"		1	1	1	1	1	1	1	1	1	1	1	1	1	1
" × 32'-0"		1	2	4	6	1	2	4	6		1	2	4	6
Separators 3"×10"×4'-0"		3				3				3			
" × 5'-0"		3				3				3			
" × 6'-0"			3				3				3		
" × 8'-0"				3				3				3	
" × 10'-0"					3				3				3
Cap 12"×14"×14'-0"		1	1	1	1	1	1	1	1	1	1	1	1	1
Drift Bolts 3/4"φ × 22"		11	13	15	19	23	12	14	16	20	24	13	15	17	21	25
Lag Screws 3/4"φ × 12"		3	3	3	3	3	3	3	3	3	3	3	3	3	3
#16 Galv. Iron 24"×20" Ea.		5	5	5	5	5	6	6	6	6	6	7	7	7	7
6 Oz. Canvas 36"×36" Ea.		10	10	10	10	10	12	12	12	12	12	14	14	14	14
#12 Galv. Iron Wire Lb.		2.5	2.5	2.5	2.5	2.5	3.0	3.0	3.0	3.0	3.0	3.5	3.5	3.5	3.5
Bearing Plate EBR Ea.														
Total Timber M.B.M.		.826	1.026	1.225	1.624	2.023	.826	1.026	1.225	1.624	2.023	.826	1.026	1.225	1.624	2.023

MATERIAL REQUIRED PER 14" OF DECK

NO	ITEM
1	8"×8"×10'-0" Bridge Tie
3	Standard Ogee Washers for 3/4"φ
1	3/4"φ × 14" Sq. Hd. Bolt with Nut
1	3/4"φ × 15"
1	Carn Rail Clip #106 25/32"φ Hole
2-4"	of 4"×8" Guard Rail Order in 14'-0" Lengths

Note! The proper number of Shims under Rail Clips are furnished by the Steel Fabricator as a part of HSR. Do not order separately. Timber per foot of Deck = 51.05 B.M.

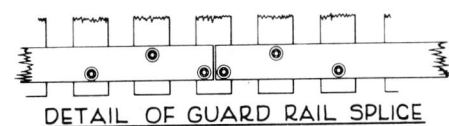

DETAIL OF GUARD RAIL SPLICE

— GENERAL NOTES —

All holes bored in wood shall be thoroughly painted with creosote before bolts are placed.

All timber shall be treated in accordance with Wabash Specifications for Treating Timber.

Pile Tops to be protected in the manner as shown on this sheet.

Bearing Plates EBR and PBR to be furnished by the steel fabricator as part of the structural steel.

The spacing of piles in the End Bents at the cap shall be the same as shown for the pier bents.

All piles in the End Bents shall be driven vertically except on a curve, where the piles shall be driven to the same batter as shown for pier bents on a curve.

In fresh fill, 2-untreated piles shall be driven to support the bulkhead timber.

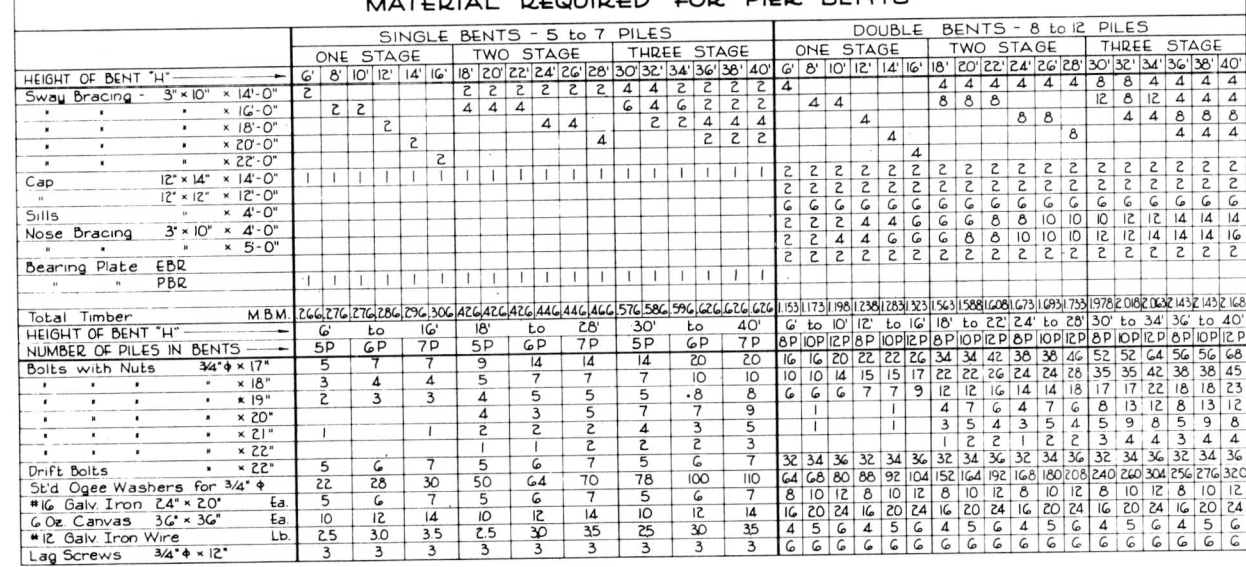

MATERIAL REQUIRED FOR PIER BENTS

		SINGLE BENTS – 5 to 7 PILES												DOUBLE BENTS – 8 to 12 PILES																		
		ONE STAGE		TWO STAGE			THREE STAGE						ONE STAGE			TWO STAGE				THREE STAGE					
HEIGHT OF BENT "H"		6'	8'	10'	12'	14'	16'	18'	20'	22'	24'	26'	28'	30'	32'	34'	36'	38'	40'	6'	8'	10'	12'	14'	16'	18'	20'	22'	24'	26'	28'	30'	32'	34'	36'	38'	40'
Sway Bracing 3"×10"×14'-0"		2						2	2	2	2	2	4	4	2	2	2	2	4						4	4	4	4	4	8	8	12	4	4	4
" × 16'-0"			2	2				4	4	4			6	4	6	2	2	4			4	4				8	8	8			4	4	8	8
" × 18'-0"					2						4	4			2	2	4	4					4						8				4	4	4
" × 20'-0"						2							4			2	2	2						4	
Cap 12"×14"×14'-0"		1	1	1	1	1	1	1	1	1	1	1	1	1	1	1	1	1	1	2	2	2	2	2	2	2	2	2	2	2	2	2	2	2	2	2	2
12"×12"×12'-0"																				2	2	2	2	2	2	2	2	2	2	2	2	2	2	2	2	2	2
Sills " × 4'-0"																				6	6	6	6	6	6	6	6	6	6	6	6	6	6	6	6	6	6
Nose Bracing 3"×10"×4'-0"																				2	2	2	2	4	6	6	6	8	8	8	8	12	12	14	14	14	14
" × 5'-0"																				2	2	4	4	6	8	8	10	10	10	12	12	14	14	14	16
Bearing Plate EBR																				2	2	2	2	2	2	2	2	2	2	2	2	2	2	2	2	2	2
" PBR		1	1	1	1	1	1	1	1	1	1	1	1	1	1	1	1	1	1	1	1	1	1	1	1	1	1	1	1	1	1	1	1	1	1	1	1
Total Timber M.B.M.		.266	.276	.276	.286	.296	.306	.426	.426	.426	.446	.446	.466	.576	.586	.596	.626	.626	.626	1.153	1.173	1.198	1.238	1.283	1.323	1.563	1.588	1.608	1.673	1.693	1.733	1.978	2.018	2.063	2.143	2.143	2.168
HEIGHT OF BENT "H"		6' to 16'		18' to 28'			30' to 40'						6' to 10'			12' to 16'			18' to 22'			24' to 28'			30' to 34'			36' to 40'		
NUMBER OF PILES IN BENTS		5P	6P	7P	5P	6P	7P	5P	6P	7P				8P	10P	12P	8P	10P	12P	8P	10P	12P	8P	10P	12P	8P	10P	12P	8P	10P	12P
Bolts with Nuts 3/4"φ × 17"		5	7	7	9	14	14	14	20	20				16	16	16	22	22	26	34	34	42	38	38	46	52	52	64	56	56	68
" × 18"		3	4	4	5	7	7	7	10	10				10	10	14	15	15	17	22	22	26	24	24	28	35	35	42	38	38	45
" × 19"		2	3	3	4	5	5	5	8	8				6	6	6	7	7	9	12	12	14	14	14	18	17	17	22	18	18	23
" × 20"					4	3	3	7	7	9							4	7	6	4	7	8	6	8	13	12	8	13	12
" × 21"		1		1	2	2	2	4	3	5				1			3	5	4	3	5	4	5	9	8	5	9	8
" × 22"					1	1	2	2	2	3							4	7	6	4	7	6	8	13	12	8	13	12
Drift Bolts " × 22"		5	6	7	5	6	7	5	6	7				32	34	36	32	34	36	32	34	36	32	34	36	32	34	36	32	34	36
St'd Ogee Washers for 3/4"φ		22	28	30	50	64	70	78	100	110				64	68	80	88	92	104	152	164	192	168	180	208	240	260	304	256	276	320
#16 Galv. Iron 24"×20" Ea.		5	6	7	5	6	7	5	6	7				8	10	12	8	10	12	8	10	12	8	10	12	8	10	12	8	10	12
6 Oz. Canvas 36"×36" Ea.		10	12	14	10	12	14	10	12	14				16	20	24	16	20	24	16	20	24	16	20	24	16	20	24	16	20	24
#12 Galv. Iron Wire Lb.		2.5	3.0	3.5	2.5	3.0	3.5	2.5	3.0	3.5				4	5	6	4	5	6	4	5	6	4	5	6	4	5	6	4	5	6
Lag Screws 3/4"φ × 12"		3	3	3	3	3	3	3	3	3				6	6	6	6	6	6	6	6	6	6	6	6	6	6	6	6	6	6

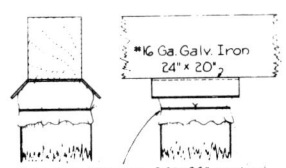

#16 Ga. Galv. Iron 24"×20"

2 Ply 6 oz Canvas 36"×36" soaked with creosote and fastened with 2 turns of #12 Galv. Iron Wire

DETAILS OF PILE PROTECTION

WABASH RAILWAY
STANDARD
I-BEAM TRESTLE
PILE BENTS AND DECK DETAILS
OFFICE OF THE CHIEF ENGINEER
ADOPTED 1-2-34

PLAN NO. 3090
CASE 12-1-2

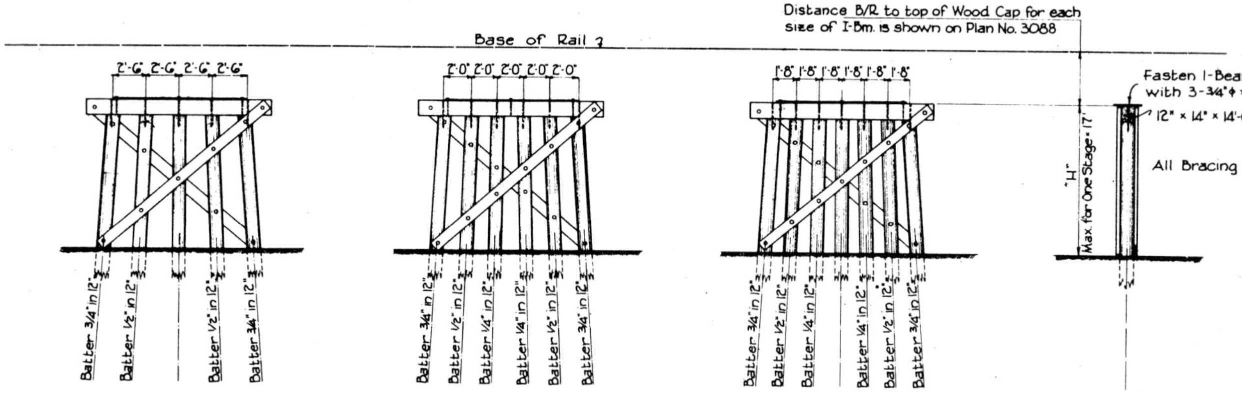
Distance B/R to top of Wood Cap for each size of I-Bm. is shown on Plan No. 3088
Base of Rail
2'-6" 2'-6" 2'-6" 2'-6"
2'-0" 2'-0" 2'-0" 2'-0" 2'-0"
1'-8" 1'-8" 1'-8" 1'-8" 1'-8" 1'-8"
Fasten 1-Bearing Pl. PBR with 3-3/4"ϕ × 12" Lag Screws
12" × 14" × 14'-0" Cap
All Bracing 3" × 10"
"H" Max. for One Stage = 17'
Batter 3/4" in 12"
Batter 1/2" in 12"
Batter 1/4" in 12"

5 PILE BENT

6 PILE BENT

7 PILE BENT

END VIEW

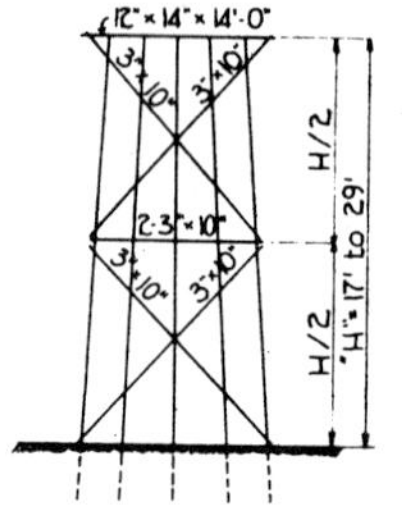
12" × 14" × 14'-0"
3" × 10"
2-3" × 10"
H/2
"H" = 17' to 29'

TWO STAGE BRACING

SINGLE BENTS WITH ONE STAGE SWAY BRACING

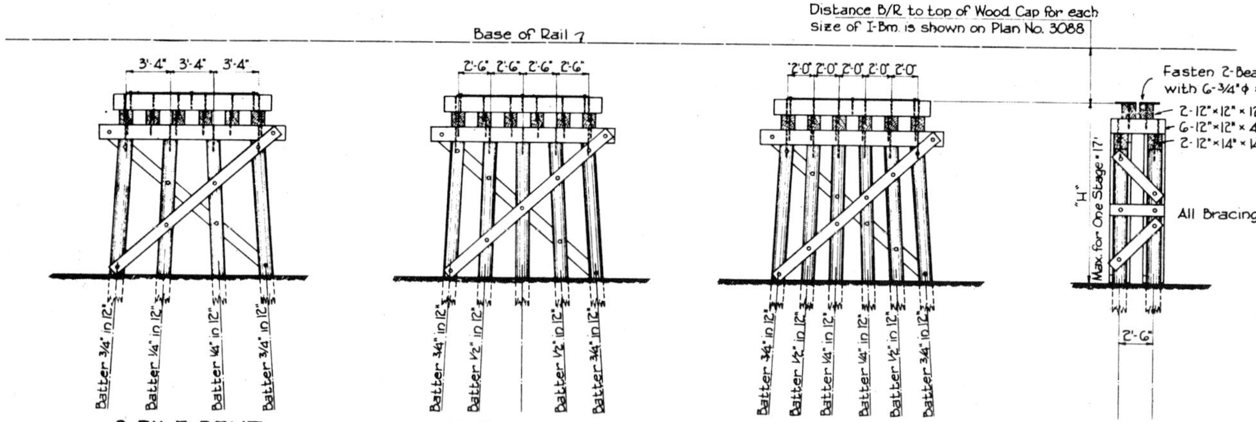
Distance B/R to top of Wood Cap for each size of I-Bm. is shown on Plan No. 3088
Base of Rail
3'-4" 3'-4" 3'-4"
2'-6" 2'-6" 2'-6" 2'-6"
2'-0" 2'-0" 2'-0" 2'-0" 2'-0"
Fasten 2-Bearing Pls. EBR with 6-3/4"ϕ × 12" Lag Screws
2-12" × 12" × 12'-0" Caps
6-12" × 12" × 4'-0"
2-12" × 14" × 14'-0" Caps
All Bracing 3" × 10"
"H" Max. for One Stage = 17'
2'-6"
Batter 3/4" in 12"
Batter 1/2" in 12"
Batter 1/4" in 12"

8 PILE BENT

10 PILE BENT

12 PILE BENT

END VIEW

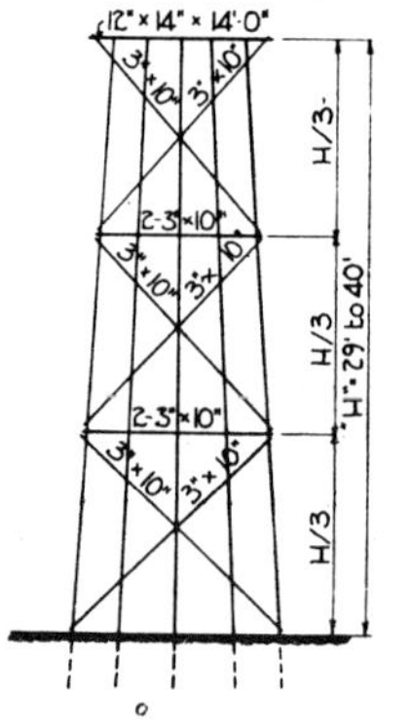
12" × 14" × 14'-0"
3" × 10"
2-3" × 10"
H/3
"H" = 29' to 40'

THREE STAGE BRACING

DOUBLE BENTS WITH ONE STAGE SWAY BRACING

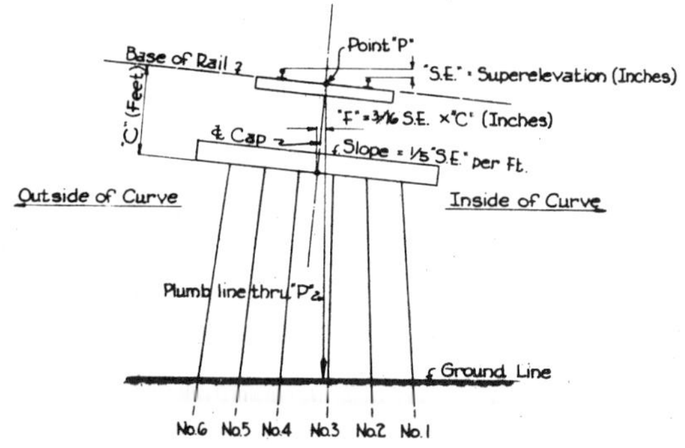
Point "P"
Base of Rail
"S.E." = Superelevation (Inches)
"C" (Feet)
"F" = 3/16 S.E. × "C" (Inches)
℄ Cap
Slope = 1/5 "S.E." per Ft.
Outside of Curve
Inside of Curve
Plumb line thru "P"
Ground Line
No.6 No.5 No.4 No.3 No.2 No.1

DIAGRAM OF BENT ON A CURVE

INSTRUCTIONS FOR DRIVING BENTS ON CURVES

Piles in bents on a curve shall be battered in accordance with the table as shown below, depending upon the superelevation of the track. Note:- Piles are numbered from the inside of curve to the outside. All batters shown underscored in the table mean that the pile shall be driven so that the top leans to the outside of the curve, and if not underscored, the pile shall lean toward the inside of the curve.

The spacing of piles at cut-off elevation shall be the same as shown for bents on tangent track. The distance from each pile to a plumb line thru ℄ Track at Base of Rail [Point "P"] at the ground line is figured in the usual way except that all piles will be moved to the outside of the curve by the distance "F" = 3/16 "S.E." × "C". See Diagram. Example: S.E. = 2", "C" = 4'-3" then "F" = 3/16 × 2" × 4 1/4 = 6/16 × 4 1/4 = 26/16 = 1 5/8"

BATTER OF PILES [INCHES PER FT.] FOR BENTS LOCATED ON CURVES

SUPER-	4 PILE BENT				5 PILE BENT					6 PILE BENT						7 PILE BENT						
ELEVATION	No.1	No.2	No.3	No.4	No.1	No.2	No.3	No.4	No.5	No.1	No.2	No.3	No.4	No.5	No.6	No.1	No.2	No.3	No.4	No.5	No.6	No.7
1/2"	3/4	1/4	5/16	7/8	3/4	3/8	1/16	1/2	7/8	3/4	7/16	1/8	3/16	9/16	7/8	3/4	1/2	3/16	1/16	5/16	5/8	7/8
1"	3/4	1/4	3/8	1	3/4	5/16	1/8	9/16	1	3/4	3/8	1/16	1/4	5/8	1	3/4	1/2	3/16	1/8	3/8	11/16	1
1 1/2"	3/4	1/8	7/16	1	3/4	5/16	1/8	9/16	1	3/4	3/8	0	5/16	11/16	1	3/4	7/16	1/8	1/8	7/16	3/4	1
2"	3/4	1/8	1/2	1 1/8	3/4	1/4	3/16	5/8	1 1/8	3/4	3/8	0	3/8	3/4	1 1/8	3/4	7/16	1/8	3/16	1/2	13/16	1 1/8
2 1/2"	3/4	1/16	9/16	1 1/4	3/4	1/4	1/4	3/4	1 1/4	3/4	3/8	0	7/16	13/16	1 1/4	3/4	7/16	1/16	1/4	9/16	7/8	1 1/4
[illegible]	[illegible]	[illegible]	[illegible]	[illegible]	[illegible]	[illegible]	[illegible]	[illegible]	[illegible]	[illegible]	[illegible]	[illegible]	[illegible]	[illegible]	[illegible]	[illegible]	[illegible]	[illegible]	[illegible]	[illegible]	[illegible]	[illegible]
3 1/2"	3/4	0	3/4	1 1/2	3/4	3/16	3/8	15/16	1 1/2	3/4	5/16	1/8	9/16	1	1 1/2	3/4	3/8	0	3/8	3/4	1 1/8	1 1/2
4"	3/4	0	3/4	1 1/2	3/4	3/16	3/8	15/16	1 1/2	3/4	5/16	1/8	5/8	1 1/16	1 1/2	3/4	3/8	0	3/8	13/16	13/16	1 1/2
4 1/2"	3/4	1/16	7/8	1 5/8	3/4	1/8	7/16	1	1 5/8	3/4	1/4	3/16	11/16	1 1/8	1 5/8	3/4	3/8	1/16	7/16	7/8	1 1/4	1 5/8
5"	3/4	1/8	15/16	1 3/4	3/4	1/8	1/2	1 1/8	1 3/4	3/4	1/4	1/4	3/4	1 1/4	1 3/4	3/4	5/16	1/16	1/2	15/16	1 3/8	1 3/4
5 1/2"	3/4	1/8	1	1 7/8	3/4	1/8	9/16	1 1/4	1 7/8	3/4	1/4	1/4	13/16	15/16	1 7/8	3/4	5/16	1/16	9/16	1	1 7/16	1 7/8
6"	3/4	3/16	1 1/16	2	3/4	1/16	5/8	15/16	2	3/4	3/16	5/16	7/8	1 7/16	2	3/4	5/16	1/13	5/8	1 1/16	1 1/2	2

— GENERAL NOTES —

General Notes on Plan No. 3090 also apply to this sheet. Bill of Material for each type of bent is shown on Plan No. 3090.

Sway Bracing to be fastened with 3/4"ϕ Bolts and St'd. O.G. Washers. Caps to be fastened with 3/4"ϕ × 22" Drift Bolts.

APPROVED ______________________ VICE-PRESIDENT

APPROVED ______________________ GENERAL MANAGER

APPROVED ______________________ CHIEF ENGINEER

WABASH RAILWAY
STANDARD
I-BEAM TRESTLE
PILE BENTS

OFFICE OF THE CHIEF ENGINEER

ADOPTED 1-2-34

PLAN NO. 3089
CASE 12-1-2

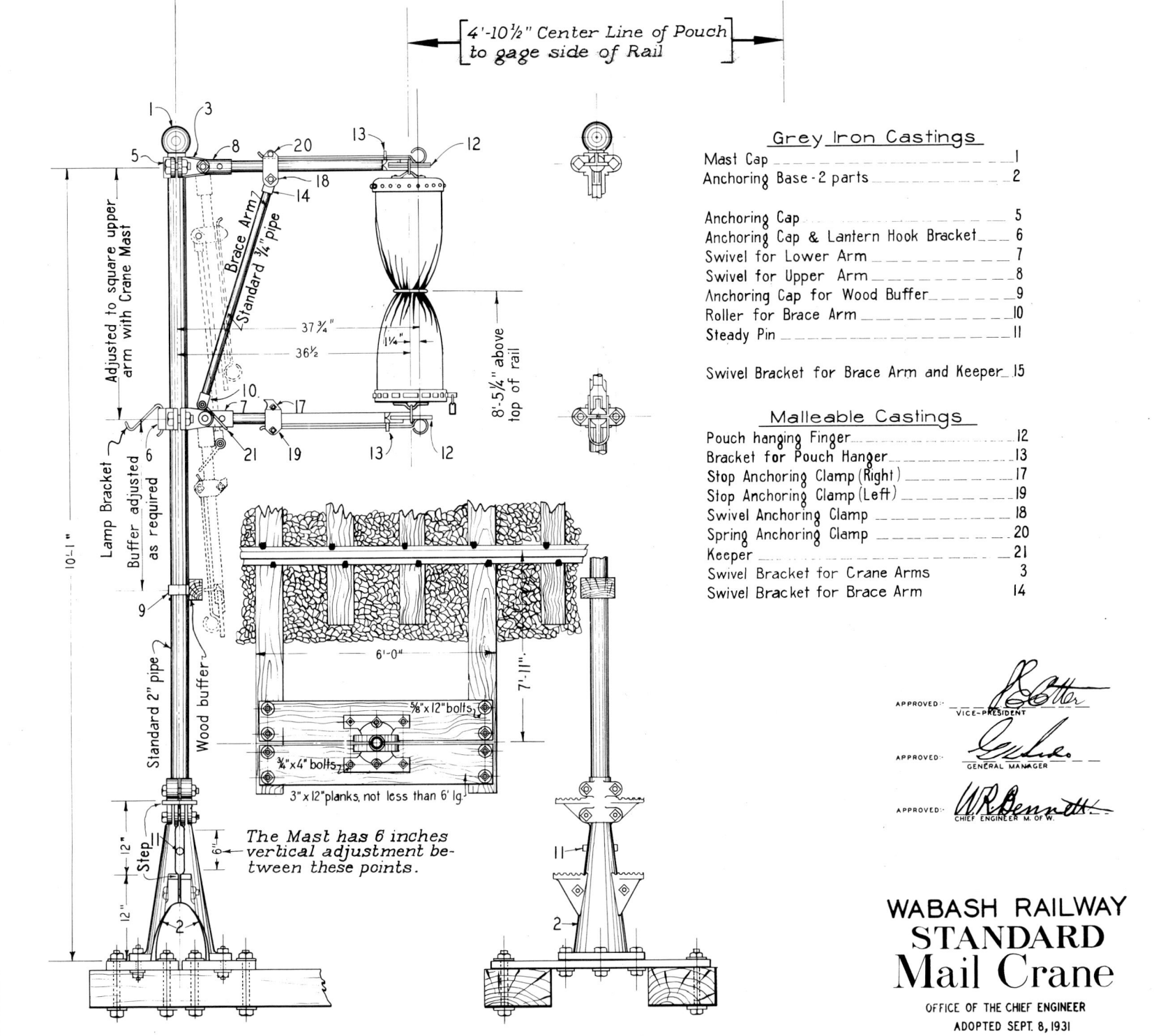

4'-10½" Center Line of Pouch to gage side of Rail

Grey Iron Castings

Mast Cap	1
Anchoring Base - 2 parts	2
Anchoring Cap	5
Anchoring Cap & Lantern Hook Bracket	6
Swivel for Lower Arm	7
Swivel for Upper Arm	8
Anchoring Cap for Wood Buffer	9
Roller for Brace Arm	10
Steady Pin	11
Swivel Bracket for Brace Arm and Keeper	15

Malleable Castings

Pouch hanging Finger	12
Bracket for Pouch Hanger	13
Stop Anchoring Clamp (Right)	17
Stop Anchoring Clamp (Left)	19
Swivel Anchoring Clamp	18
Spring Anchoring Clamp	20
Keeper	21
Swivel Bracket for Crane Arms	3
Swivel Bracket for Brace Arm	14

Adjusted to square upper arm with Crane Mast

Brace Arm Standard ¾" pipe

37¾"

36½"

1¼"

8'-5¼" above top of rail

Lamp Bracket

Buffer adjusted as required

10'-1"

Standard 2" pipe

Wood buffer

6'-0"

7'-11"

⅝" x 12" bolts

¾" x 4" bolts

3" x 12" planks, not less than 6' lg.

12" Step

6"

The Mast has 6 inches vertical adjustment between these points.

APPROVED: _____ VICE-PRESIDENT

APPROVED: _____ GENERAL MANAGER

APPROVED: W.R. Bennett CHIEF ENGINEER M. OF W.

WABASH RAILWAY STANDARD Mail Crane

OFFICE OF THE CHIEF ENGINEER
ADOPTED SEPT. 8, 1931

PLAN NO. 3042

11

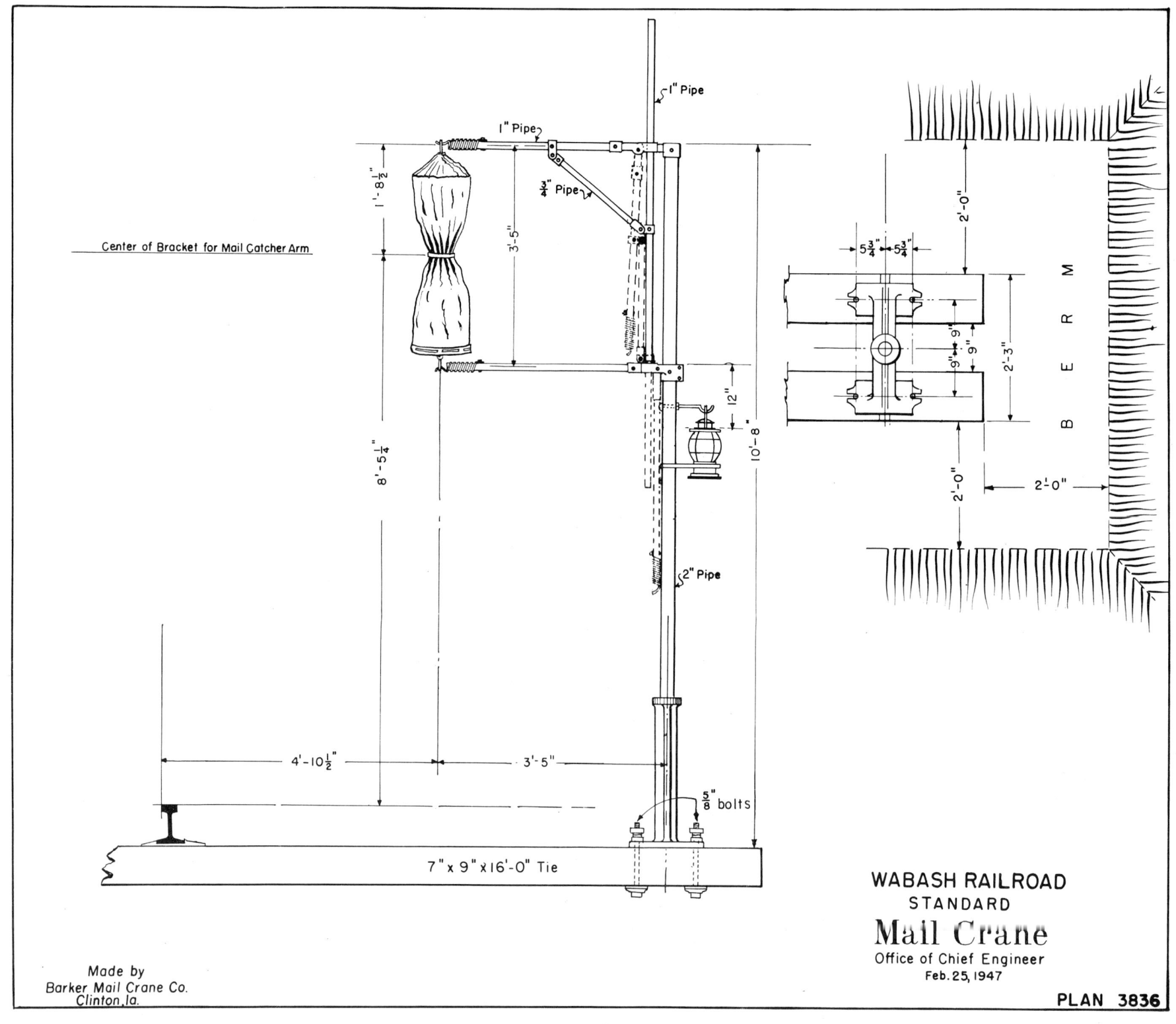

Center of Bracket for Mail Catcher Arm

1" Pipe

1" Pipe

3/4" Pipe

1'-8½"

3'-5"

8'-5¼"

12"

10'-8"

2" Pipe

4'-10½"

3'-5"

5/8" bolts

7"x 9"x16'-0" Tie

2'-0"

5¾" 5¾"

9" 9"

2'-3"

9" 9"

2'-0"

2'-0"

B E R M

WABASH RAILROAD
STANDARD
Mail Crane
Office of Chief Engineer
Feb. 25, 1947

PLAN 3836

Made by
Barker Mail Crane Co.
Clinton, Ia.

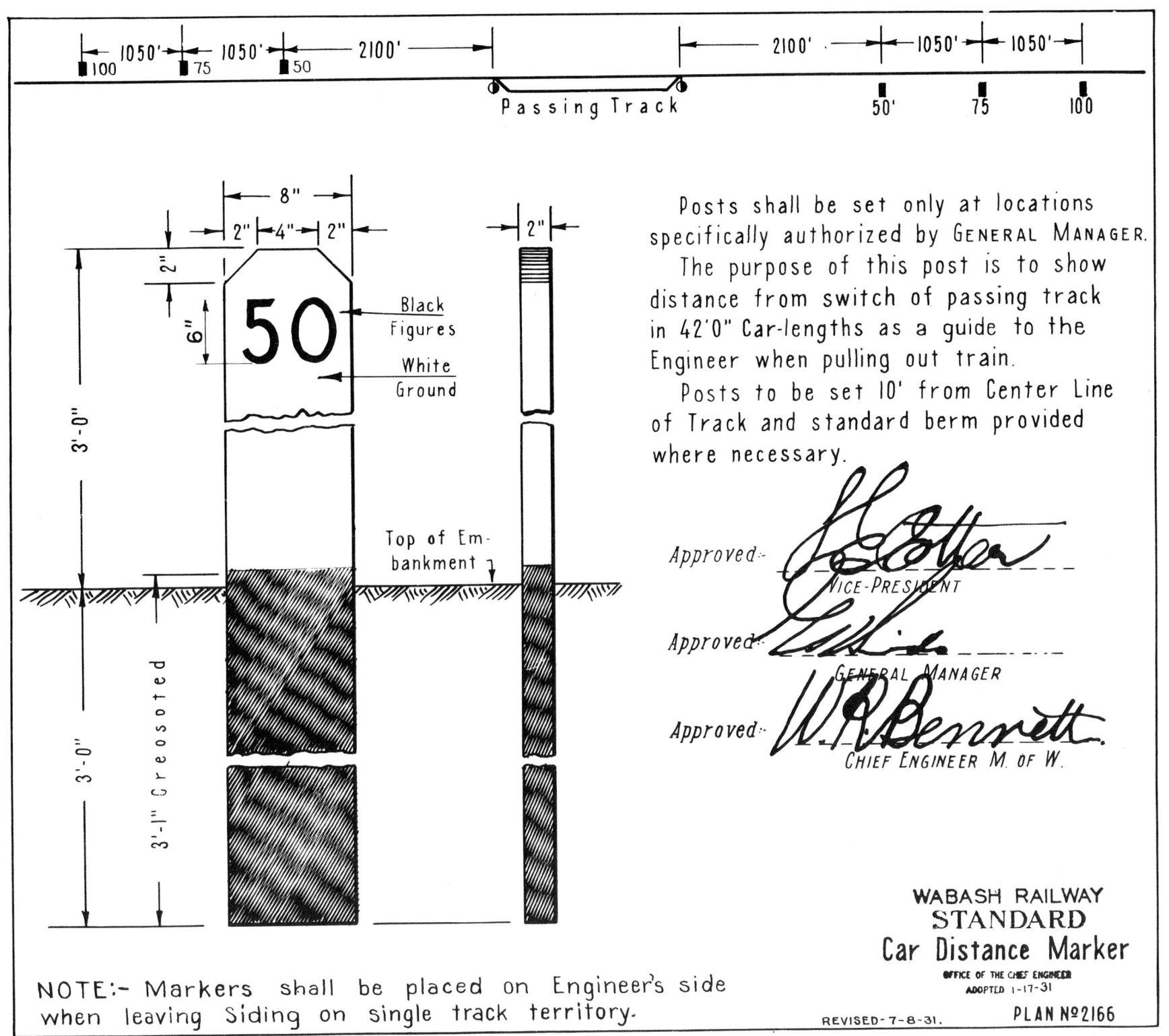

Posts shall be set only at locations specifically authorized by GENERAL MANAGER.

The purpose of this post is to show distance from switch of passing track in 42'0" Car-lengths as a guide to the Engineer when pulling out train.

Posts to be set 10' from Center Line of Track and standard berm provided where necessary.

Approved:- _____
VICE-PRESIDENT

Approved:- _____
GENERAL MANAGER

Approved:- _____
CHIEF ENGINEER M. OF W.

Black Figures

White Ground

Top of Embankment

3'-0"

3'-0"

3'-1" Creosoted

8"

2" 4" 2"

2"

6"

50

2"

WABASH RAILWAY
STANDARD
Car Distance Marker

OFFICE OF THE CHIEF ENGINEER
ADOPTED 1-17-31

REVISED-7-8-31.

PLAN N.º 2166

CASE NO. 5-1-1

NOTE:- Markers shall be placed on Engineer's side when leaving Siding on single track territory.

Passing Track

1050'   1050'   2100'   2100'   1050'   1050'
100   75   50   50'   75   100

13

SAFETY FIRST

THIS GANG HAS NOT HAD

A REPORTABLE INJURY

FOR_____   _____DAYS

HELP KEEP RECORD CLEAR

½"
1"
½"
1"
½"
1"
½"
1"
½"
1"
12"
½"
1"
½"
1"
½"
1"
½"
1"
½"

18"

Background-Flat black
Letters & border-White

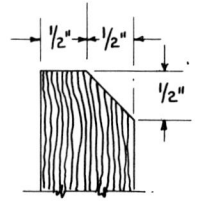

½" ½"
½"

Section "A-A"

Approved - _~S.L.Potter~_
Vice-President

Approved - _~W.A.Air~_
General Manager

Approved - _~W.R.Bennett~_
Chief Engineer M of W.

WABASH RAILWAY
STANDARD
SAFETY FIRST SIGN FOR
TOOL HOUSES
OFFICE OF THE CHIEF ENGINEER M. OF W
ADOPTED 9-26-1930

PLAN NO. 2157

14

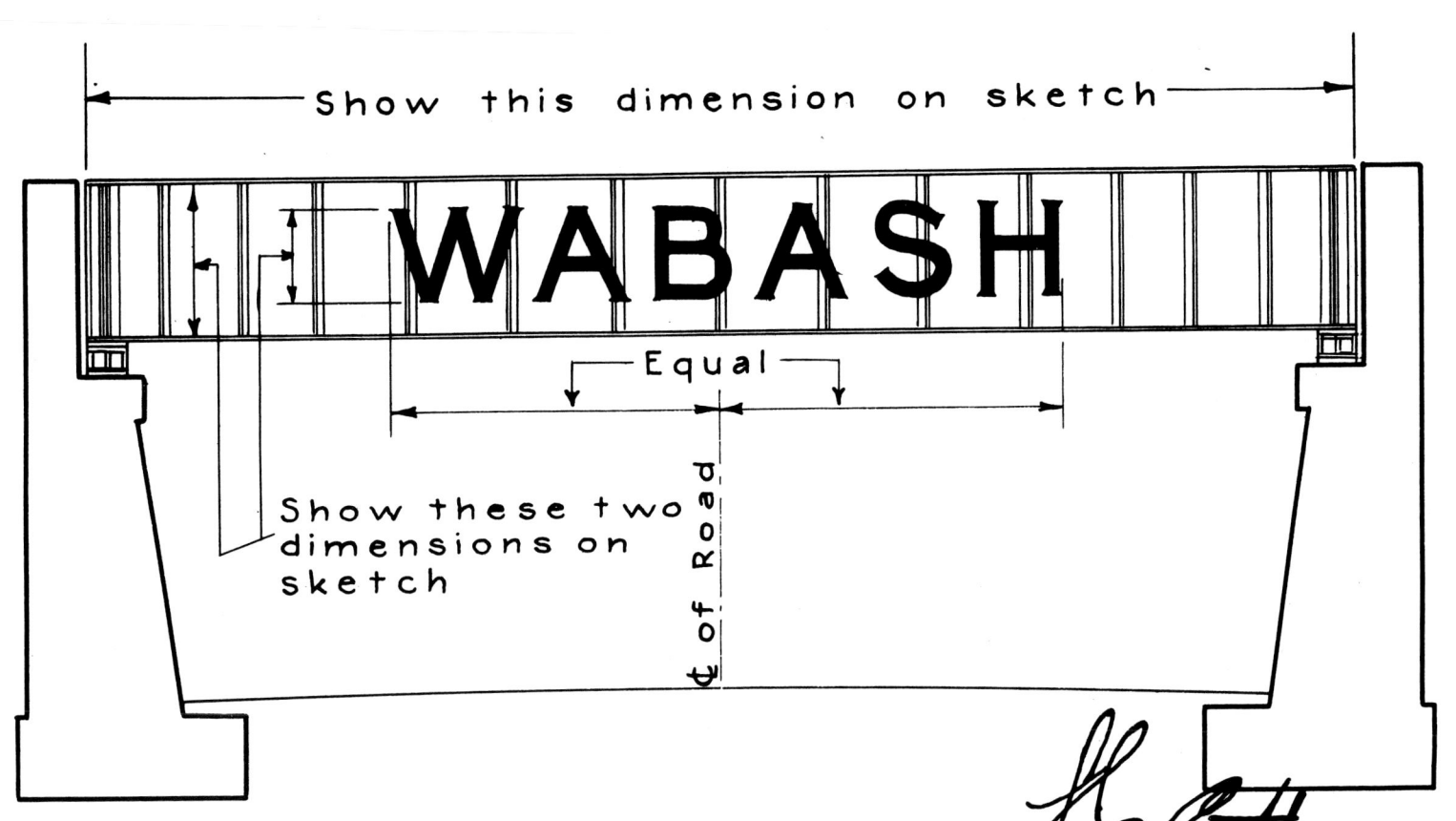

Show this dimension on sketch

WABASH

Equal

Show these two dimensions on sketch

⊄ of Road

Proportions and spacing of word "WABASH" are in accordance with instructions for painting "STATION SIGNS" as given in Chief Engineer's Drawing #1950-Case #5-1-1

Four copies of sketch showing proposed sign to be submitted to Chief Engineer M. of W. for approval before starting work.

Approved:- _____
Vice-President

Approved:- _____
General Manager

Approved:- _____
Chief Engineer M. of W.

WABASH RAILWAY
STANDARD
SIGN FOR BRIDGES

OFFICE OF THE CHIEF ENGINEER M. OF W.
ADOPTED APRIL 8, 1931

PLAN NO. 1952

J.C.W.

15

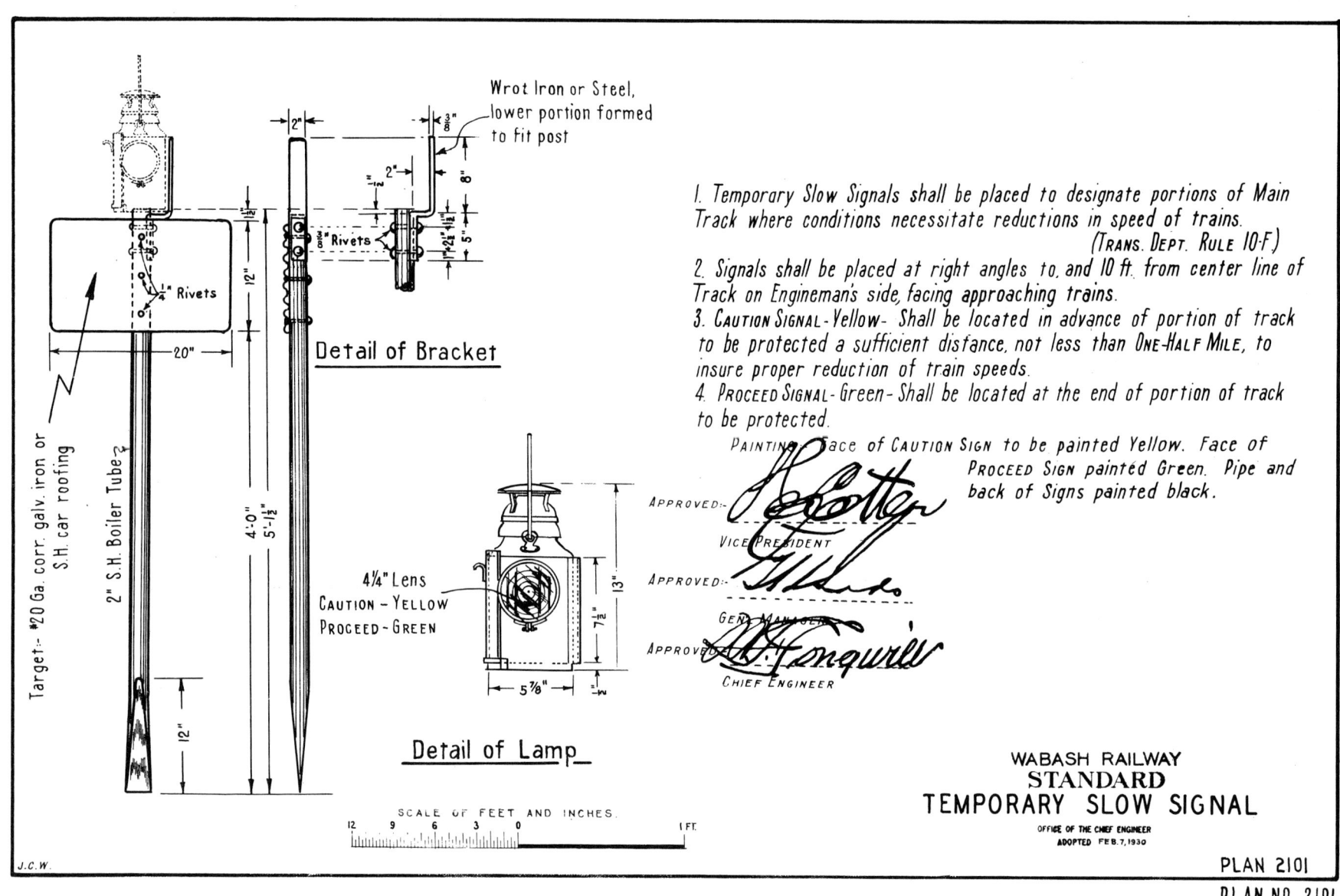

Wrot Iron or Steel,
lower portion formed
to fit post

Detail of Bracket

Target:- #20 Ga. corr. galv. iron or S.H. car roofing

2" S.H. Boiler Tube

¼" Rivets

20"

¼" Rivets

4¼" Lens
Caution – Yellow
Proceed – Green

Detail of Lamp

SCALE OF FEET AND INCHES.
12 9 6 3 0   1 FT.

J.C.W.

1. Temporary Slow Signals shall be placed to designate portions of Main Track where conditions necessitate reductions in speed of trains.
(Trans. Dept. Rule 10-F.)

2. Signals shall be placed at right angles to, and 10 ft. from center line of Track on Engineman's side, facing approaching trains.

3. Caution Signal - Yellow - Shall be located in advance of portion of track to be protected a sufficient distance, not less than One-Half Mile, to insure proper reduction of train speeds.

4. Proceed Signal - Green - Shall be located at the end of portion of track to be protected.

Painting - Face of Caution Sign to be painted Yellow. Face of Proceed Sign painted Green. Pipe and back of Signs painted black.

APPROVED:-
Vice President

APPROVED:-
Genl Manager

APPROVED:-
Chief Engineer

WABASH RAILWAY
STANDARD
TEMPORARY SLOW SIGNAL

OFFICE OF THE CHIEF ENGINEER
ADOPTED FEB. 7, 1930

PLAN 2101

PLAN NO. 2101
CASE NO. 5-1-1

16

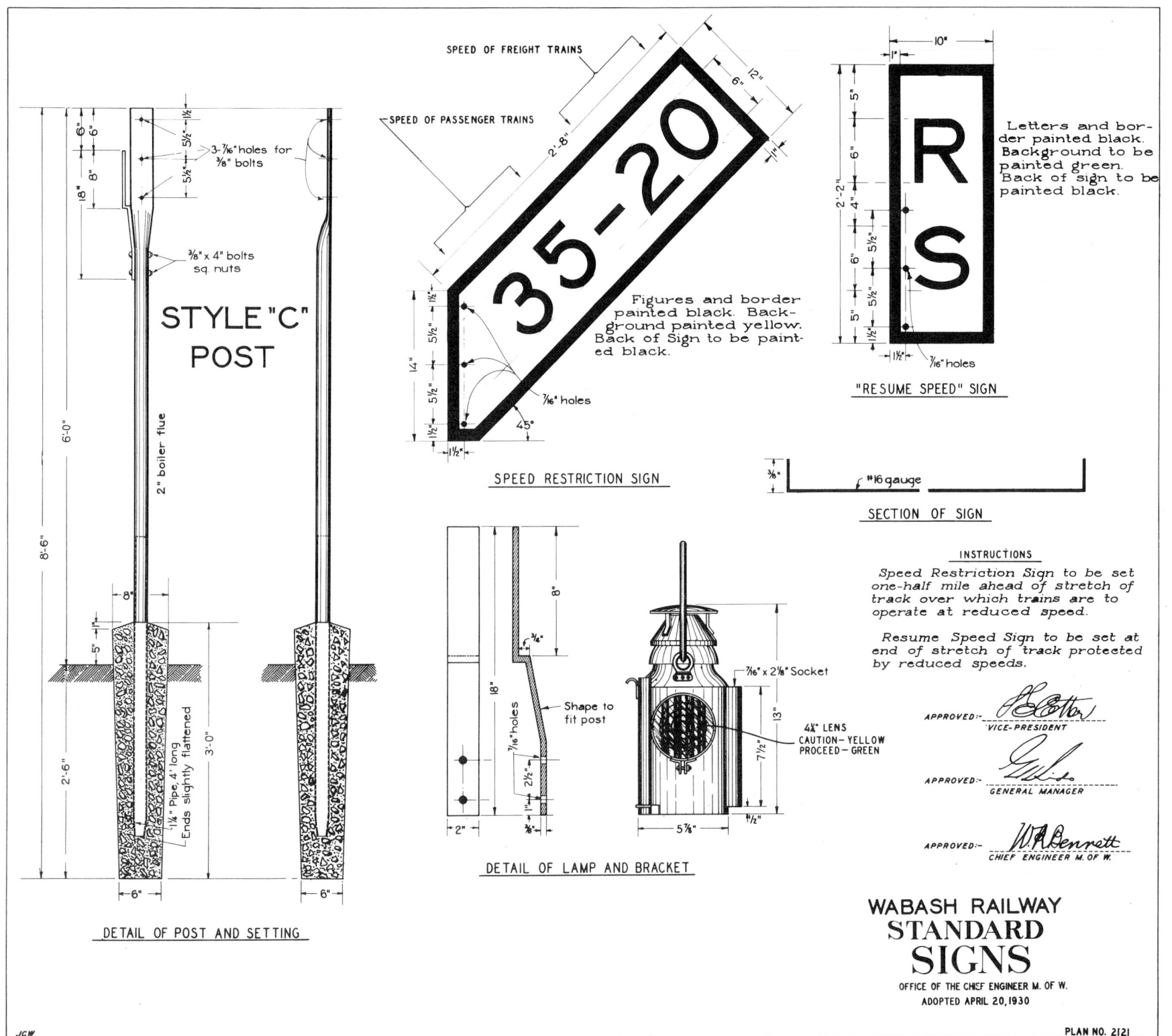

STYLE "C" POST

3-7/16" holes for 3/8" bolts

3/8" x 4" bolts sq. nuts

2" boiler flue

1¼" Pipe, 4' long
Ends slightly flattened

DETAIL OF POST AND SETTING

SPEED OF FREIGHT TRAINS

SPEED OF PASSENGER TRAINS

35-20

Figures and border painted black. Background painted yellow. Back of Sign to be painted black.

7/16" holes

45°

SPEED RESTRICTION SIGN

R
S

Letters and border painted black. Background to be painted green. Back of sign to be painted black.

7/16" holes

"RESUME SPEED" SIGN

#16 gauge

SECTION OF SIGN

INSTRUCTIONS

Speed Restriction Sign to be set one-half mile ahead of stretch of track over which trains are to operate at reduced speed.

Resume Speed Sign to be set at end of stretch of track protected by reduced speeds.

Shape to fit post

7/16" holes

DETAIL OF LAMP AND BRACKET

7/16" x 2⅛" Socket

4¼" LENS
CAUTION—YELLOW
PROCEED—GREEN

APPROVED:- _____
VICE-PRESIDENT

APPROVED:- _____
GENERAL MANAGER

APPROVED:- W. A. Bennett
CHIEF ENGINEER M. OF W.

WABASH RAILWAY
STANDARD
SIGNS
OFFICE OF THE CHIEF ENGINEER M. OF W.
ADOPTED APRIL 20, 1930

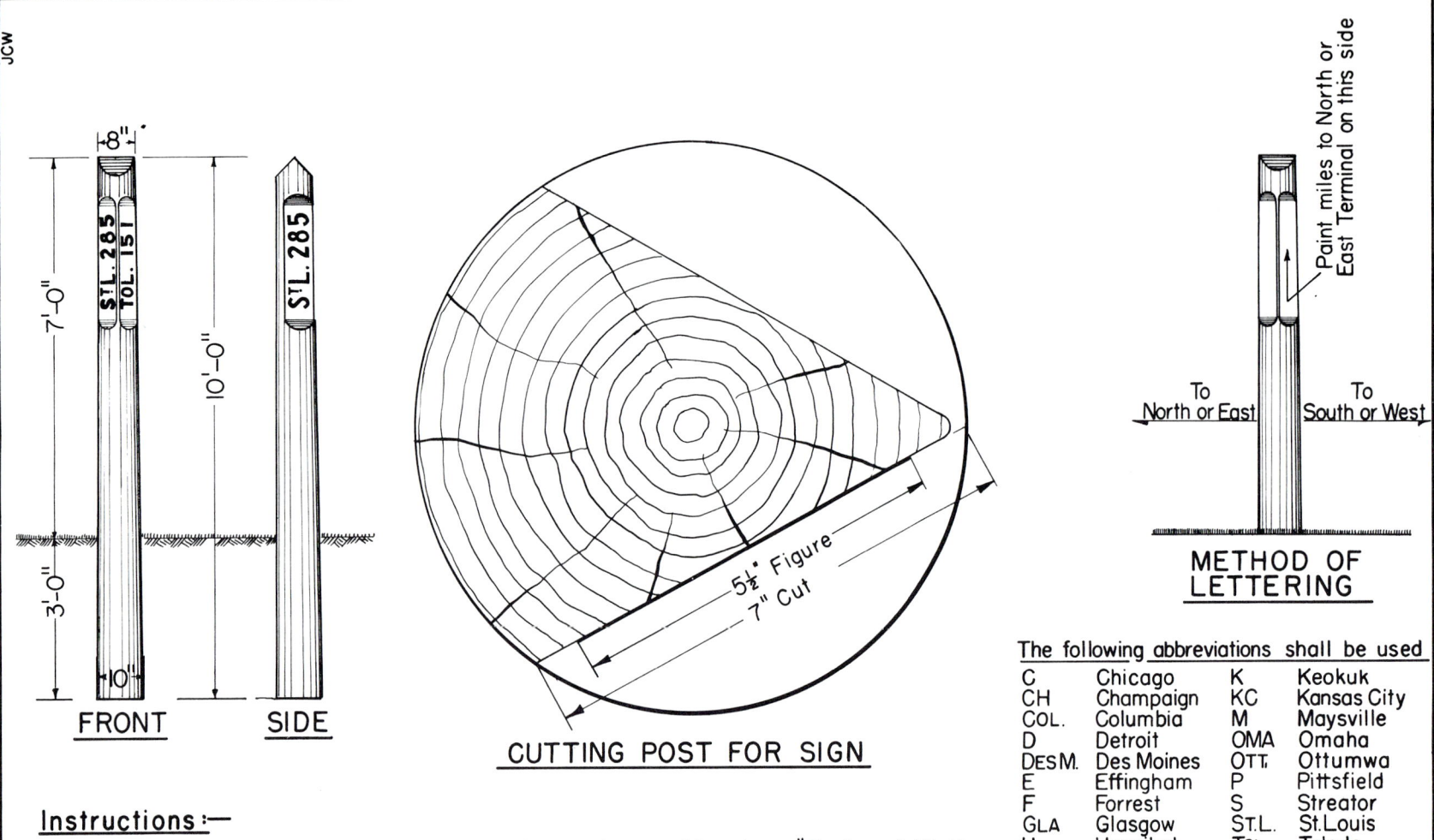

FRONT   **SIDE**

St'L. 285
TOL. 151
St'L. 285

8"
7'-0"
10'-0"
3'-0"
10"

5½" Figure
7" Cut

CUTTING POST FOR SIGN

Paint miles to North or East Terminal on this side

To North or East   To South or West

METHOD OF LETTERING

Instructions:—

For the purpose of locating Mile Posts the WABASH is considered an "East and West Line", and the Mile Posts are to be located on the South side of track. When facing the front of Sign, the distance to North or East Terminal is on Right side of Post, and the distance to South or West Terminal is on Left side of Post.

Terminals to be shown on the various lines are as follows:—

The following abbreviations shall be used

C	Chicago	K	Keokuk
CH	Champaign	KC	Kansas City
COL.	Columbia	M	Maysville
D	Detroit	OMA	Omaha
DES M.	Des Moines	OTT.	Ottumwa
E	Effingham	P	Pittsfield
F	Forrest	S	Streator
GLA	Glasgow	ST.L.	St. Louis
H	Hannibal	TOL.	Toledo

LINE	EAST TER.	WEST TER.	LINE	EAST TER.	WEST TER.
Toledo—New Haven via Defiance	Toledo	St. Louis	Maysville–Pittsfield	Maysville	Pittsfield
Detroit–Chicago	Detroit	Chicago	Hannibal–Moberly	Hannibal (only one shown)	
Maumee–Montpelier	Toledo	St. Louis	St. Louis–Moberly	St. Louis	Kansas City
Montpelier–St. Louis	Detroit	St. Louis	St. Louis–Ferguson (Levee Line)	St. Louis	Kansas City
Sidney–Champaign	Detroit	Champaign			
Chicago–Bement	Chicago	St. Louis	Centralia–Columbia	St. Louis	Columbia
Forrest–Streator	Forrest	Streator	Moberly–Des Moines	St. Louis	Des Moines
Bement–Effingham	Chicago	Effingham	Moulton Ottumwa	St. Louis	Ottumwa
Decatur–Hannibal	Detroit	Hannibal	Salisbury–Glasgow	St. Louis	Glasgow
Bluffs–Keokuk	Detroit	Keokuk	Brunswick–Omaha	St. Louis	Omaha
			Moberly–Kansas City	St. Louis	Kansas C.

WABASH RAILWAY STANDARD MILE POST

Office of the Chief Engineer
May 7, 1940

PLAN 3381
10-2-2

JCW

18

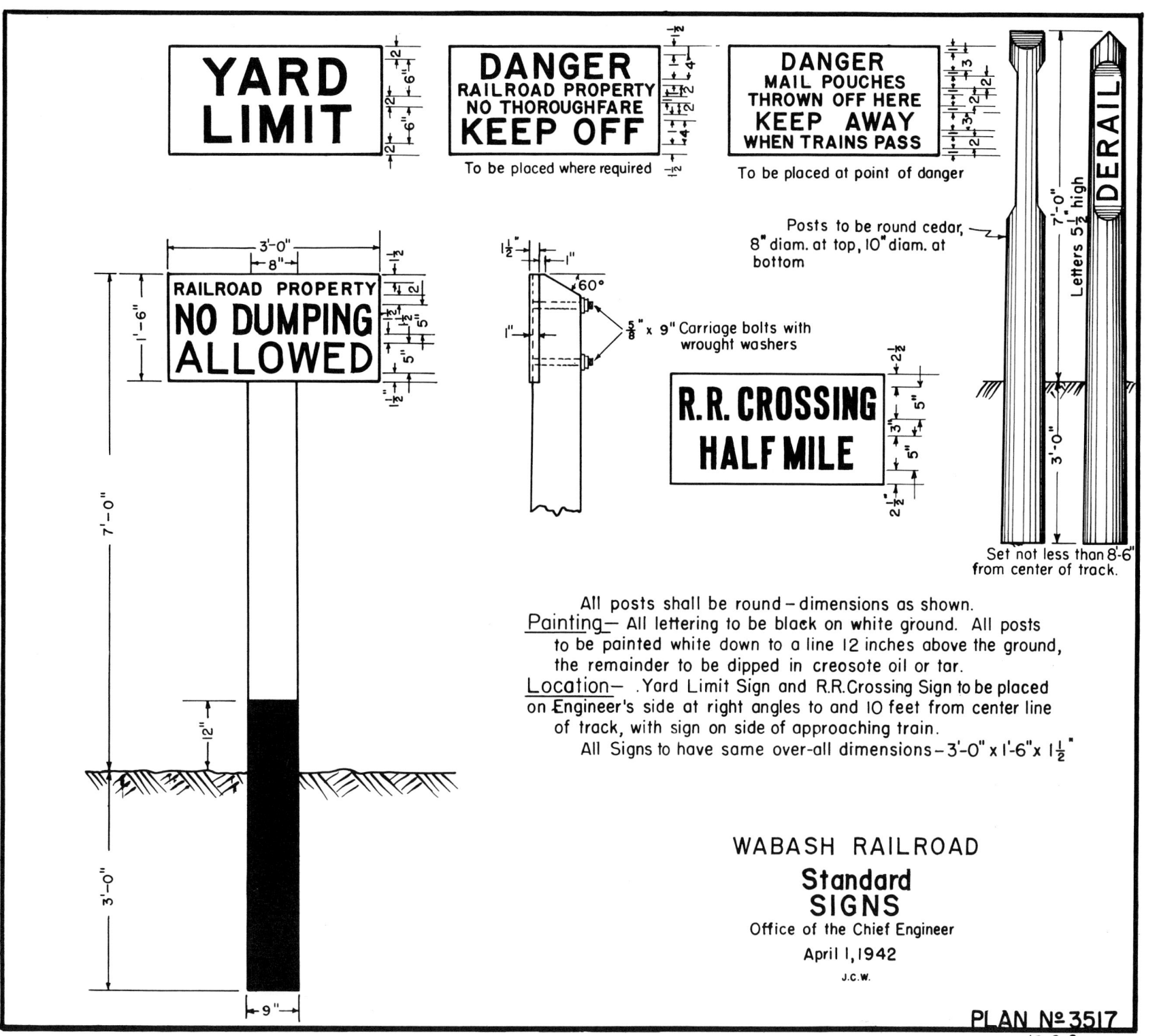

YARD LIMIT

DANGER
RAILROAD PROPERTY
NO THOROUGHFARE
KEEP OFF

To be placed where required

DANGER
MAIL POUCHES
THROWN OFF HERE
KEEP AWAY
WHEN TRAINS PASS

To be placed at point of danger

DERAIL

Letters 5½" high

7'-0" high

3'-0"

Set not less than 8'-6" from center of track.

Posts to be round cedar, 8" diam. at top, 10" diam. at bottom

3'-0"
8"

RAILROAD PROPERTY
NO DUMPING
ALLOWED

1'-6"

7'-0"

12"

3'-0"

9"

1½" 1"
60°
1"
⅝" x 9" Carriage bolts with wrought washers

R.R. CROSSING
HALF MILE

2½"
3" 5"
2½"

All posts shall be round — dimensions as shown.

Painting— All lettering to be black on white ground. All posts to be painted white down to a line 12 inches above the ground, the remainder to be dipped in creosote oil or tar.

Location— Yard Limit Sign and R.R. Crossing Sign to be placed on Engineer's side at right angles to and 10 feet from center line of track, with sign on side of approaching train.

All Signs to have same over-all dimensions—3'-0" x 1'-6" x 1½"

WABASH RAILROAD
Standard
SIGNS
Office of the Chief Engineer
April 1, 1942

J.C.W.

PLAN No 3517
10-2-2

19

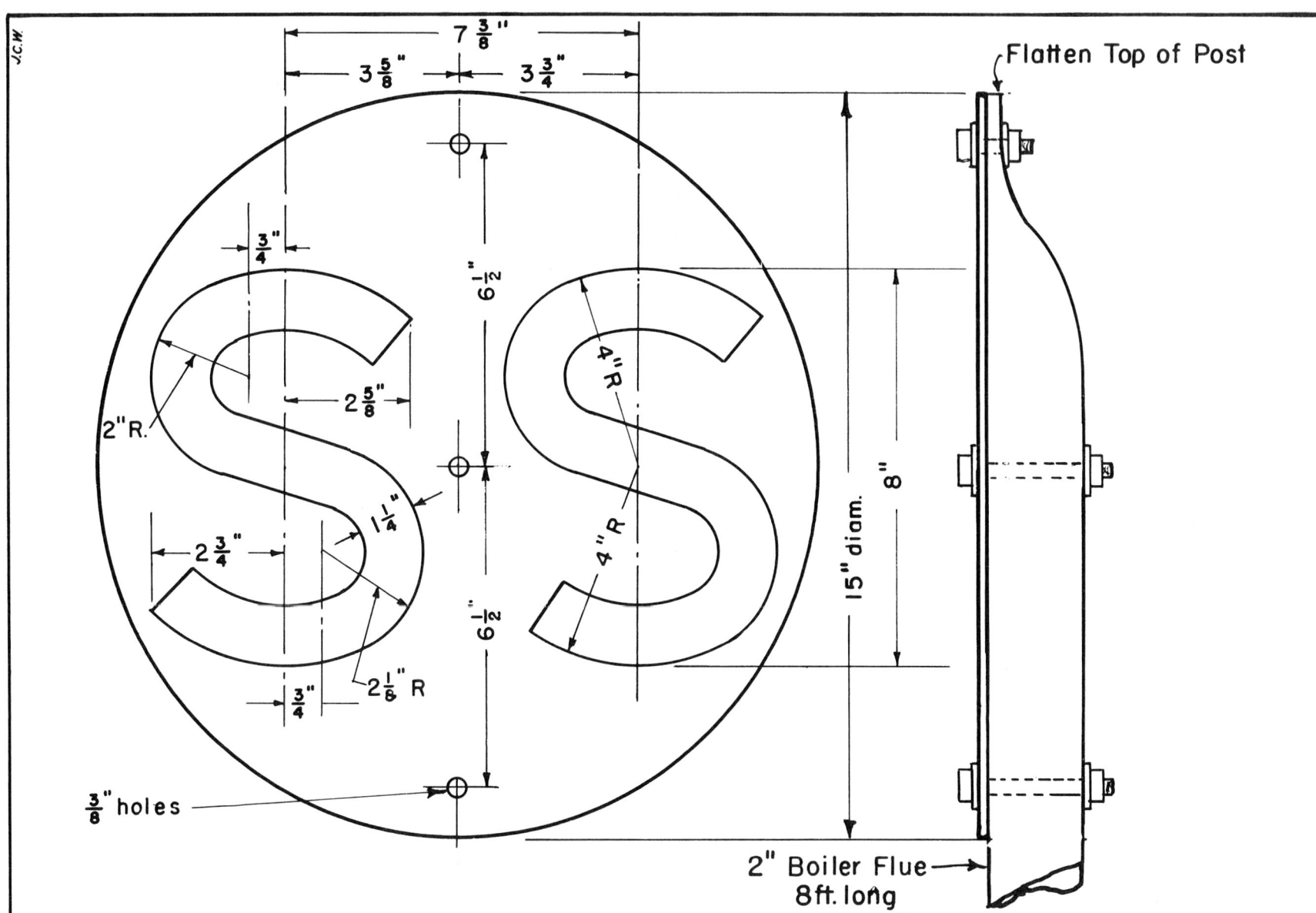

Flatten Top of Post

7 3/8"
3 5/8" 3 3/4"
3/4"
6 1/2"
2" R.
2 5/8"
1 1/4"
2 3/4"
4" R
4" R
6 1/2"
3/4"
2 1/8" R
3/8" holes

15" diam.
8"

2" Boiler Flue
8ft. long

Sign shall be made of #12 sheet metal, painted both
sides with black letters on white background
Mount Sign on 2" boiler flue, 8 ft. long. Set post on switch
stand side of track, approximately 3 ft. out from switch
stand at end of No.I headblock.   Place sign at right-angles
to track.
Stencil for letters to be cut from full-size template PLAN 3419

WABASH RAILWAY
Standard
SIGN
FOR
SPRING SWITCHES
OFFICE OF CHIEF ENGINEER
DEC.3,1940
PLAN 3418
CASE 10-2-2

20

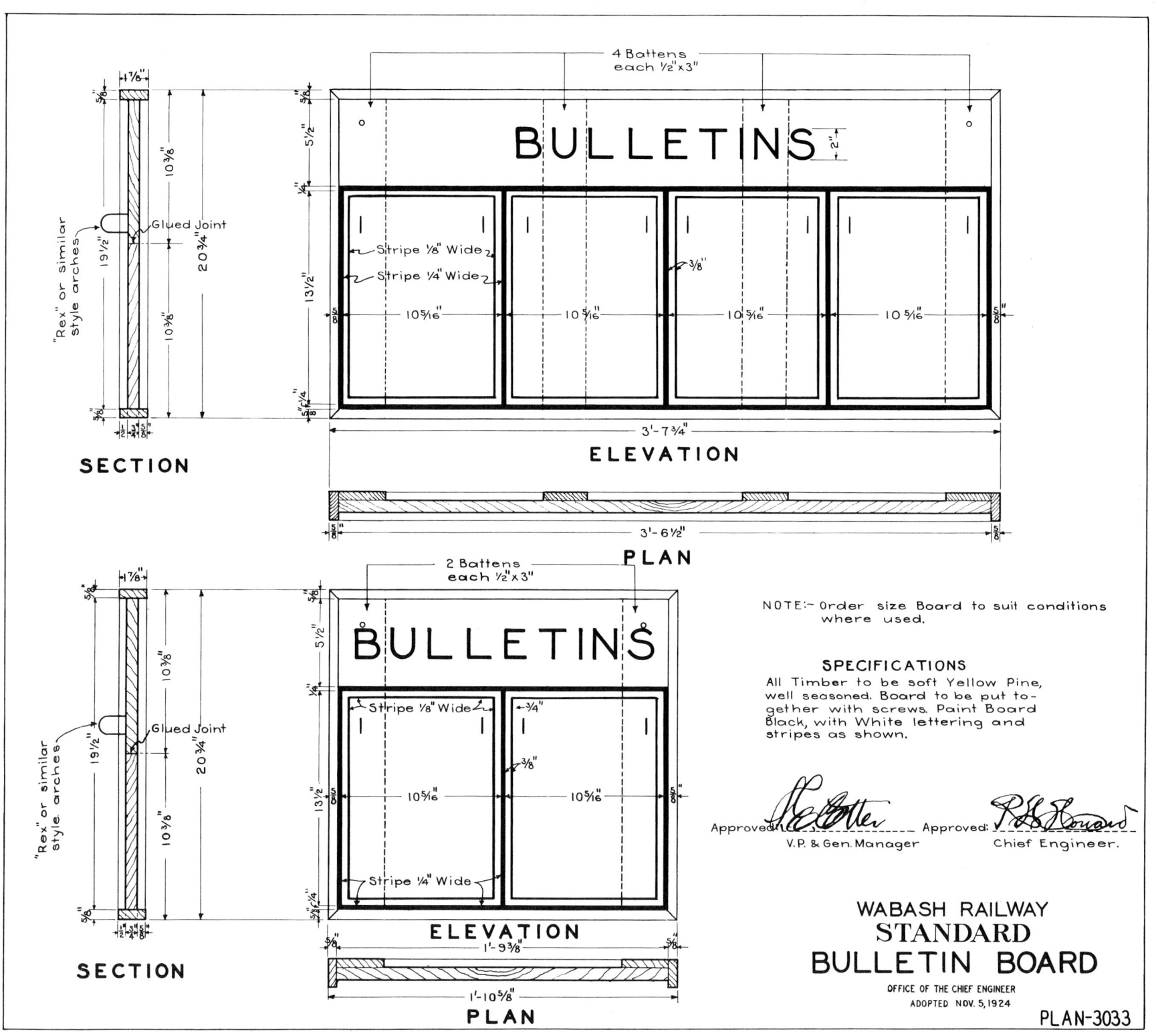

SECTION

ELEVATION

PLAN

4 Battens each ½"x3"

BULLETINS

Stripe ⅛" Wide
Stripe ¼" Wide
10⁵⁄₁₆" 10⁵⁄₁₆" 10⁵⁄₁₆" 10⁵⁄₁₆"
3'- 7¾"
3'- 6½"

"Rex" or similar style arches
Glued Joint

SECTION

ELEVATION

PLAN

2 Battens each ½"x3"

BULLETINS

Stripe ⅛" Wide
Stripe ¼" Wide
10⁵⁄₁₆" 10⁵⁄₁₆"
1'- 9⅜"
1'- 10⅝"

"Rex" or similar style arches
Glued Joint

NOTE:- Order size Board to suit conditions where used.

SPECIFICATIONS
All Timber to be soft Yellow Pine, well seasoned. Board to be put together with screws. Paint Board Black, with White lettering and stripes as shown.

Approved: _____ Approved: _____
V.P. & Gen. Manager   Chief Engineer.

WABASH RAILWAY
STANDARD
BULLETIN BOARD
OFFICE OF THE CHIEF ENGINEER
ADOPTED NOV. 5, 1924

PLAN-3033

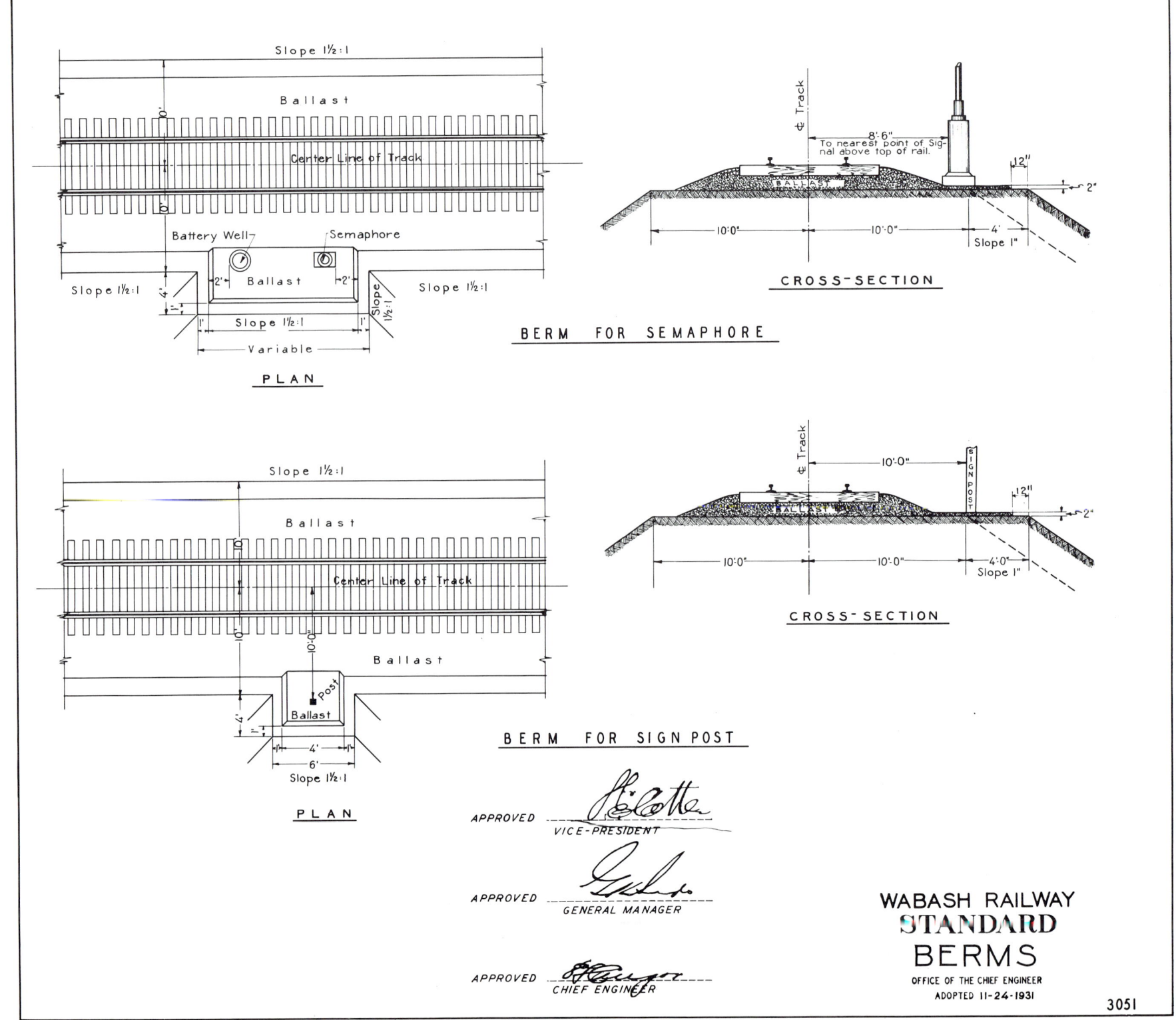

Slope 1½:1

Ballast

Center Line of Track

Battery Well   Semaphore

2' Ballast 2'

Slope 1½:1   4'   Slope 1½:1   Slope 1½:1

1'   Slope 1½:1   1'

Variable

PLAN

₵ Track

8'·6"
To nearest point of Sig-
nal above top of rail.

12"

2"

10'·0"   10'·0"   4'
Slope 1"

CROSS-SECTION

BERM FOR SEMAPHORE

Slope 1½:1

Ballast

Center Line of Track

Ballast

Post

Ballast

4'

4'

6'

Slope 1½:1

PLAN

BERM FOR SIGN POST

₵ Track

10'·0"

SIGN POST

12"

2"

10'·0"   10'·0"   4'·0"
Slope 1"

CROSS-SECTION

APPROVED _____
VICE-PRESIDENT

APPROVED _____
GENERAL MANAGER

APPROVED _____
CHIEF ENGINEER

WABASH RAILWAY
STANDARD
BERMS
OFFICE OF THE CHIEF ENGINEER
ADOPTED 11-24-1931

3051

22

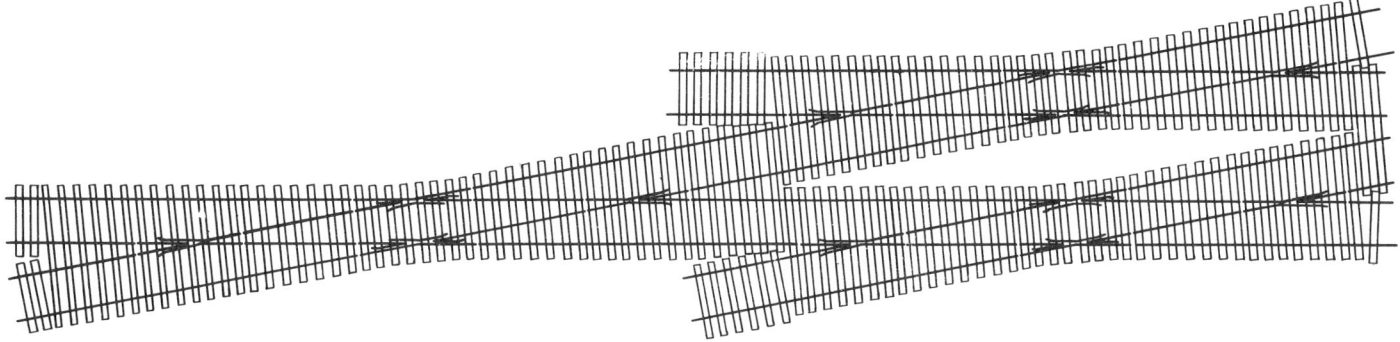

Angles 8°-10' to 14°-15'

DRAINAGE :- Crossing installation must be so drained
that all water will be diverted away
from the roadbed.

BALLAST :- A minimum depth of 12" of rock, slag or
washed gravel to be used below bot-
tom of tie.

CROSSING TIES :- Crossing ties must be kept tamped to
provide full bearing; spaced about
20" C. to C., using 7"x 9" Ties.

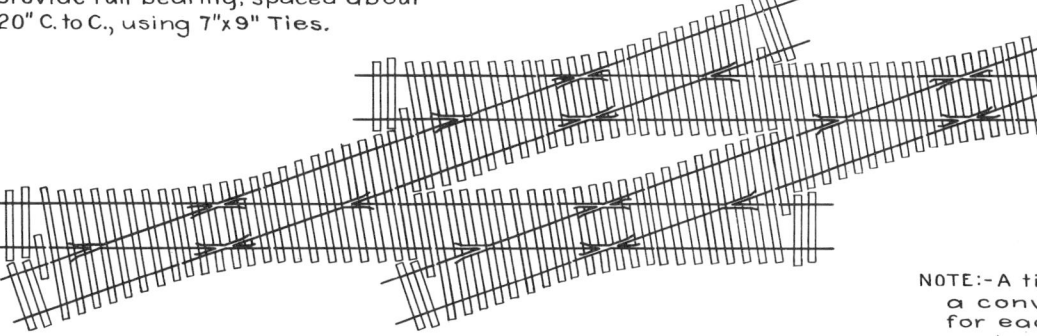

Angles 14°-15' to 25°-0'

NOTE:- A tie layout plan shall be made to
a convenient scale by Division Engineer
for each Crossing, and the exact lengths
and number of ties required determined
from this plan.

WABASH RAILWAY
STANDARD
TIE LAYOUT FOR CROSSINGS
ANGLES 8°-10' TO 25°-0'
OFFICE OF THE CHIEF ENGINEER
ADOPTED 11-24-1931

3052

Approved: _____
Vice President

Approved: _____
Gen. Manager

Approved: _____
Chief Engineer

23

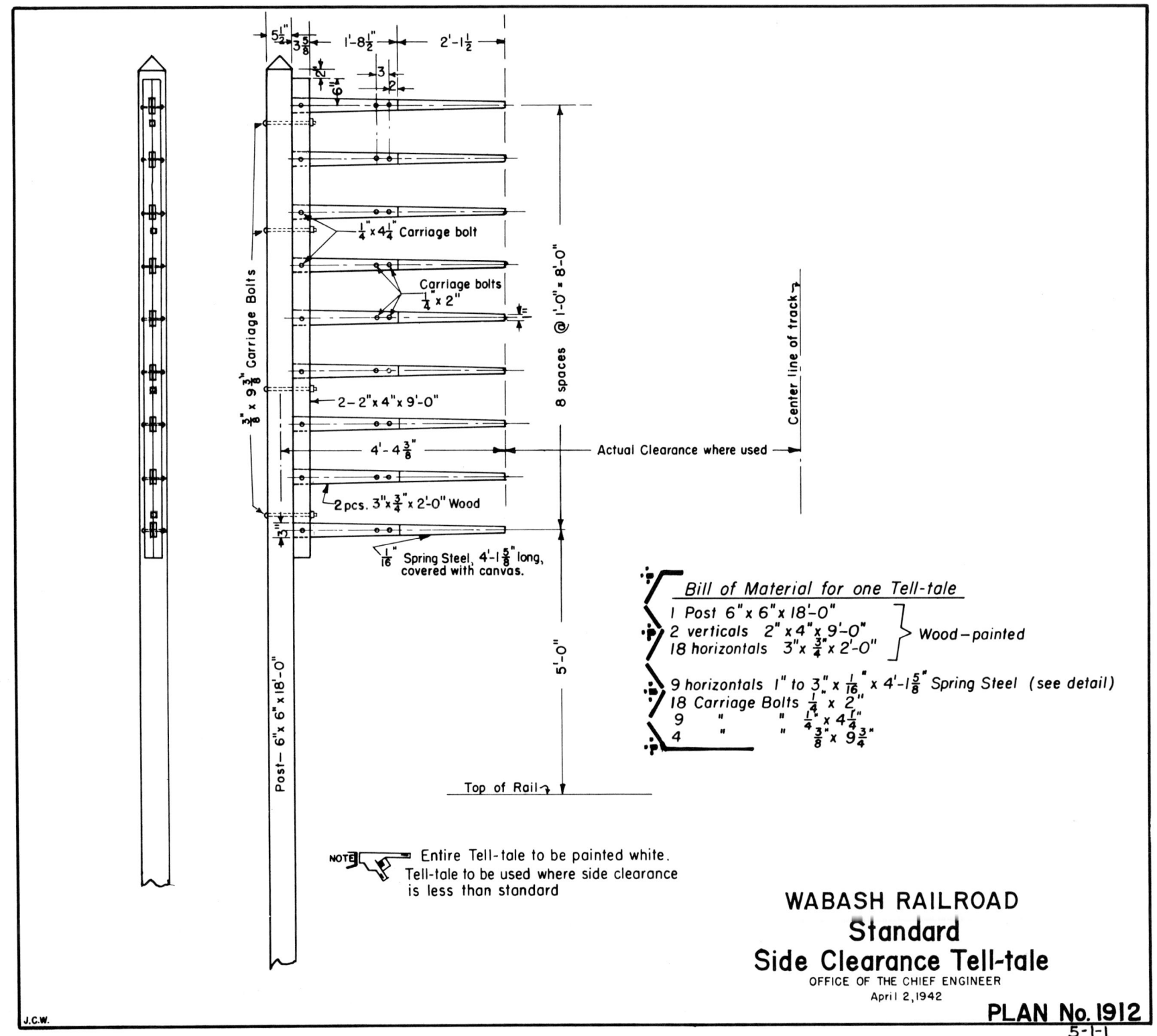

Bill of Material for one Tell-tale

1 Post 6" x 6" x 18'-0"
2 verticals 2" x 4" x 9'-0"   } Wood – painted
18 horizontals 3" x $\frac{3}{4}$" x 2'-0"

9 horizontals 1" to 3" x $\frac{1}{16}$" x 4'-1$\frac{5}{8}$" Spring Steel (see detail)
18 Carriage Bolts $\frac{1}{4}$" x 2"
9   "   " $\frac{1}{4}$" x 4$\frac{1}{4}$"
4   "   " $\frac{3}{8}$" x 9$\frac{3}{4}$"

NOTE: Entire Tell-tale to be painted white.
Tell-tale to be used where side clearance
is less than standard

$\frac{1}{4}$" x 4$\frac{1}{4}$" Carriage bolt

Carriage bolts $\frac{1}{4}$" x 2"

2 – 2" x 4" x 9'-0"

2 pcs. 3" x $\frac{3}{4}$" x 2'-0" Wood

$\frac{1}{16}$" Spring Steel, 4'-1$\frac{5}{8}$" long,
covered with canvas.

$\frac{3}{8}$" x 9$\frac{3}{4}$" Carriage Bolts

Post – 6" x 6" x 18'-0"

8 spaces @ 1'-0" = 8'-0"

Center line of track

Actual Clearance where used

4'-4$\frac{3}{8}$"

5'-0"

Top of Rail

WABASH RAILROAD
Standard
Side Clearance Tell-tale
OFFICE OF THE CHIEF ENGINEER
April 2, 1942

PLAN No. 1912
5-1-1

24   J.C.W.

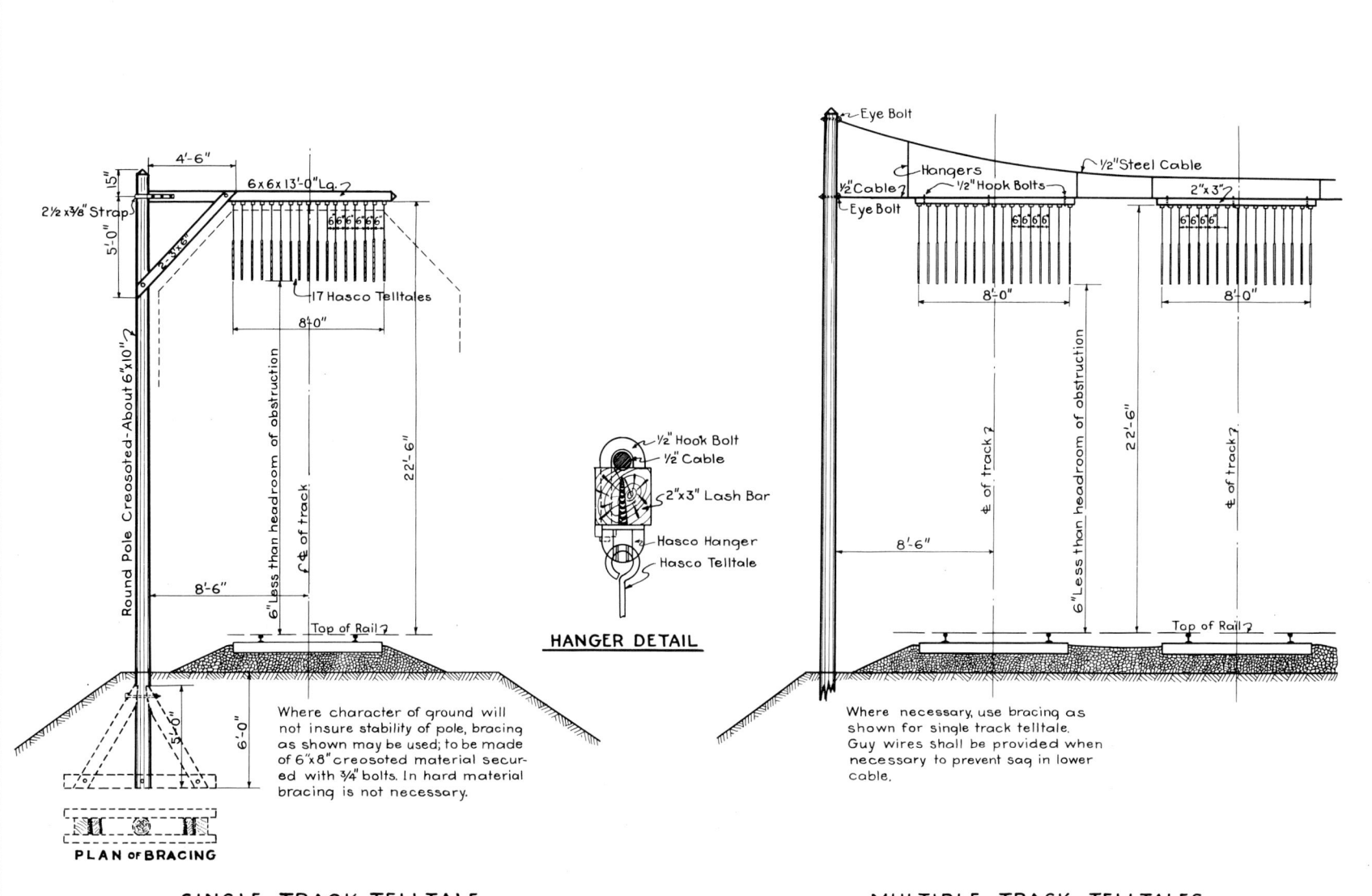

SINGLE TRACK TELLTALE

4'-6"

15"

2½ x ⅜" Strap

6 x 6 x 13'-0" Lg.

17 Hasco Telltales

8'-0"

Round Pole Creosoted-About 6"x10"

5'-0"

22'-6"

6" Less than headroom of obstruction

℄ of track

8'-6"

Top of Rail

3'-6"

6'-0"

Where character of ground will not insure stability of pole, bracing as shown may be used; to be made of 6"x8" creosoted material secured with ¾" bolts. In hard material bracing is not necessary.

PLAN of BRACING

HANGER DETAIL

½" Hook Bolt
½" Cable
2"x3" Lash Bar
Hasco Hanger
Hasco Telltale

MULTIPLE TRACK TELLTALES

Eye Bolt
Hangers
½" Steel Cable
½" Cable
½" Hook Bolts
Eye Bolt
2"x3"

8'-0"

8'-0"

22'-6"

6" Less than headroom of obstruction

℄ of track

℄ of track

℄ of track

8'-6"

Top of Rail

Where necessary, use bracing as shown for single track telltale. Guy wires shall be provided when necessary to prevent sag in lower cable.

Approved:
Vice President

Approved:
Gen. Manager.

Approved:
W.R.Bennett
Chief Engineer M. of W.

WABASH RAILWAY
STANDARD
OVERHEAD TELLTALE
OFFICE OF THE CHIEF ENGINEER M. OF W.
ADOPTED JUNE 2, 1931

PLAN Nº 3012

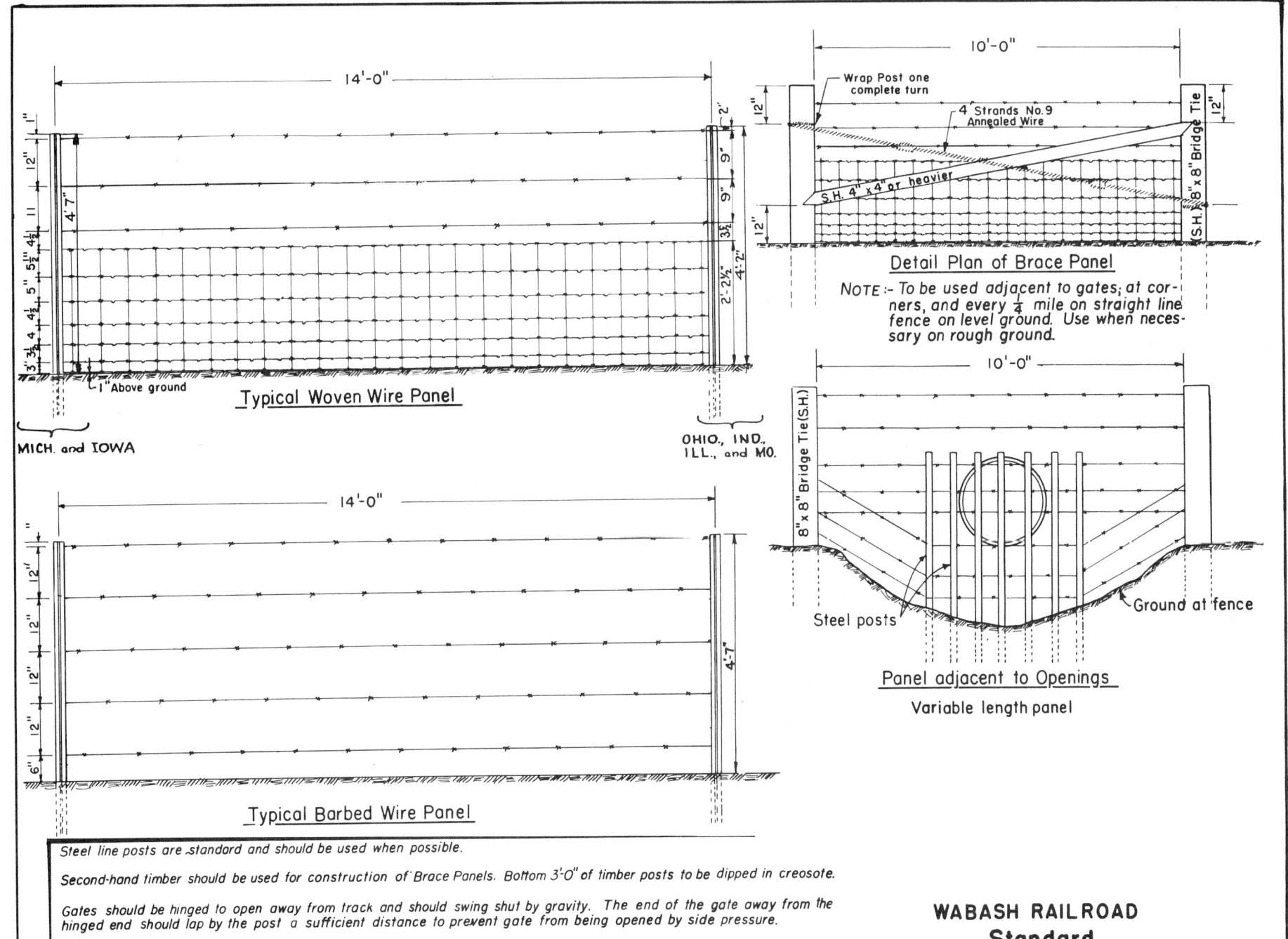

14'-0"

1" Above ground

MICH. and IOWA

OHIO., IND., ILL., and MO.

Typical Woven Wire Panel

10'-0"

Wrap Post one complete turn

4 Strands No.9 Annealed Wire

S.H. 4" x 4" or heavier

S.H. 8" x 8" Bridge Tie

Detail Plan of Brace Panel

NOTE:- To be used adjacent to gates; at corners, and every $\frac{1}{4}$ mile on straight line fence on level ground. Use when necessary on rough ground.

14'-0"

4'-7"

Typical Barbed Wire Panel

10'-0"

8" x 8" Bridge Tie(S.H.)

Steel posts

Ground at fence

Panel adjacent to Openings

Variable length panel

Steel line posts are standard and should be used when possible.

Second-hand timber should be used for construction of Brace Panels. Bottom 3'-0" of timber posts to be dipped in creosote.

Gates should be hinged to open away from track and should swing shut by gravity. The end of the gate away from the hinged end should lap by the post a sufficient distance to prevent gate from being opened by side pressure.

Longitudinal wires should be stretched uniformly tight and parallel; stays shall be straight and vertical. Wires shall be placed on the side of the post away from the track except that on curves of 1° or more the wires shall be placed on the outside of the curve

WABASH RAILROAD
Standard
RIGHT-OF-WAY FENCE
Office of Chief Engineer
April 18, 1946
J.C.W.

PLAN 3785
10-2-2

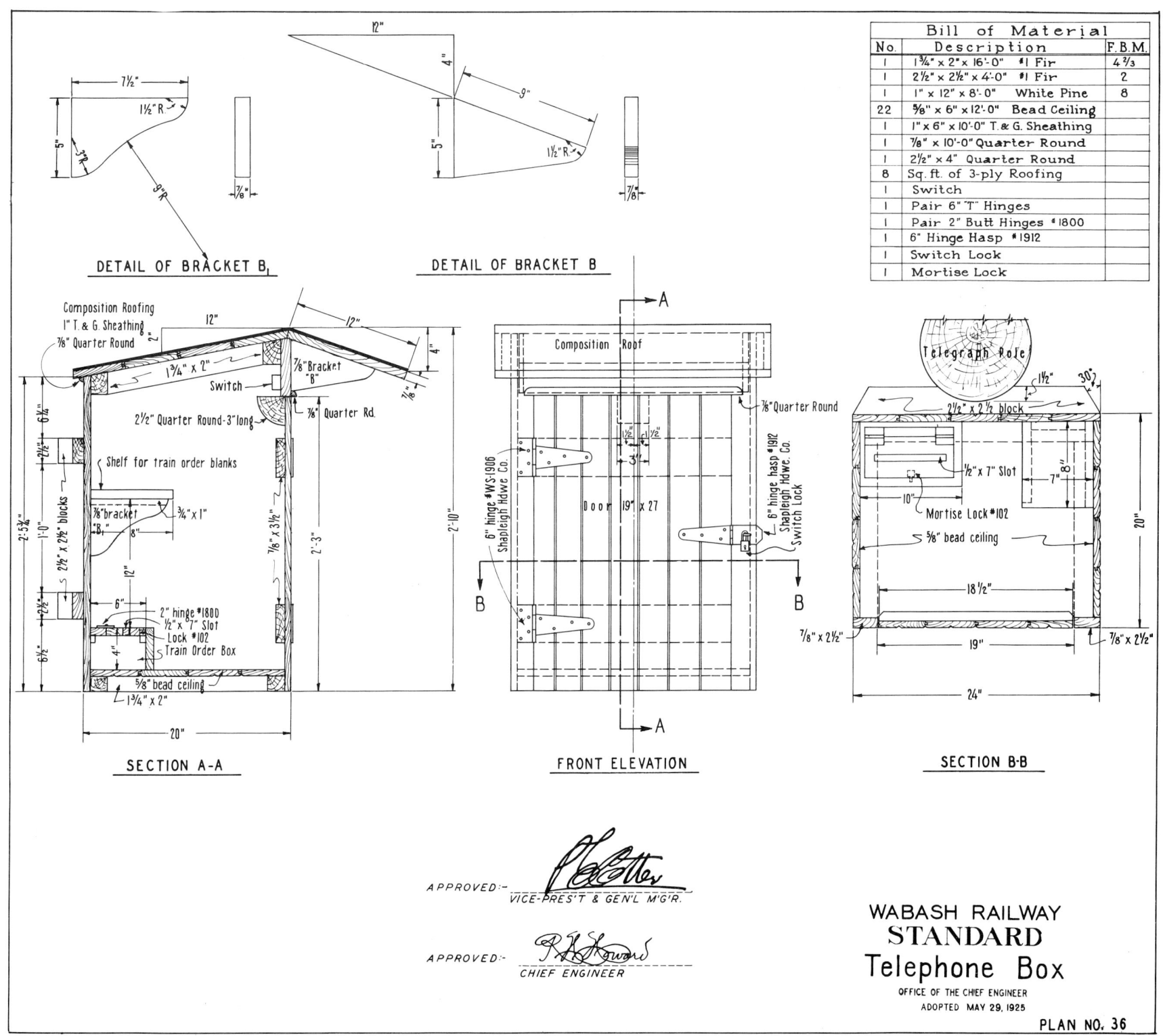

DETAIL OF BRACKET B₁

DETAIL OF BRACKET B

Bill of Material

No.	Description	F.B.M.
1	1¾" x 2" x 16'-0" #1 Fir	4⅔
1	2½" x 2½" x 4'-0" #1 Fir	2
1	1" x 12" x 8'-0" White Pine	8
22	⅝" x 6" x 12'-0" Bead Ceiling	
1	1" x 6" x 10'-0" T. & G. Sheathing	
1	⅞" x 10'-0" Quarter Round	
1	2½" x 4" Quarter Round	
8	Sq. ft. of 3-ply Roofing	
1	Switch	
1	Pair 6" "T" Hinges	
1	Pair 2" Butt Hinges #1800	
1	6" Hinge Hasp #1912	
1	Switch Lock	
1	Mortise Lock	

SECTION A-A

FRONT ELEVATION

SECTION B-B

APPROVED:-

VICE-PRES'T & GEN'L M'G'R.

APPROVED:-

CHIEF ENGINEER

WABASH RAILWAY
STANDARD
Telephone Box

OFFICE OF THE CHIEF ENGINEER
ADOPTED MAY 29, 1925

PLAN NO. 36

27

DRAINAGE:- Crossing installation must be so drained that all water will be diverted away from the roadbed.

BALLAST:- A minimum depth of 12" of rock, slag or washed gravel to be used below bottom of tie.

CROSSING TIES:- Crossing ties must be kept tamped to provide full bearing; spaced about 20" C. to C., using 7"x 9" Ties.

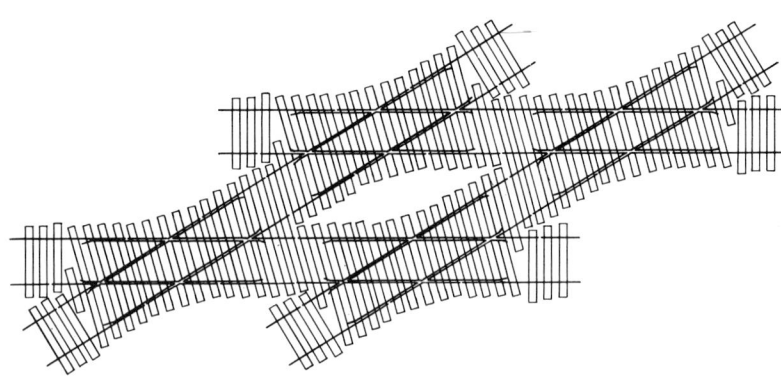

Angles 25°-0' to 35°-0'

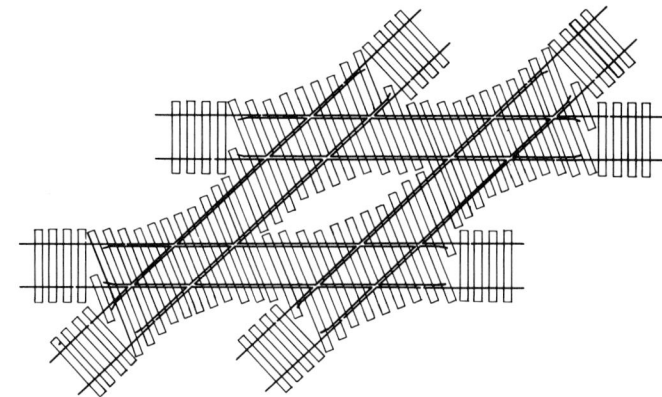

Angles 35°-0' to 50°-0'

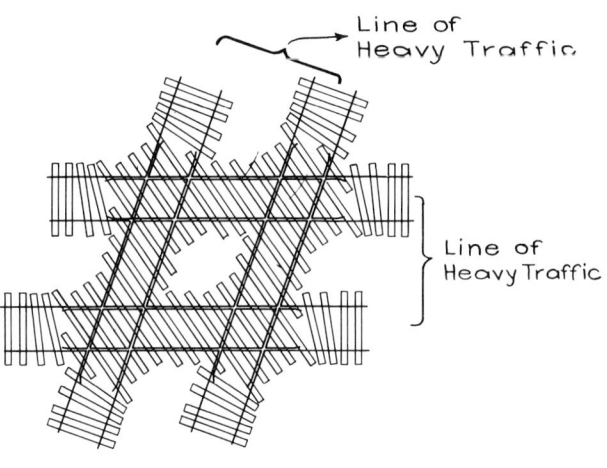

Line of Heavy Traffic

Line of Heavy Traffic

Type 1

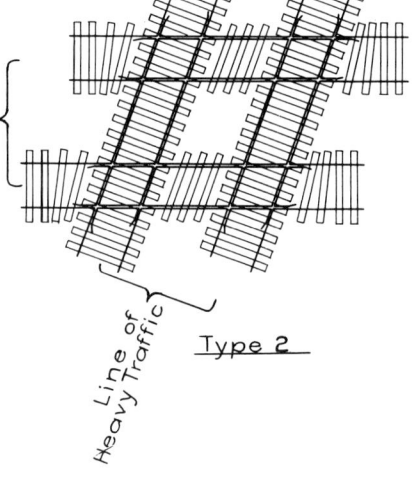

Line of Light Traffic

Line of Heavy Traffic

Type 2

Angles 50°-0' to 90°-0'

NOTE:- A tie layout plan shall be made to a convenient scale by Division Engineer for each Crossing, and the exact lengths and number of ties required determined from this plan.

NOTE:- Type 1 should be used unless traffic over one line is very light, then type 2 may be used.

Approved:
_J.E.C....._
Vice President.

Approved:
_G.B....._
Gen. Manager.

Approved:
_E.A....._
Chief Engineer

WADAOH RAILWAY
STANDARD
TIE LAYOUT FOR CROSSINGS
ANGLES 25°-0' TO 90°-0'
OFFICE OF THE CHIEF ENGINEER
ADOPTED 11-24-1931

3053

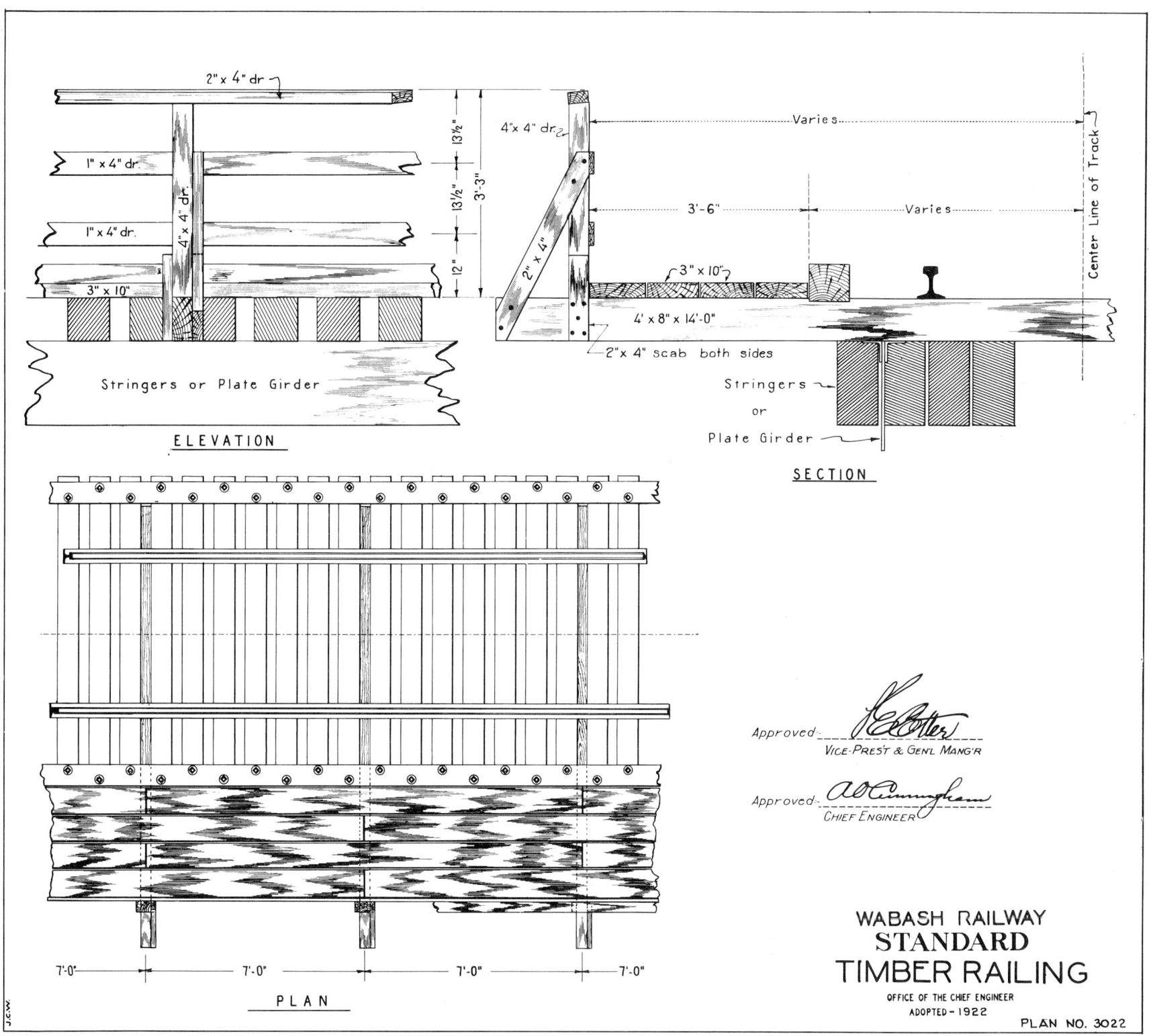

ELEVATION

SECTION

2" x 4" dr

1" x 4" dr.

1" x 4" dr.

4" x 4" dr.

3" x 10"

Stringers or Plate Girder

13½"
13½"
12"
3'-3"

4" x 4" dr.

2" x 4"

2" x 4" scab both sides

3" x 10"

4' x 8" x 14'-0"

Varies

Varies

3'-6"

Center Line of Track

Stringers
or
Plate Girder

PLAN

7'-0"   7'-0"   7'-0"   7'-0"

Approved: _____
VICE-PREST & GENL MANG'R

Approved: _____
CHIEF ENGINEER

WABASH RAILWAY
STANDARD
TIMBER RAILING
OFFICE OF THE CHIEF ENGINEER
ADOPTED - 1922
PLAN NO. 3022

J.C.W.

29

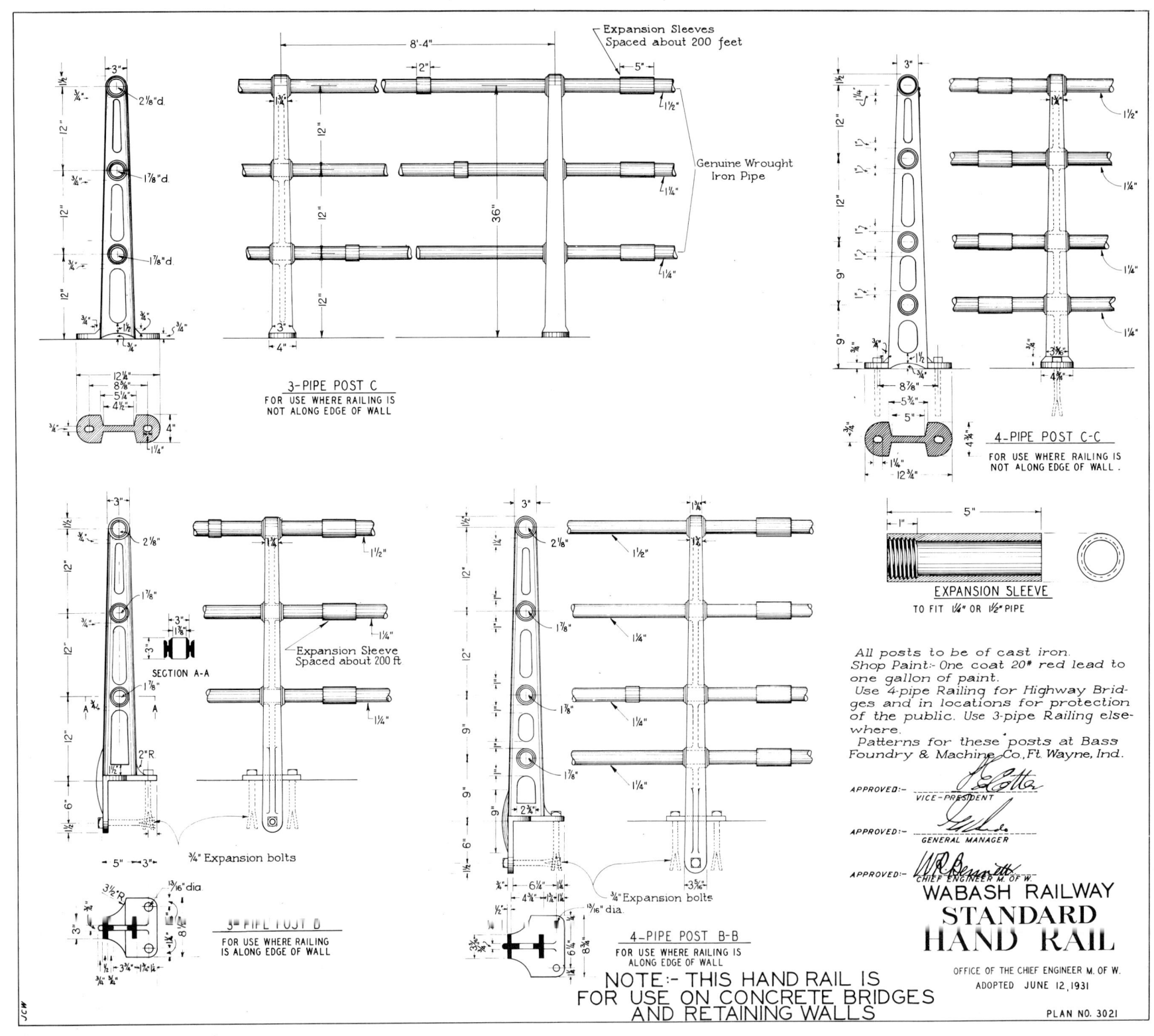

3-PIPE POST C
FOR USE WHERE RAILING IS
NOT ALONG EDGE OF WALL

4-PIPE POST C-C
FOR USE WHERE RAILING IS
NOT ALONG EDGE OF WALL.

SECTION A-A

3-PIPE POST B
FOR USE WHERE RAILING
IS ALONG EDGE OF WALL

4-PIPE POST B-B
FOR USE WHERE RAILING
IS ALONG EDGE OF WALL

Expansion Sleeves
Spaced about 200 feet

Genuine Wrought
Iron Pipe

Expansion Sleeve
Spaced about 200 ft

¾" Expansion bolts

¾" Expansion bolts

EXPANSION SLEEVE
TO FIT 1¼" OR 1½" PIPE

All posts to be of cast iron.
Shop Paint:- One coat 20# red lead to
one gallon of paint.
Use 4-pipe Railing for Highway Bridges and in locations for protection
of the public. Use 3-pipe Railing else-
where.
Patterns for these posts at Bass
Foundry & Machine Co, Ft. Wayne, Ind.

APPROVED:-
VICE-PRESIDENT

APPROVED:-
GENERAL MANAGER

APPROVED:-
CHIEF ENGINEER M. OF W.

WABASH RAILWAY
STANDARD
HAND RAIL

OFFICE OF THE CHIEF ENGINEER M. OF W.
ADOPTED JUNE 12, 1931

PLAN NO. 3021

NOTE:- THIS HAND RAIL IS
FOR USE ON CONCRETE BRIDGES
AND RETAINING WALLS

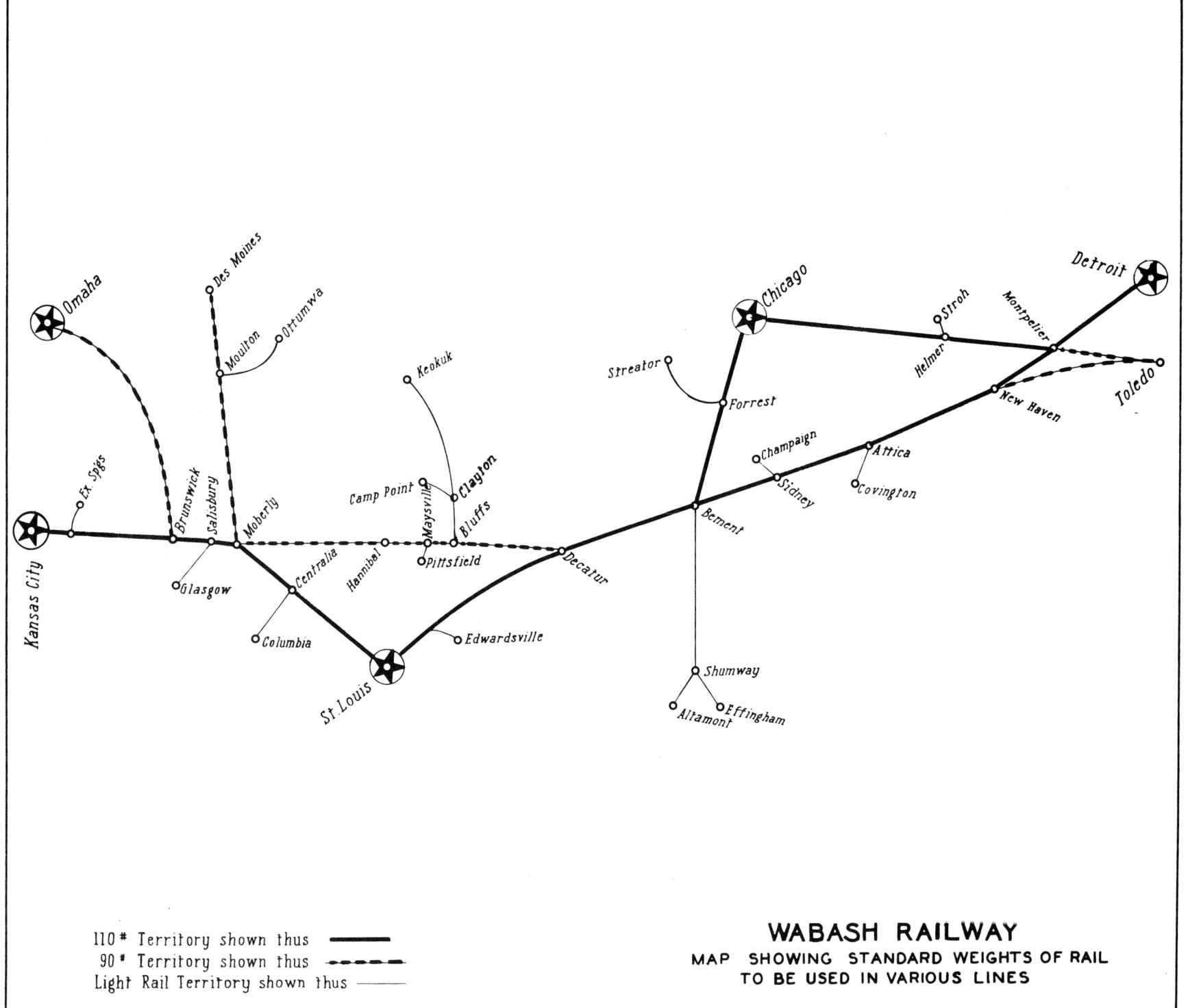

WABASH RAILWAY

MAP SHOWING STANDARD WEIGHTS OF RAIL
TO BE USED IN VARIOUS LINES

110 # Territory shown thus ——————
90 # Territory shown thus —-—-—-—
Light Rail Territory shown thus ——————

Omaha
Des Moines
Moulton
Ottumwa
Keokuk
Ex. Sp'gs
Brunswick
Salisbury
Moberly
Glasgow
Camp Point
Clayton
Maysville
Bluffs
Centralia
Hannibal
Pittsfield
Columbia
Edwardsville
Decatur
Kansas City
St. Louis
Streator
Forrest
Chicago
Champaign
Sidney
Attica
Covington
Bement
Stroh
Helmer
Montpelier
New Haven
Detroit
Toledo
Shumway
Altamont
Effingham

J.C.W.

3039-A

31

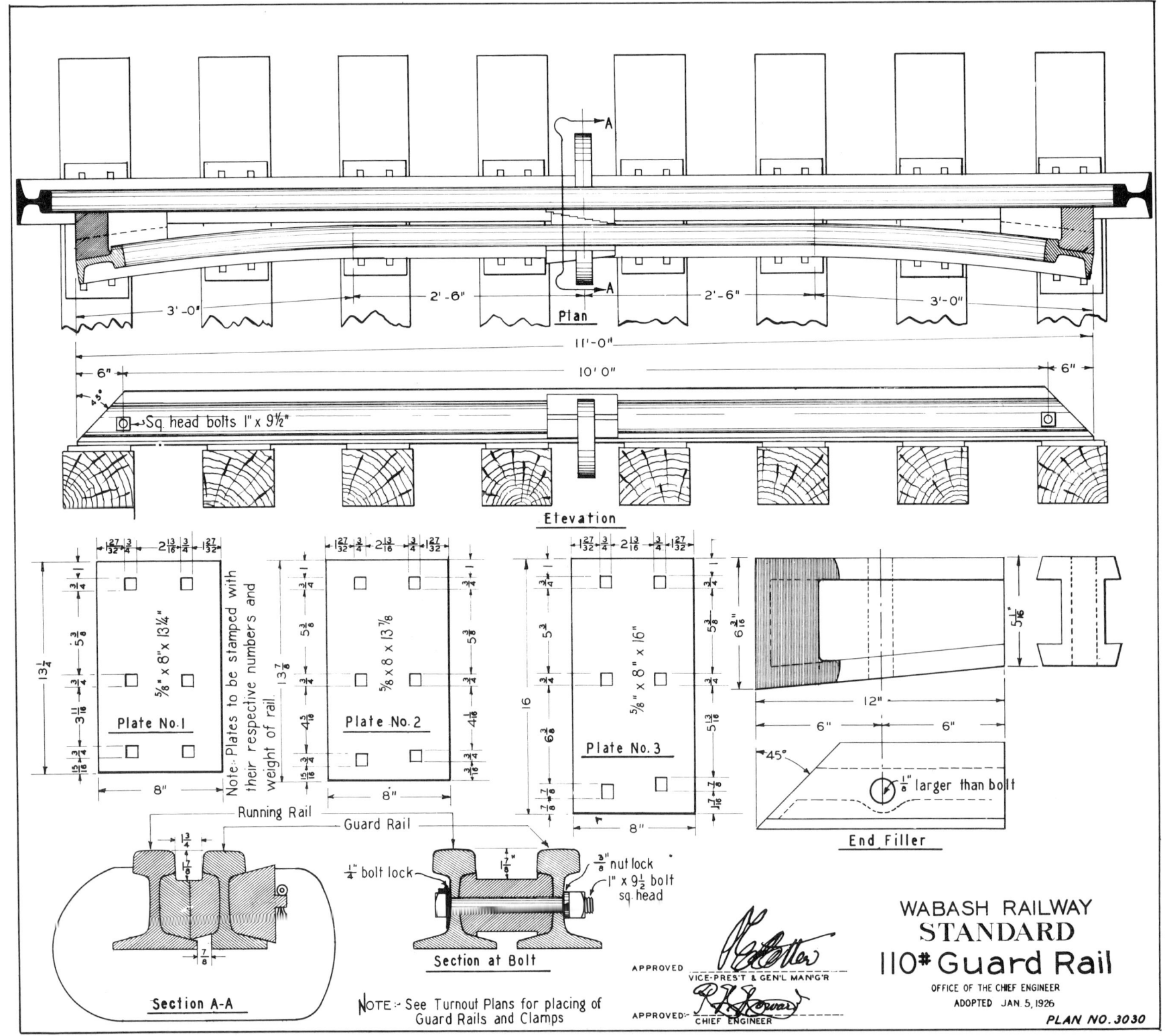

Plan

3'-0"   2'-6"   2'-6"   3'-0"

11'-0"

6"   10' 0"   6"

45°

Sq. head bolts 1" x 9½"

Elevation

Note:- Plates to be stamped with their respective numbers and weight of rail.

1²⁷⁄₃₂ ³⁄₄ 2¹³⁄₁₆ 1²⁷⁄₃₂

⅝" x 8" x 13¼"

13¼

8"

Plate No. 1

1²⁷⁄₃₂ ³⁄₄ 2¹³⁄₁₆ ³⁄₄ 1²⁷⁄₃₂

⅝ x 8 x 13⅞

13⅞

8"

Plate No. 2

1²⁷⁄₃₂ ³⁄₄ 2¹³⁄₁₆ ³⁄₄ 1²⁷⁄₃₂

⅝" x 8" x 16"

16

8"

Plate No. 3

6³⁄₁₆"

5¹⁄₁₆"

12"

6"   6"

45°

⅛" larger than bolt

End Filler

Running Rail

Guard Rail

1³⁄₄"

1⅞"

⁷⁄₈

Section A-A

¼" bolt lock

1⅞"

³⁄₈" nut lock

1" x 9½" bolt sq. head

Section at Bolt

NOTE:- See Turnout Plans for placing of Guard Rails and Clamps

APPROVED
VICE-PRES'T & GEN'L MAN'G'R

APPROVED:-
CHIEF ENGINEER

WABASH RAILWAY
STANDARD
110# Guard Rail

OFFICE OF THE CHIEF ENGINEER
ADOPTED JAN. 5, 1926

PLAN NO. 3030

32

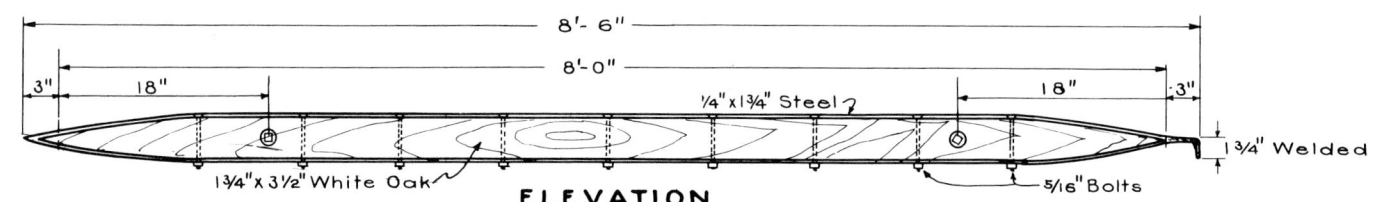

8'- 6"

8'-0"

3" 18" ¼"x1¾" Steel 18" 3"

1¾" Welded

1¾" x 3½" White Oak 5/16" Bolts

ELEVATION

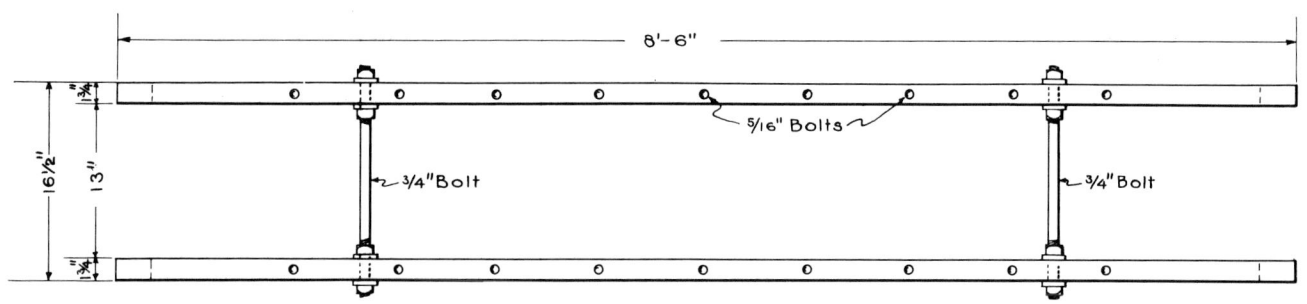

8'- 6"

16½" 13"

5/16" Bolts

¾" Bolt ¾" Bolt

PLAN

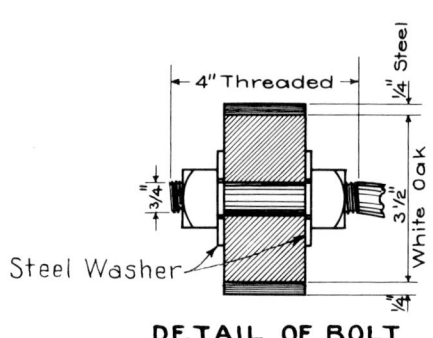

4" Threaded ¼ Steel

¾" 3½" White Oak

Steel Washer ¼

DETAIL OF BOLT

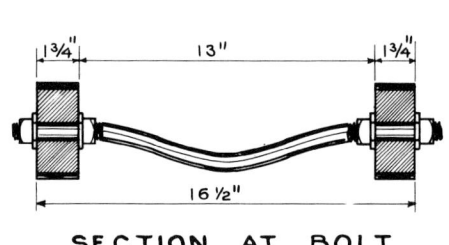

1¾" 13" 1¾"

16½"

SECTION AT BOLT

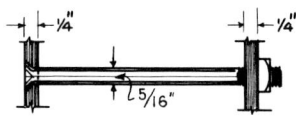

¼" ¼"

5/16"

DETAIL OF BOLT

SPECIFICATIONS

Side Rails to be of best quality well seasoned white oak dressed free from knots and other imperfections. Curved steel braces to have 4" thredded at both ends with nuts on both sides of each rail to form shoulders. Woodwork to have natural oil finish, Steel to be painted black.

Approved:

~Vice President~

Approved:

Gen. Manager

Approved:

Chief Engineer

WABASH RAILWAY
STANDARD
FREIGHT HOUSE SKIDS

OFFICE OF THE CHIEF ENGINEER
ADOPTED DEC. 11, 1917
REVISED 12-26-23 PLAN 3034

33

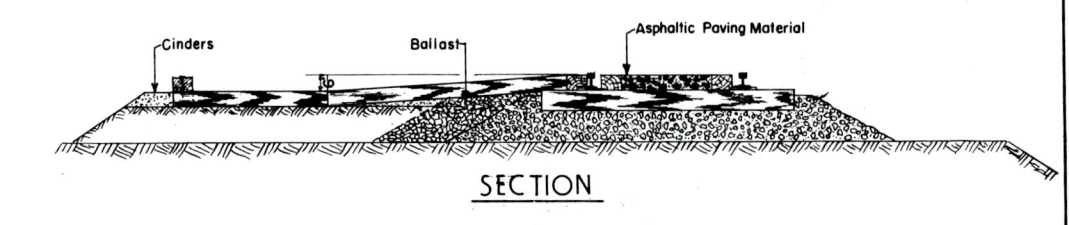

Cinders   Ballast   Asphaltic Paving Material

SECTION

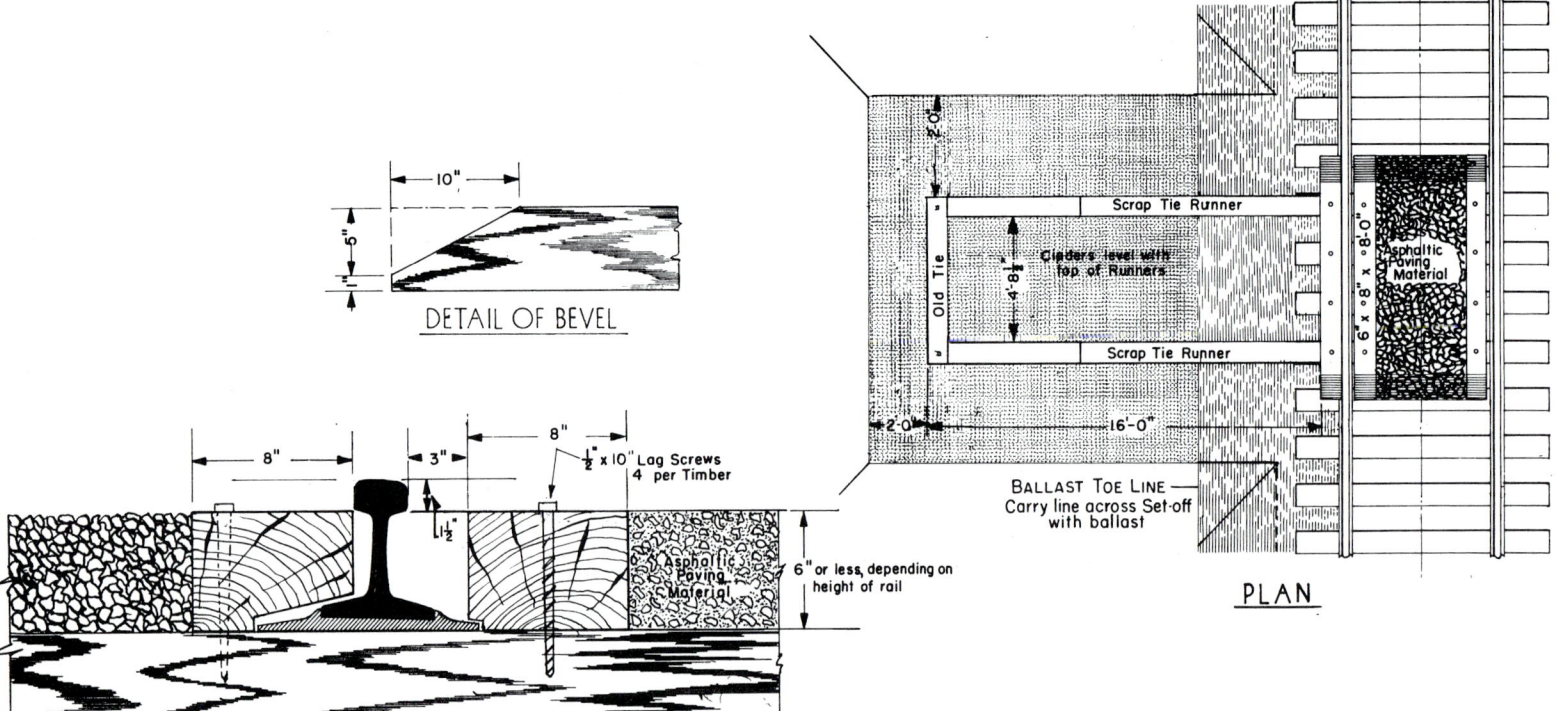

10"

DETAIL OF BEVEL

Scrap Tie Runner

Cinders level with top of Runners

Old Tie   4'-8"

Scrap Tie Runner

2'-0"   16'-0"

Asphaltic Paving Material

6" x 8" x 8'-0"

BALLAST TOE LINE
Carry line across Set-off
with ballast

PLAN

8"   3"   8"

½" x 10" Lag Screws
4 per Timber

1½"

Asphaltic Paving Material

6" or less, depending on
height of rail

SECTION A-A

Flangeway ties to be sized to place top 1½"
below top of rail. Ties to be dapped to clear
tie-plates and spikes.

WABASH RAILROAD
Standard
TRACK CAR SET-OFF
Office of the Chief Engineer
Apr. 24, 1947

3847

34

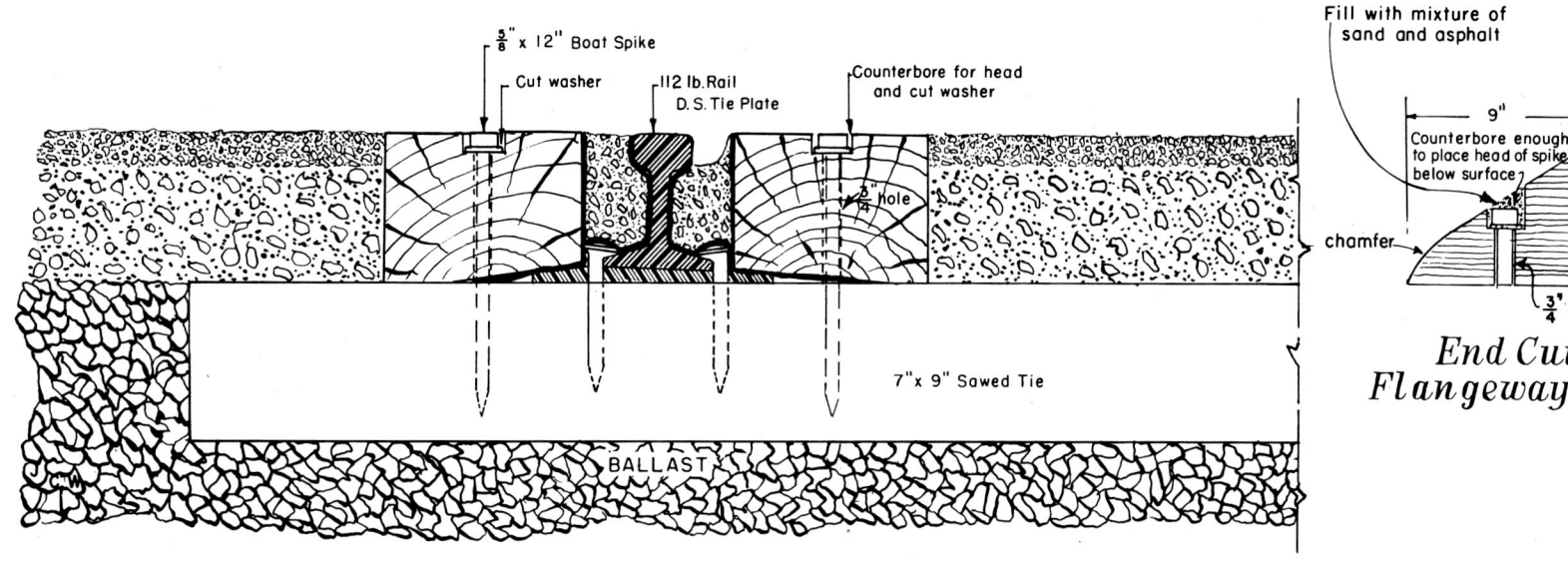

Half Section

$\frac{5}{8}$" x 12" Boat Spike

Cut washer

112 lb. Rail
D.S. Tie Plate

Counterbore for head
and cut washer

$\frac{3}{4}$" hole

7"x 9" Sawed Tie

BALLAST

Fill with mixture of
sand and asphalt

9"

Counterbore enough
to place head of spike
below surface

chamfer

$\frac{3}{4}$" hole

End Cut
Flangeway Ties

7"x 9" sawed ties shall be placed against back of spikes,
with corners chamfered enough to clear tie plates.

Flangeway ties shall be spiked to every second tie as
shown on plan.

Fill to within $1\frac{1}{2}$" from top of flangeway with clean ballast
and tamp. Sprinkle top of ballast course with asphalt. Apply
finish surface mixture and tamp to level with top of flangeway ties. Space between flangeway ties and rail to be
filled with surface mixture.

Surfaces shown by heavy lines to be painted with asphalt
before filling crossing.

All holes to be $\frac{3}{4}$" and prebored through flangeway ties
only.

Flangeway ties must be cut so ends will be even with
edge of track ties.

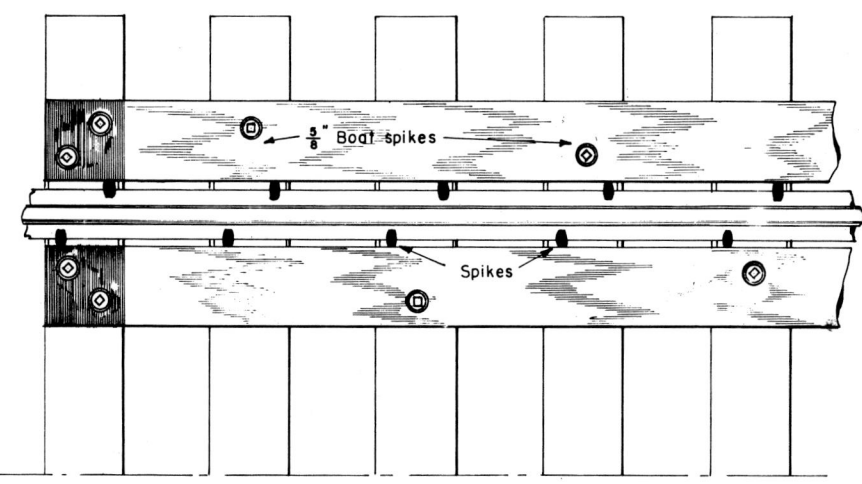

$\frac{5}{8}$" Boat spikes

Spikes

Part Plan

**Wabash Railway
Standard
Highway Crossing**

Office of the Chief Engineer
June 12, 1941

PLAN NO. 3438

35

2-3-2

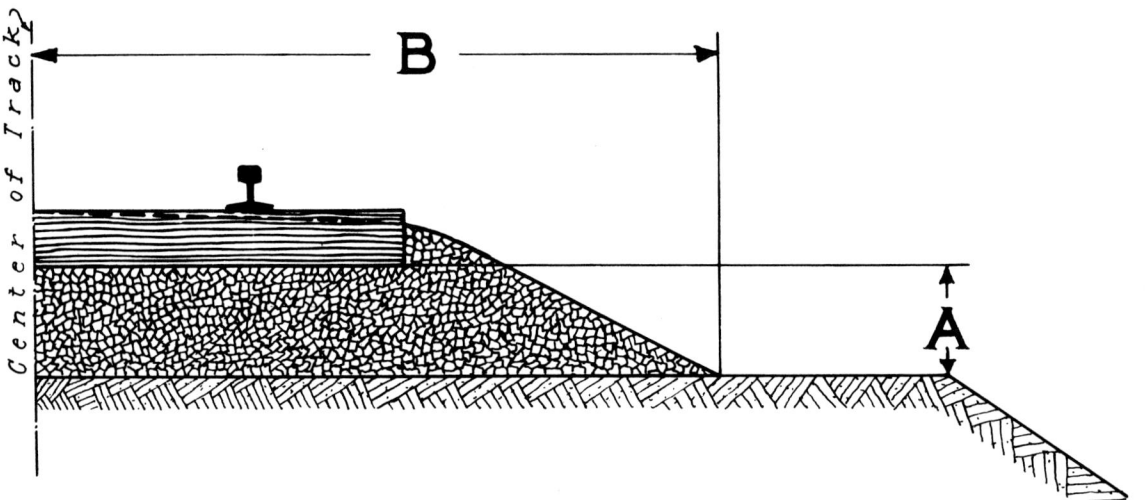

In establishing the toe line of Rock Ballast, the distance between the bottom of tie and top of roadbed, measured at the shoulder, will establish "B", the distance from center of track to toe line.

In order to maintain a uniform toe line over long stretches of track, the following table shall be used.

When "A" is	"B" is
6 in. or less	6 ft. 3 in.
7 in. to 12 in.	6 ft. 9 in.
Over 12 in.	7 ft. 3 in.

Change in location of toe line shall be made at bridges, station grounds, curves or other locations where it will not be noticeable.

WABASH RAILWAY
Location of
Rock Ballast Toe Line
OFFICE OF THE CHIEF ENGINEER M. of W.
MAY 12, 1931

1791-A

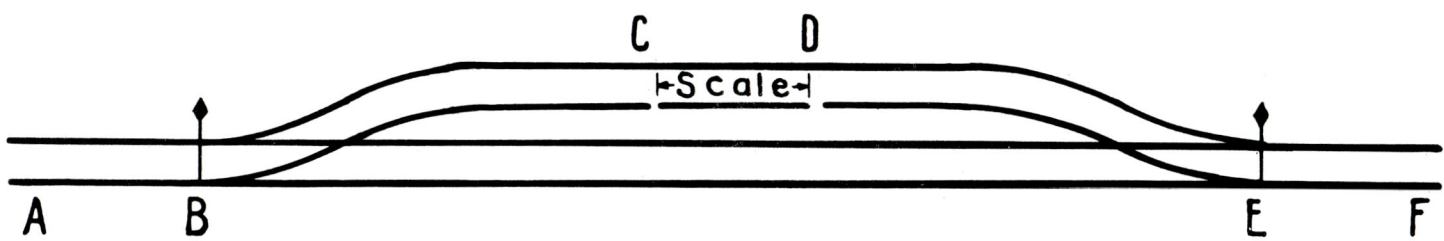

C   D

Scale

A   B   E   F

If Train is moving from A toward F, proper procedure is for Train to take path A-B-E-F, until last car has cleared point E, then back up over Scale C-D, returning to A-F via B. This method obviates one-half the wear which results from taking path A-B-C-D-E-F and then backing up over Scale C-D.

If Train is moving from F toward A, proper procedure is for Train to take path F-E-B-A, until last car has cleared point B, then back up over Scale C-D, returning to A-F via E.

NOTE:
For movement over 4 section Scales, see instructions "Form 950"

Approved: _____
Vice President.

Approved: _____
General Manager

Approved: _____
Chief Engineer M. of W.

WABASH RAILWAY
STANDARD
MOVEMENT OVER
2-SECTION SCALES
OFFICE OF THE CHIEF ENGINEER M OF W
ADOPTED

PLAN Nº 1890

37

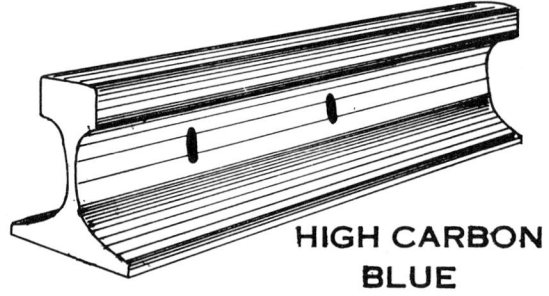

HIGH CARBON
BLUE

Use only on Curves unless otherwise instructed.

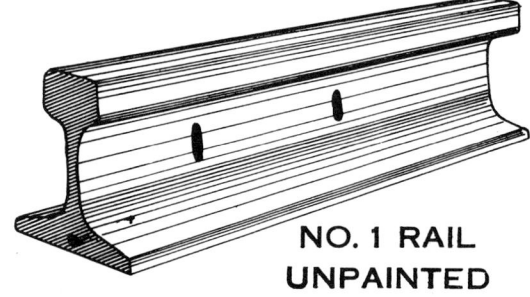

NO. 1 RAIL
UNPAINTED

For general usage, as has been done heretofore.

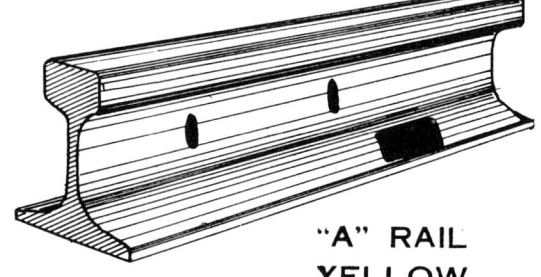

"A" RAIL
YELLOW

Use on tangent track only, preferably at places of slow speed.

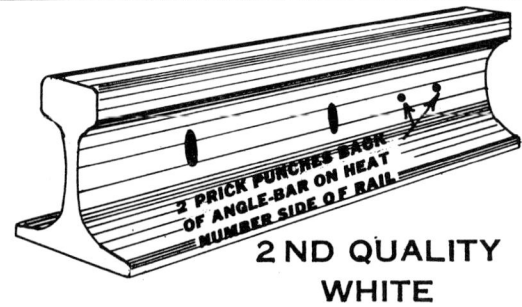

2 PRICK PUNCHES BACK OF ANGLE-BAR ON HEAT NUMBER SIDE OF RAIL

2ND QUALITY
WHITE

Use in Yards, Passing Tracks, Turnouts, (back of Frog) etc.

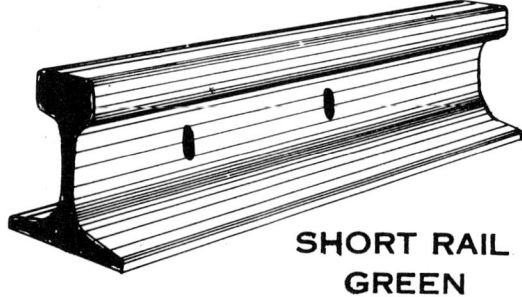

SHORT RAIL
GREEN

Use in making connections in Yards and Turnouts, and Curve Compensation.

3 PRICK PUNCHES BACK OF ANGLE-BAR ON HEAT NUMBER SIDE OF RAIL

SPECIAL RAIL
BROWN

Use only as personally directed by Asst. Chief Engineer.

NOTE:- PRICK PUNCHES ARE ON ONE END OF RAIL ONLY

REVISIONS		
DATE	BY	DESCRIPTION

J.C.W.

WARNING! Special rails contain interior defects and should never be placed in high speed main or other important tracks

"A" RAIL is rail from top of ingot in a heat where no defects were developed by tests

Rail painted in two colors to be used only as directed by Asst. Chief Engineer

WABASH RAILWAY
ST. LOUIS, MO.
STANDARD
90 LB. RAIL CLASSIFICATION

OFFICE OF CHIEF ENGINEER
NO SCALE   MAY 4, 1925
APPROVED   APPROVED

CHIEF ENGINEER   V. P. & GEN'L MANGR.
PLAN NO. 35

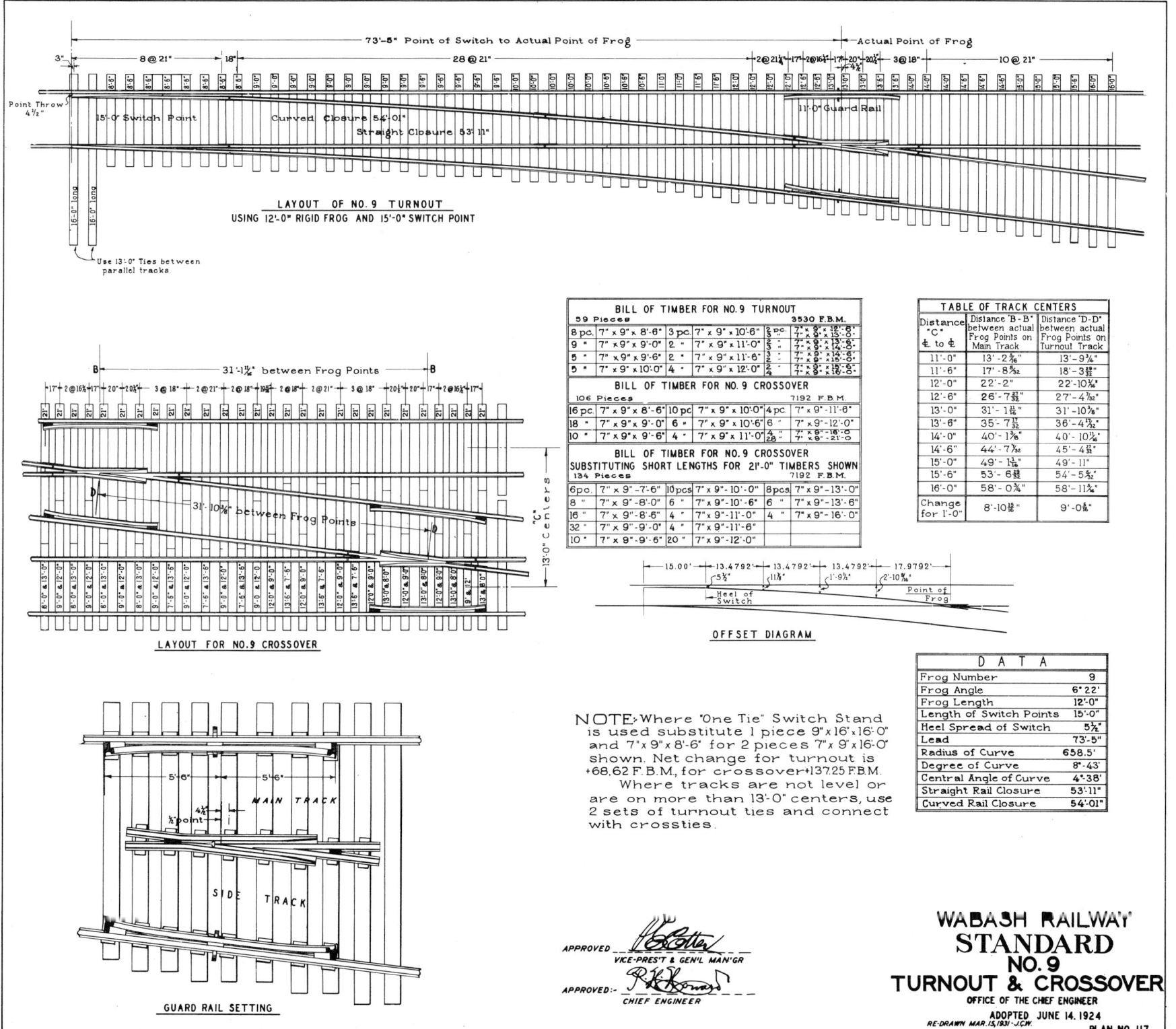

LAYOUT OF NO. 9 TURNOUT
USING 12'-0" RIGID FROG AND 15'-0" SWITCH POINT

73'-5" Point of Switch to Actual Point of Frog

Actual Point of Frog

Point Throw 4½"

15'-0" Switch Point

Curved Closure 54'-0½"
Straight Closure 53'-11"

11'-0" Guard Rail

16'-0" long

Use 13'-0" Ties between parallel tracks

LAYOUT FOR NO.9 CROSSOVER

31'-1½" between Frog Points

31'-10⅜" between Frog Points

13'-0" Centers

GUARD RAIL SETTING

MAIN TRACK
SIDE TRACK

5'-6"   5'-6"
4½" point
½" point

OFFSET DIAGRAM

15.00'   13.4792'   13.4792'   13.4792'   17.9792'

Heel of Switch   Point of Frog

BILL OF TIMBER FOR NO. 9 TURNOUT					
59 Pieces				3530 F.B.M.	
8 pc.	7" x 9" x 8'-6"	3 pc.	7" x 9" x 10'-6"	2	7" x 9" x 12'-6"
9 "	7" x 9" x 9'-0"	2	7" x 9" x 11'-0"	5	7" x 9" x 13'-0"
5 "	7" x 9" x 9'-6"	2	7" x 9" x 11'-6"	1	7" x 9" x 14'-6"
5 "	7" x 9" x 10'-0"	4	7" x 9" x 12'-0"	2	7" x 9" x 15'-6"
				2	7" x 9" x 16'-0"

BILL OF TIMBER FOR NO. 9 CROSSOVER					
106 Pieces				7192 F.B.M.	
16 pc.	7" x 9" x 8'-6"	10 pc	7" x 9" x 10'-0"	4 pc.	7" x 9" x 12'-0"
18 "	7" x 9" x 9'-0"	6 "	7" x 9" x 10'-6"		
10 "	7" x 9" x 9'-6"	4 "	7" x 9" x 11'-0"	4	7" x 9" x 16'-0"
				28	7" x 9" x 21'-0"

BILL OF TIMBER FOR NO. 9 CROSSOVER					
SUBSTITUTING SHORT LENGTHS FOR 21'-0" TIMBERS SHOWN					
134 Pieces				7192 F.B.M.	
6 pc.	7" x 9" x 7'-6"	10 pcs	7" x 9" x 10'-0"	8 pcs	7" x 9" x 13'-0"
8 "	7" x 9" x 8'-0"	6 "	7" x 9" x 10'-6"	6 "	7" x 9" x 13'-6"
16 "	7" x 9" x 8'-6"	4 "	7" x 9" x 11'-0"	4 "	7" x 9" x 16'-0"
32 "	7" x 9" x 9'-0"	4 "	7" x 9" x 11'-6"		
10 "	7" x 9" x 9'-6"	20 "	7" x 9" x 12'-0"		

TABLE OF TRACK CENTERS		
Distance "C" ℄ to ℄	Distance 'B-B' between actual Frog Points on Main Track	Distance 'D-D' between actual Frog Points on Turnout Track
11'-0"	13'-2 9/16"	13'-9¾"
11'-6"	17'-8 5/32"	18'-3 21/32"
12'-0"	22'-2"	22'-10¾"
12'-6"	26'-7 47/32"	27'-4 3/32"
13'-0"	31'-1 11/16"	31'-10⅜"
13'-6"	35'-7 11/32"	36'-4 11/32"
14'-0"	40'-1 ⅞"	40'-10⅛"
14'-6"	44'-7 7/32"	45'-4 21/32"
15'-0"	49'-1 1/16"	49'-11"
15'-6"	53'-6 21/32"	54'-5 5/32"
16'-0"	58'-0 ¾"	58'-11 5/32"
Change for 1'-0"	8'-10 9/16"	9'-0 5/16"

DATA	
Frog Number	9
Frog Angle	6° 22'
Frog Length	12'-0"
Length of Switch Points	15'-0"
Heel Spread of Switch	5½"
Lead	73'-5"
Radius of Curve	658.5'
Degree of Curve	8°-43'
Central Angle of Curve	4°-38'
Straight Rail Closure	53'-11"
Curved Rail Closure	54'-0½"

NOTE:- Where "One Tie" Switch Stand is used substitute 1 piece 9" x 16" x 16'-0" and 7" x 9" x 8'-6" for 2 pieces 7" x 9" x 16'-0" shown. Net change for turnout is +68.62 F.B.M. for crossover +137.25 F.B.M.
   Where tracks are not level or are on more than 13'-0" centers, use 2 sets of turnout ties and connect with crossties.

APPROVED _____
VICE-PREST & GEN'L MAN'GR

APPROVED :- _____
CHIEF ENGINEER

WABASH RAILWAY
STANDARD
NO. 9
TURNOUT & CROSSOVER
OFFICE OF THE CHIEF ENGINEER
ADOPTED JUNE 14, 1924
RE-DRAWN MAR. 13, 1931 · J.C.W.
PLAN NO. 117

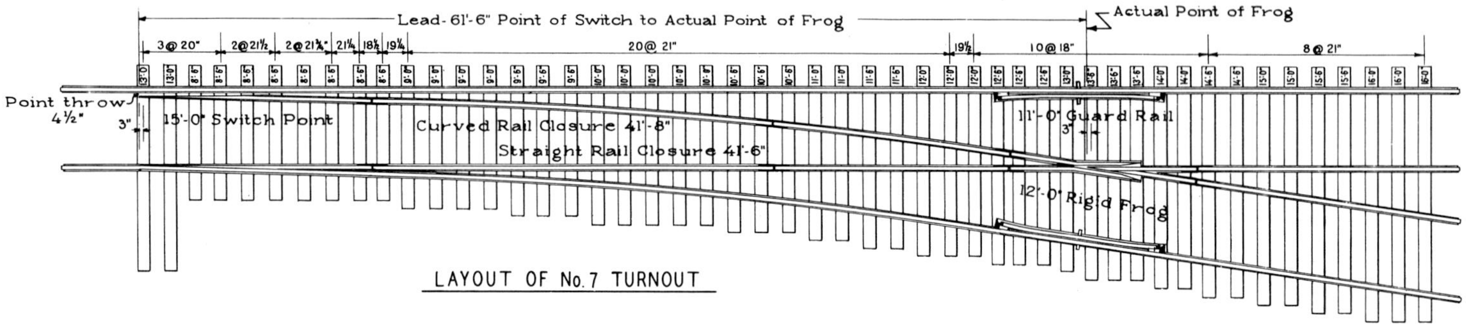
Lead-61'-6" Point of Switch to Actual Point of Frog
Actual Point of Frog
3@20"
2@21½
2@21¾
21¼
18¾
19¼
20@21"
19½
10@18"
8@21"
Point throw 4½"
3"
15'-0" Switch Point
Curved Rail Closure 41'-8"
Straight Rail Closure 41'-6"
11'-0" Guard Rail
12'-0" Rigid Frog

LAYOUT OF No. 7 TURNOUT

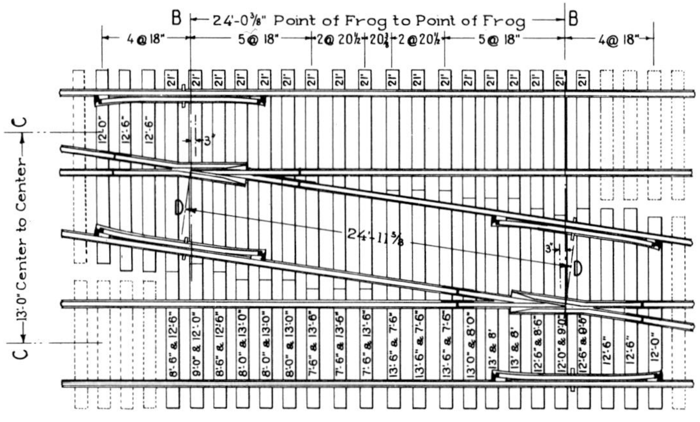
B
24'-0⅜" Point of Frog to Point of Frog
B
4@18"
5@18"
2@20½
20½
2@20½
5@18"
4@18"
C
13'-0" Center to Center
C
D
24'-11⅝
D
3"

LAYOUT OF No. 7 CROSS-OVER

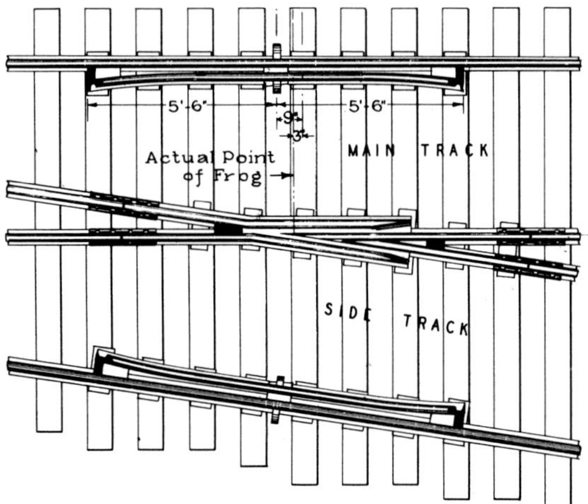
5'-6"
5'-6"
9"
3"
Actual Point of Frog
MAIN TRACK
SIDE TRACK

GUARD RAIL SETTING

BILL OF TIMBER FOR NO. 7 TURNOUT — 50 PIECES — 3034.5 F.B.M.							
8 pcs	7" x 9" x 8'-6"	3 pcs	7" x 9" x 10'-6"	3 pcs	7" x 9" x 12'-6"	2 pcs	7" x 9" x 14'-6"
4 pcs	7" x 9" x 9'-0"	2 pcs	7" x 9" x 11'-0"	3 pcs	7" x 9" x 13'-0"	2 pcs	7" x 9" x 15'-0"
3 pcs	7" x 9" x 9'-6"	2 pcs	7" x 9" x 11'-6"	3 pcs	7" x 9" x 13'-6"	2 pcs	7" x 9" x 15'-6"
5 pcs	7" x 9" x 10'-0"	3 pcs	7" x 9" x 12'-0"	2 pcs	7" x 9" x 14'-0"	3 pcs	7" x 9" x 16'-0"

BILL OF TIMBER FOR NO. 7 CROSS-OVER — 88 PIECES — 5744 F.B.M.							
16pcs	7" x 9" x 8'-6"	6pcs	7" x 9" x 10'-6"	4pcs	7" x 9" x 12'-6"		
8pcs	7" x 9" x 9'-0"	4pcs	7" x 9" x 11'-0"	4pcs	7" x 9" x 13'-0"		
6pcs	7" x 9" x 9'-6"	4pcs	7" x 9" x 11'-6"	18pcs	7" x 9" x 21'-0"		
10pcs	7" x 9" x 10'-0"	8pcs	7" x 9" x 12'-0"				

BILL OF TIMBER FOR NO. 7 CROSS OVER SUBSTITUTING SHORT LENGTHS FOR 21'-0" TIMBERS SHOWN — 106 PIECES — 5744 F.B.M.							
6pcs	7" x 9" x 7'-6"	6pcs	7" x 9" x 9'-6"	4pcs	7" x 9" x 11'-6"	6 pcs	7" x 9" x 13'-6"
6pcs	7" x 9" x 8'-0"	10pcs	7" x 9" x 10'-0"	10pcs	7" x 9" x 12'-0"		
20pcs	7" x 9" x 8'-6"	6pcs	7" x 9" x 10'-6"	8pcs	7" x 9" x 12'-6"		
10pcs	7" x 9" x 9'-0"	4pcs	7" x 9" x 11'-0"	10pcs	7" x 9" x 13'-0"		

DATA	
Frog Number	7
Frog Angle	8°-10'-16"
Frog Length	12'-0"
Length of Switch Points	15'-0"
Heel Spread of Switch	5½"
Lead	61'-6"
Radius of Curve	365.09'
Degree of Curve	15°-45'
Central Angle of Curve	6°-30'
Straight Rail Closure	41'-6"
Curved Rail Closure	41'-8"

TABLE OF TRACK CENTERS

Distance C ℄ to ℄	Distance B-B between actual frog points on Main Track	Distance D-D between actual frog points on Turnout Track
11'-0"	10'-10¼"	10'-10¾"
11'-6"	13'-7⅛"	14'-5"
12'-0"	17'-0⅞"	17'-11⅛"
12'-6"	20'-6⅝"	21'-5⅞"
13'-0"	24'-0⅜	24'-11⅝"
13'-6"	27'-6¼"	28'-5¾"
14'-0"	31'-0"	32'-0"
14'-6"	34'-5¾"	35'-6¼"
15'-0"	37'-11⅝"	39'-0½"
15'-6"	41'-5⅜"	42'-6⅝"
16'-0"	44'-11⅝"	46'-0⅞"
For change of 1 foot	6'-11⅝"	7'-0½"
	6.9687'	7.0417'

Where "One Tie" Switch Stand is used, substitute 1 piece 9" x 16" x 16'-0" and 1 piece 7" x 9" x 8'-6" for 2 pieces 7" x 9" x 13'-0" shown. Net change for turnout +100.12 F.B.M., for Cross-over +200.25 F.B.M.

Where tracks are not level or are on more than 13'-0" centers use 2 sets of turnout ties and connect with cross-ties.

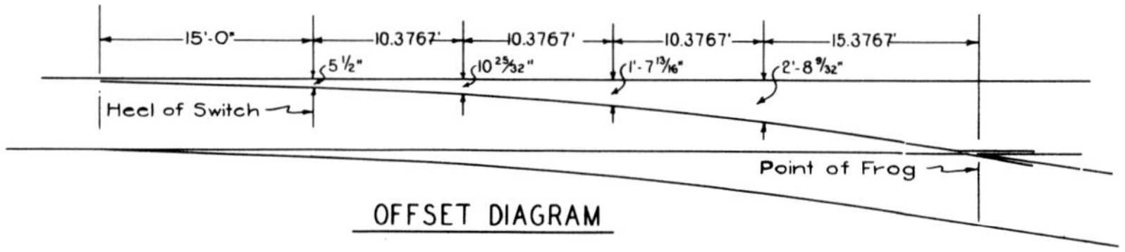
15'-0"
10.3767'
10.3767'
10.3767'
15.3767'
5½"
10 23/32"
1'-7 13/16"
2'-8 9/32"
Heel of Switch
Point of Frog

OFFSET DIAGRAM

APPROVED:- VICE-PRES'T & GEN'L MAN'GR

APPROVED:- CHIEF ENGINEER

WABASH RAILWAY
STANDARD
No. 7 TURNOUT & CROSS-OVER
12'-0" RIGID FROG 15'-0" SWITCH POINT

OFFICE OF THE CHIEF ENGINEER

ADOPTED JUNE 30, 1924

J.C.W. RE-DRAWN 3-20-31 PLAN NO. 118

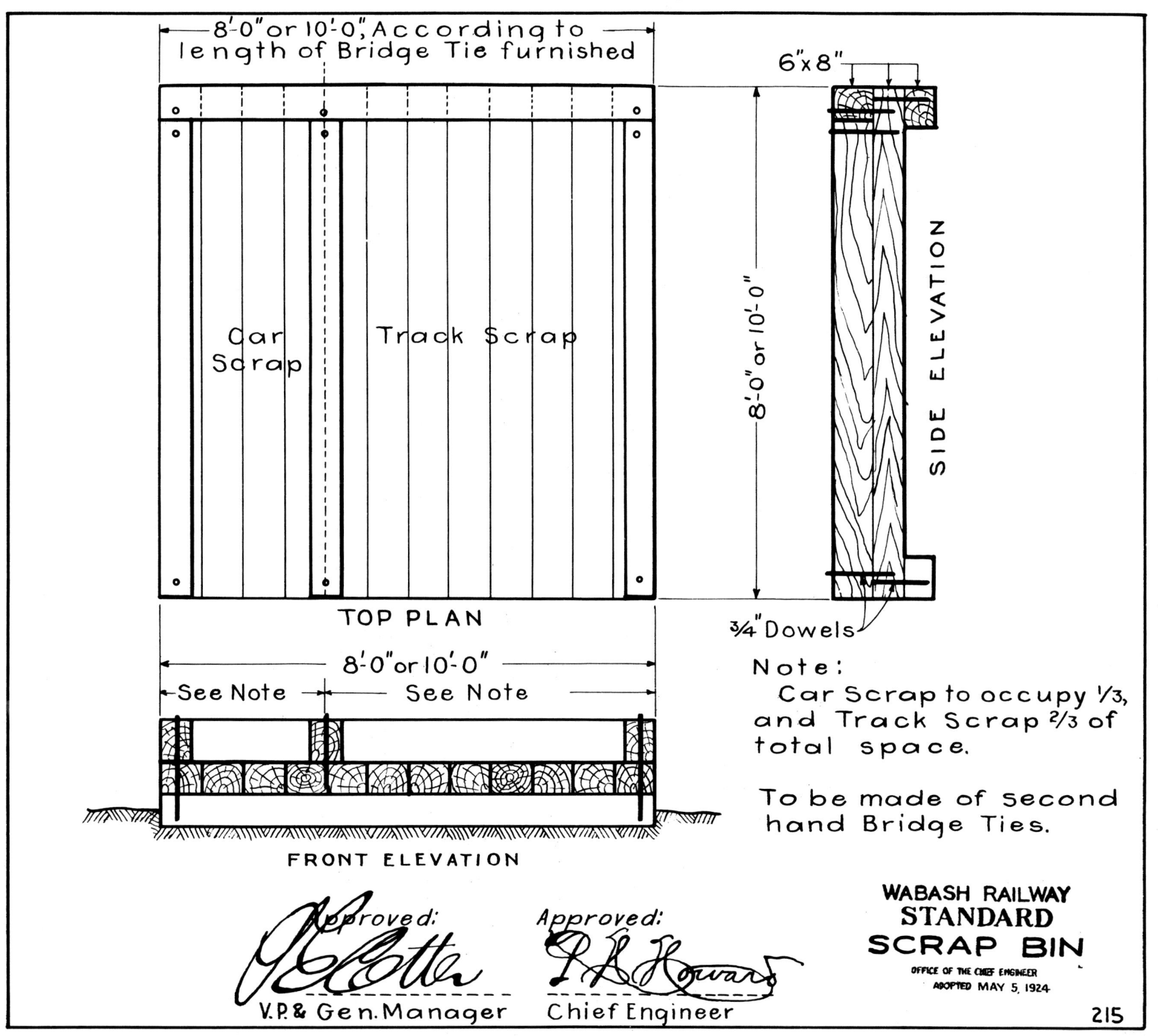

8'-0" or 10'-0" According to length of Bridge Tie furnished

6"x 8"

8'-0" or 10'-0"

Car Scrap

Track Scrap

TOP PLAN

SIDE ELEVATION

¾" Dowels

8'-0" or 10'-0"

See Note   See Note

FRONT ELEVATION

Note:
  Car Scrap to occupy ⅓, and Track Scrap ⅔ of total space.

To be made of second hand Bridge Ties.

Approved:
GG Cotter
V.P. & Gen. Manager

Approved:
P B Howard
Chief Engineer

WABASH RAILWAY
STANDARD
SCRAP BIN
OFFICE OF THE CHIEF ENGINEER
ADOPTED MAY 5, 1924

215

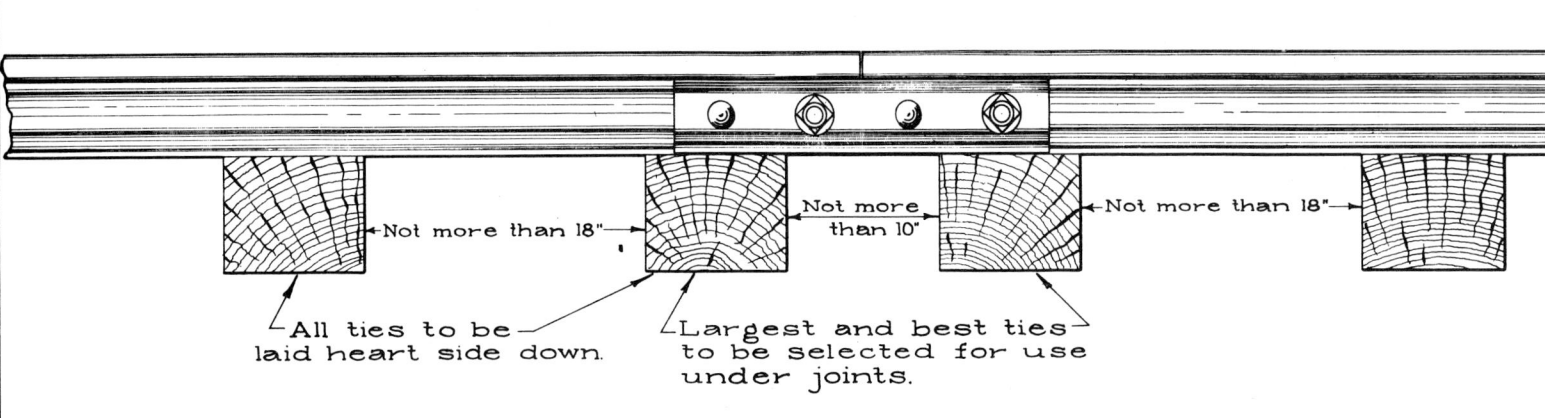

Not more than 18" | Not more than 10" | Not more than 18"

All ties to be laid heart side down.

Largest and best ties to be selected for use under joints.

NUMBER OF TIES PER RAIL LENGTH AND PER MILE						
Class of Track	39' Rail		33' Rail		30' Rail	
	Per Rail	Per Mile	Per Rail	Per Mile	Per Rail	Per Mile
Main Line - Main Track	24	3250	20	3200	18	3168
Sidings and Passing Tracks	22	2979	18	2880	16	2816
Branch Lines - Main Track	22	2979	18	2880	16	2816
Sidings and Passing Tracks	20	2708	16	2560	14	2464
Yards & Term. Heavy Duty Tk	22	2979	18	2880	16	2816
" " " Light " "	20	2708	16	2560	14	2464

APPROVED :- _____
VICE-PRES'T & GEN'L M'G'R

APPROVED _____
CHIEF ENGINEER

WABASH RAILWAY
STANDARD
FOR TIE RENEWALS

OFFICE OF THE CHIEF ENGINEER
ADOPTED FEB. 3, 1928

Re-drawn Apr. 14, 1931 - J.C.W.

PLAN NO. 230

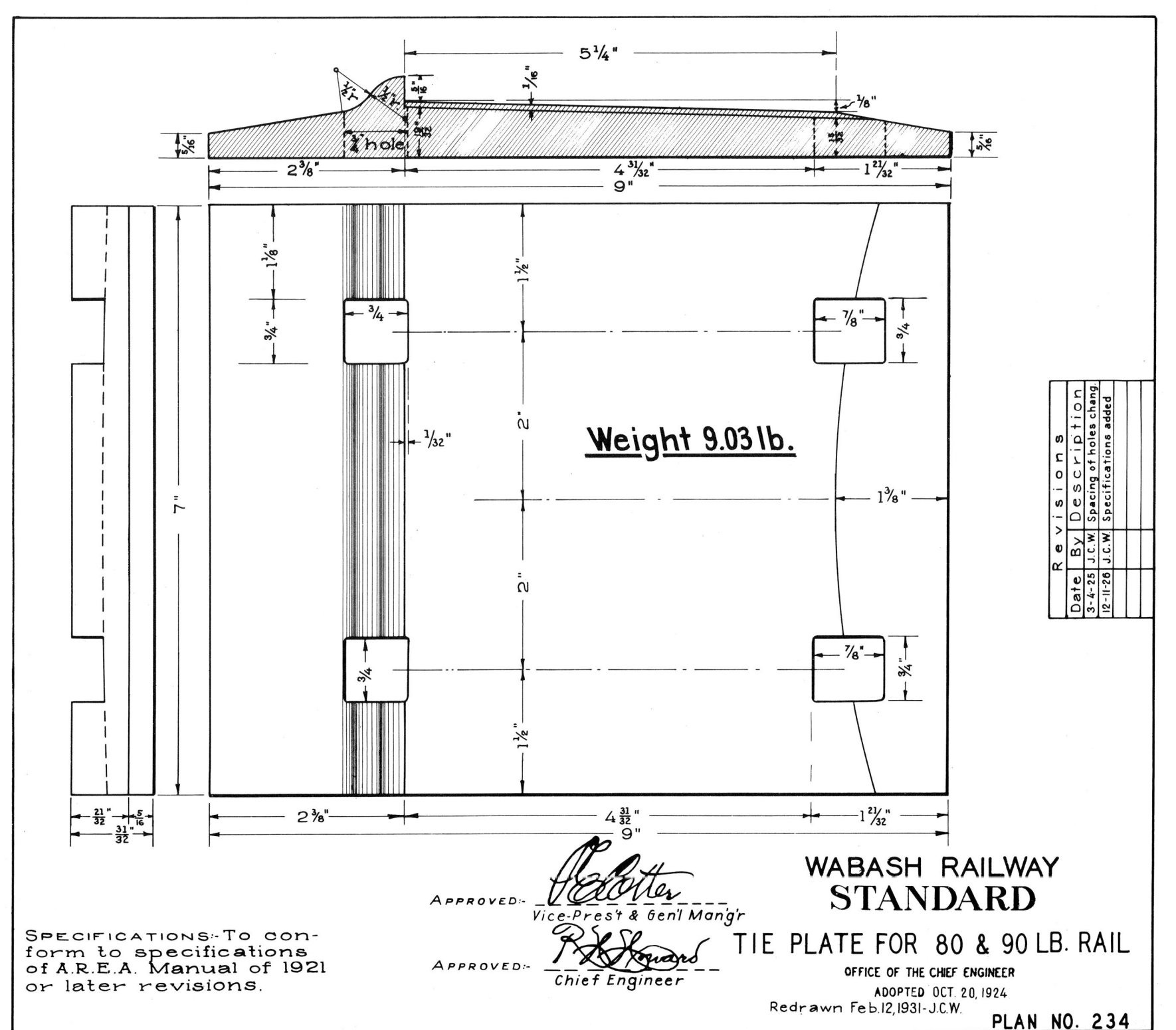

Weight 9.03 lb.

SPECIFICATIONS:- To con-
form to specifications
of A.R.E.A. Manual of 1921
or later revisions.

Revisions				
Date	By	Description		
3-4-25	J.C.W.	Spacing of holes chang.		
12-11-26	J.C.W.	Specifications added		

APPROVED:- _R.E. Potter_
Vice-Pres't & Gen'l Mang'r

APPROVED:- _R.L. Sheppard_
Chief Engineer

WABASH RAILWAY
STANDARD

TIE PLATE FOR 80 & 90 LB. RAIL

OFFICE OF THE CHIEF ENGINEER
ADOPTED OCT. 20, 1924
Redrawn Feb. 12, 1931 - J.C.W.

PLAN NO. 234

43

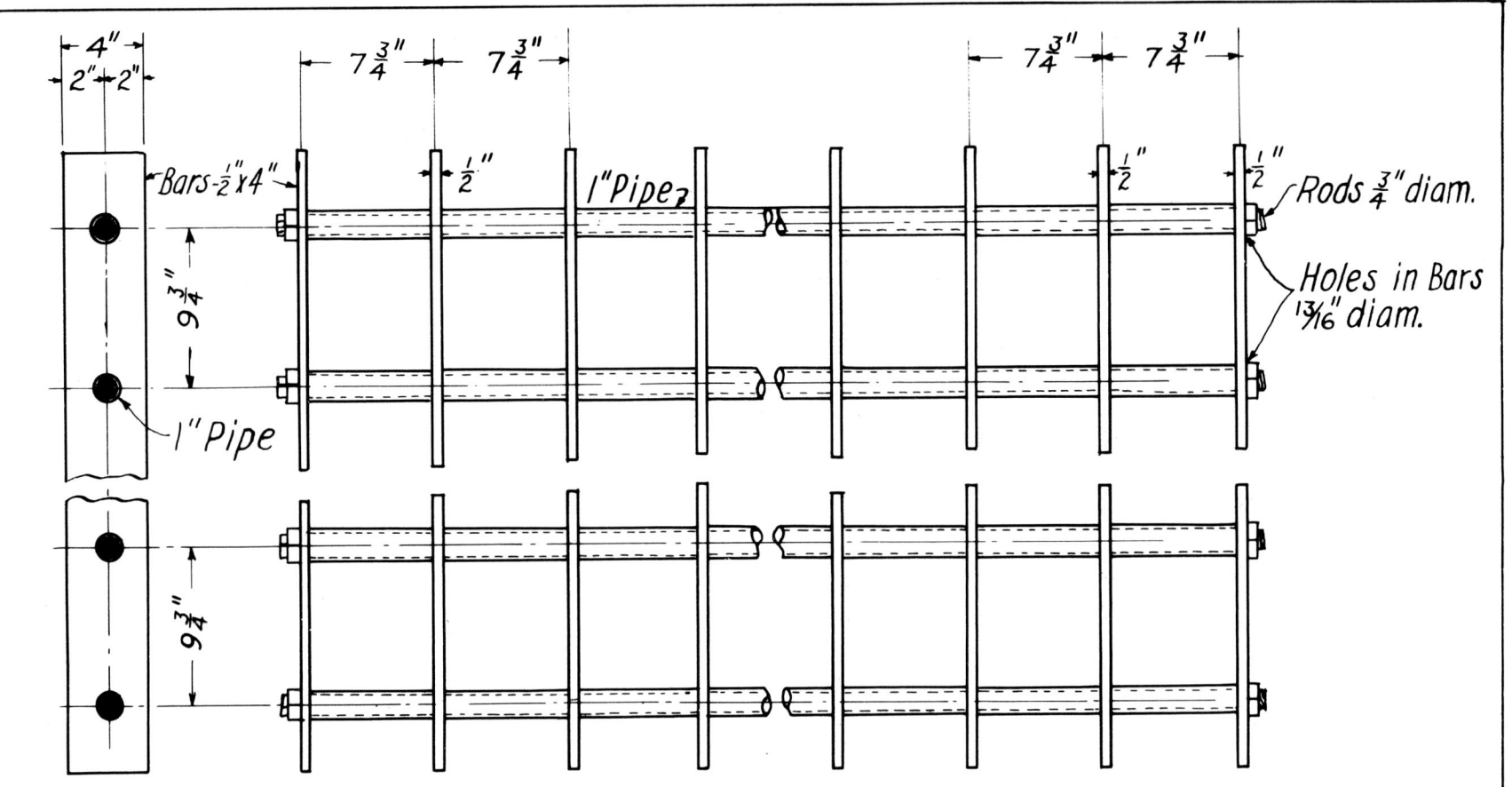

4"
2"–2"

7¾"   7¾"   7¾"   7¾"

Bars–½"x4"   ½"   I"Pipe⌐   ½"   ½"   Rods ¾" diam.

9¾"

Holes in Bars
13⁄16" diam.

I" Pipe

9¾"

NOTE:– No opening shall be larger than Shown.

Approved: Approved: Approved:

(signature)   *(signature)*   *(signature)*

‑‑‑‑‑‑‑‑‑‑‑‑‑‑‑‑   ‑‑‑‑‑‑‑‑‑‑‑‑‑‑‑   ‑‑‑‑‑‑‑‑‑‑‑‑‑‑‑‑
V.P. & Gen'l. Mang'r.   Chief Engineer   Supt. of Motive Power.

WABASH RAILWAY
STANDARD
BREAKER BARS FOR
COAL CHUTES
OFFICE OF THE CHIEF ENGINEER
ADOPTED – APRIL, 1 ST, 1926

T.W.C.

264

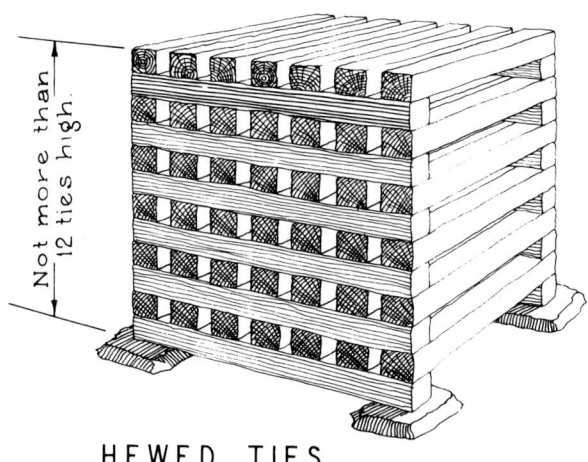

Not more than 12 ties high.

HEWED TIES

Two bottom ties to be not less than six (6) inches above ground, supported on stone or sound wood sills.
Face of Piles to be not less than 10 feet from nearest rail of any track
To be piled in alternating layers of 2 and 7 ties.
Piles must be at least 5 feet apart

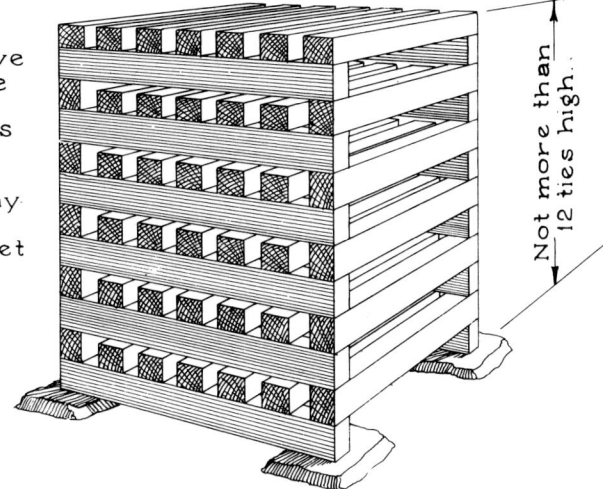

Not more than 12 ties high.

SAWED TIES

PILING UNTREATED TIES FOR INSPECTION AND SEASONING

Not more than 8 ties high, nor less than 3 ties high

Treated ties piled for storage on right of way shall be stacked as compactly as possible, with face of pile not less than 10 feet from nearest rail of any track.
Piles shall be not less than 15 feet apart.

Where ties for maintenance are unloaded along track, to be used within a short time they may be stored as shown above, parallel to track, with nearest tie not less than 5'-0" from nearest rail.
Piles shall contain 3, 6, or 10 ties, but not more than 10

PILING TREATED TIES FOR STORAGE

Approved _____
Vice-President

Approved _____
Gen'l Manager

Approved _____
Chief Engineer M. of W.

WABASH RAILWAY
STANDARD
METHOD OF PILING TIES
OFFICE OF THE CHIEF ENGINEER M. OF W.
ADOPTED FEB. 18, 1931
PLAN NO. 399

W.E.G - J.C.W.

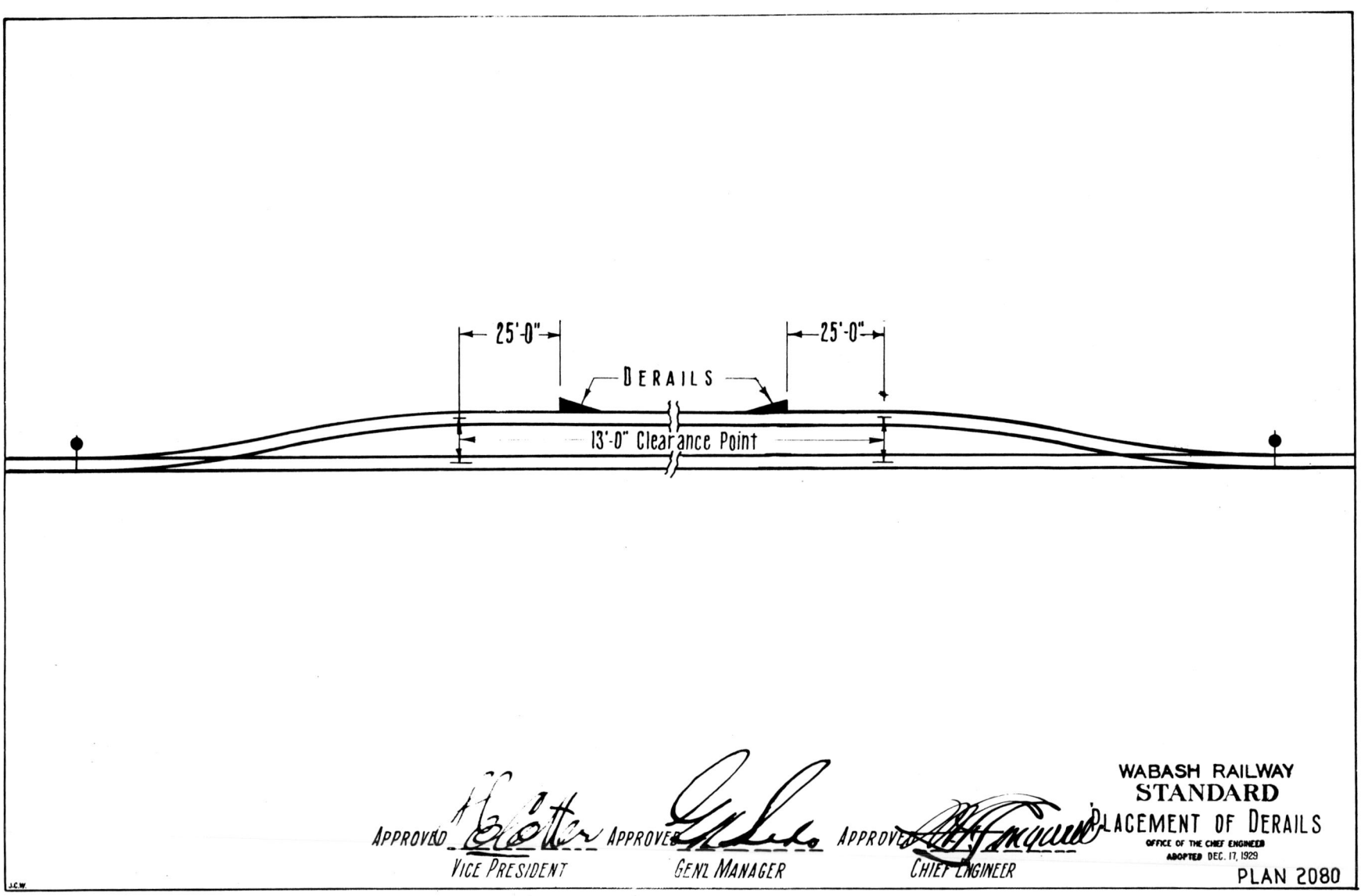

WABASH RAILWAY
STANDARD
PLACEMENT OF DERAILS
OFFICE OF THE CHIEF ENGINEER
ADOPTED DEC. 17, 1929

PLAN 2080

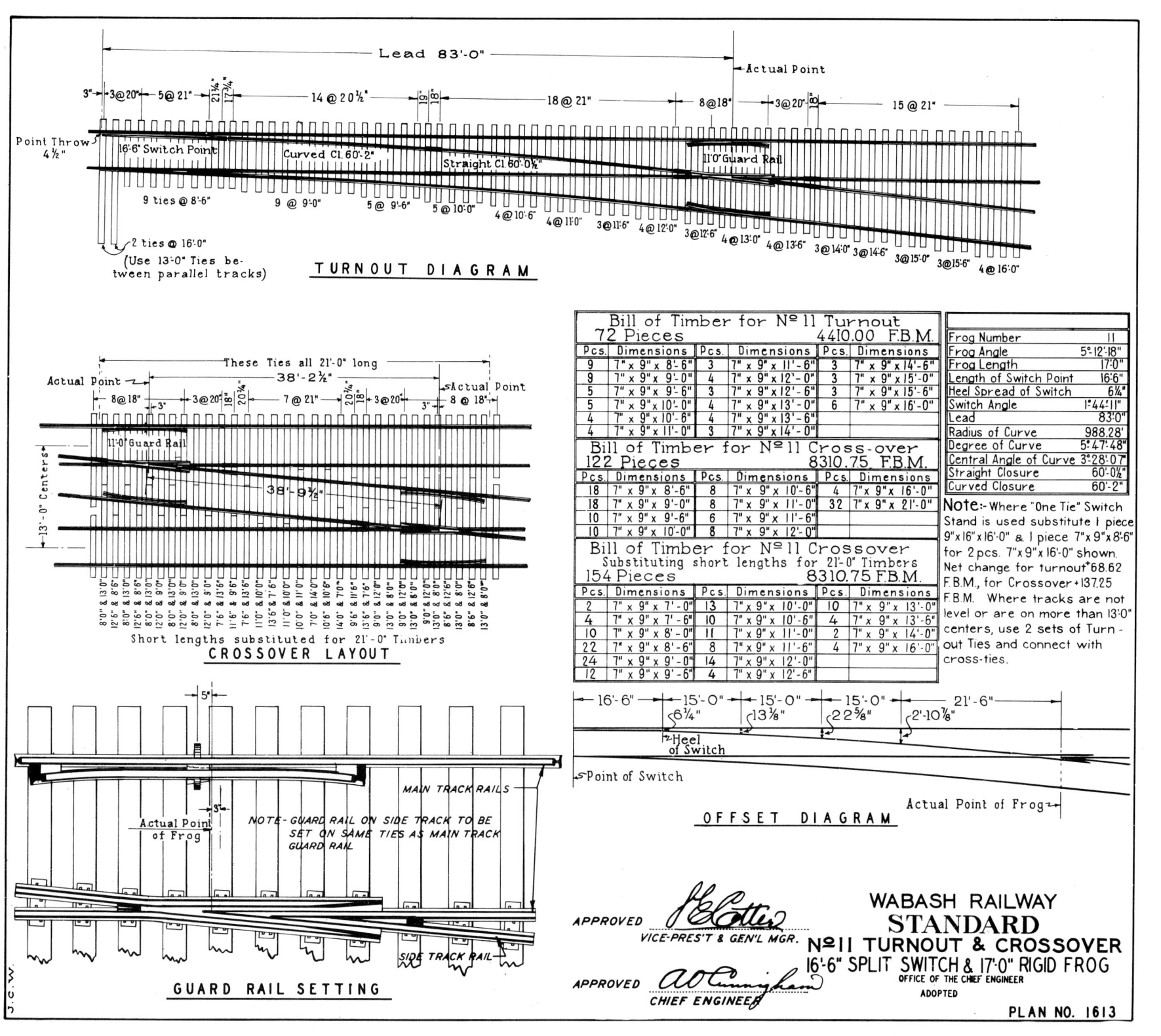

TURNOUT DIAGRAM

CROSSOVER LAYOUT

GUARD RAIL SETTING

OFFSET DIAGRAM

WABASH RAILWAY STANDARD Nº11 TURNOUT & CROSSOVER
16'-6" SPLIT SWITCH & 17'-0" RIGID FROG

PLAN NO. 1613

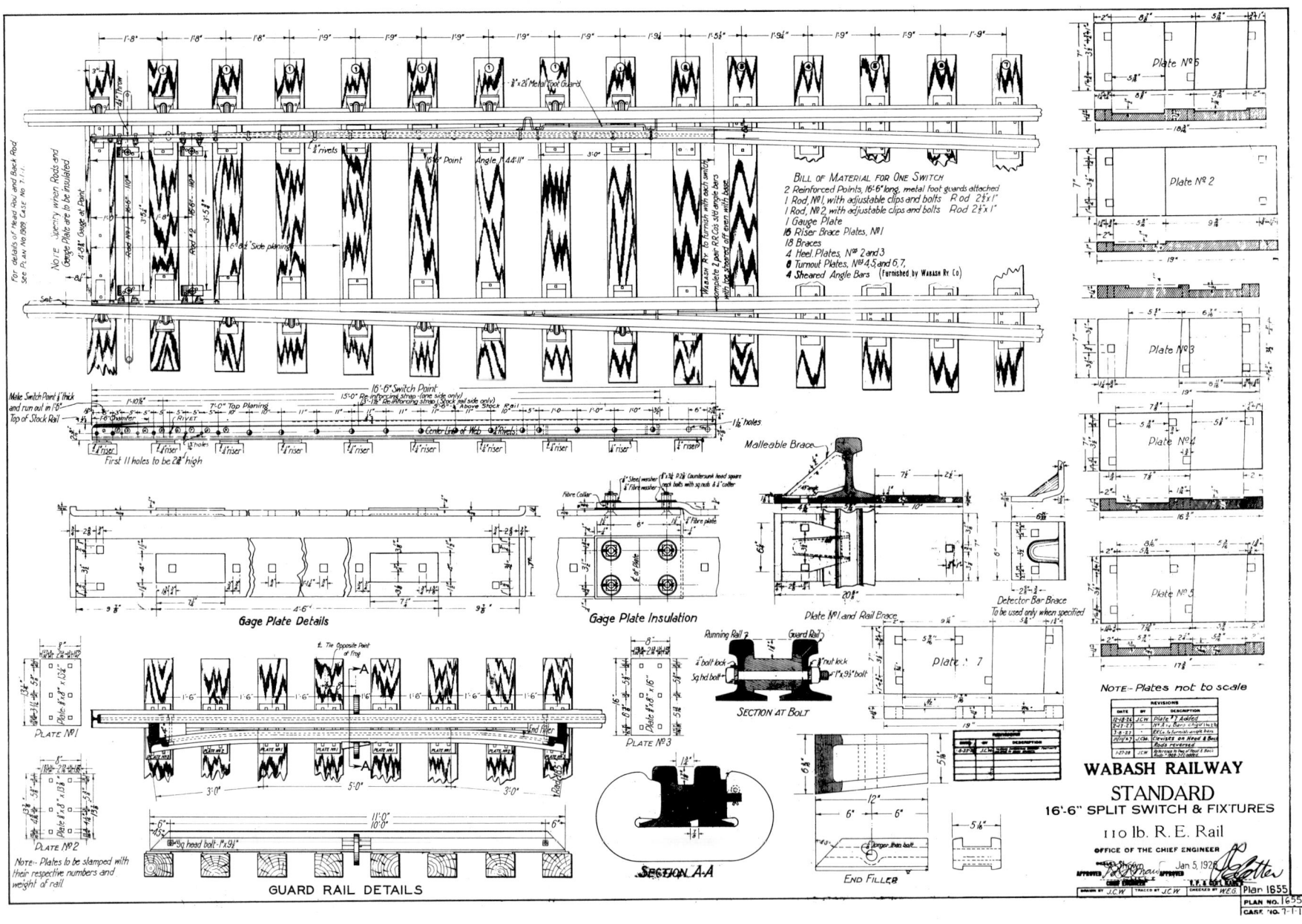

BILL OF MATERIAL FOR ONE SWITCH
2 Reinforced Points, 16'-6" long, metal foot guards attached
1 Rod, No. 1, with adjustable clips and bolts   Rod 2⅛"x1"
1 Rod, No. 2, with adjustable clips and bolts   Rod 2⅛"x1"
1 Gauge Plate
16 Riser Brace Plates, No. 1
18 Braces
4 Heel Plates, No. 2 and 3
8 Turnout Plates, No. 4, 5 and 6, 7,
4 Sheared Angle Bars (Furnished by Wabash Ry Co)

Gage Plate Details

Gage Plate Insulation

Malleable Brace

Plate No. 1 and Rail Brace

Detector Bar Brace
To be used only when specified

GUARD RAIL DETAILS

SECTION A-A

SECTION AT BOLT

Plate No. 7

END FILLER

Plate No. 1

Plate No. 2

Note- Plates to be stamped with
their respective numbers and
weight of rail.

Plate No. 6

Plate No. 2

Plate No. 3

Plate No. 4

Plate No. 5

NOTE- Plates not to scale

WABASH RAILWAY
STANDARD
16'-6" SPLIT SWITCH & FIXTURES
110 lb. R. E. Rail
OFFICE OF THE CHIEF ENGINEER
Jan 5, 1928
Plan 1655

PLAN NO. 1655
CASE NO. 7-1-1

48

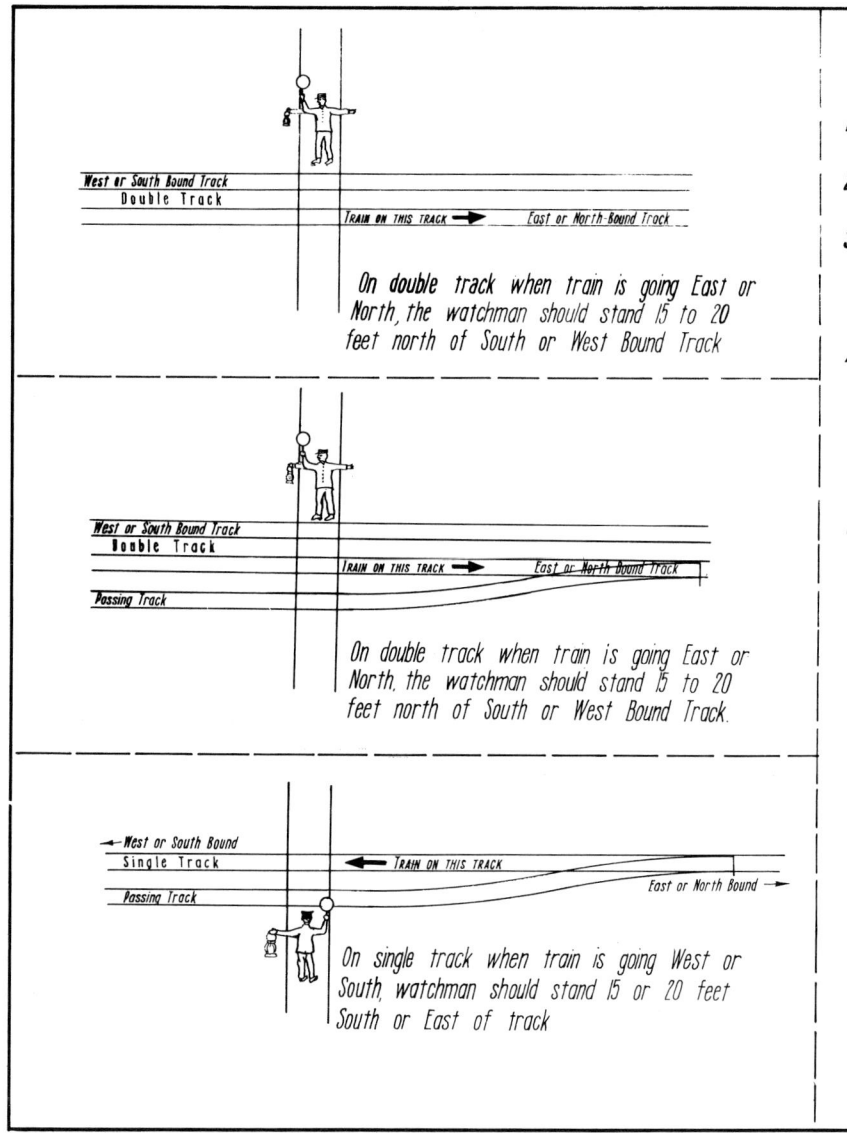

West or South Bound Track
Double Track

TRAIN ON THIS TRACK ➡ East or North-Bound Track

On **double** track when train is going East or North, the watchman should stand 15 to 20 feet north of South or West Bound Track

West or South Bound Track
Double Track

TRAIN ON THIS TRACK ➡ East or North Bound Track

Passing Track

On **double** track when train is going East or North, the watchman should stand 15 to 20 feet north of South or West Bound Track.

◀ West or South Bound
Single Track

◀ TRAIN ON THIS TRACK

Passing Track

East or North Bound ➡

On single track when train is going West or South, watchman should stand 15 or 20 feet South or East of track

---

Stop Sign by day and Red Light by night, held in position shown in diagrams on the left.

1. **NEVER** use your Stop Signal for any other signal than that for which it is intended:- **A SIGNAL TO STOP**

2. Stand in the **MIDDLE OF THE STREET**, 15 to 20 feet from the track, not on the sidewalk or edge of the street

3. **IN NO CASE** stand on the tracks, or close enough to be struck by a passing train
   Stand **FACING** the tracks, with **BOTH** arms extended, holding Stop Sign in one hand.

4. On double track when train is going East over crossing the watchman should stand north of the west bound track to protect the highway. When the train is going west, he should stand south of the eastbound track. On single track crossing, where train is going east, watchman should stand 15 to 20 feet north of main track. When train is going west he should stand 15 to 20 feet south of main track.

5. The stop sign for night indication used by crossing watchman should be an ordinary lantern with a red globe, held as indicated by dotted outlines.

6. Crossing gates at all crossings where operated at night should have suspended on the gates at either side of the tracks a shielded red lantern, either the A.R.A. standard crossing-gate lantern per circular 2091, or shielded red lantern of some other approved type, which will show a red light to all approaching roadway traffic.

Approved:- _____
Gen'l Sup't, Eastern Dist.

Approved _____
Gen'l Sup't, Western Dist.

WABASH RAILWAY
ST. LOUIS, MO.
STANDARD
RULES FOR CROSSING FLAGMEN
OFFICE OF THE CHIEF ENGINEER
Scale :- None   May 26, 1927
Approved _____ Approved _____
Chief Engineer   V-P & Gen'l Man'gr
DRAWN BY J.C.W.   TRACED BY J.C.W.   **PLAN- 1657**

PLAN NO. 1657
CASE NO. 5-3-1

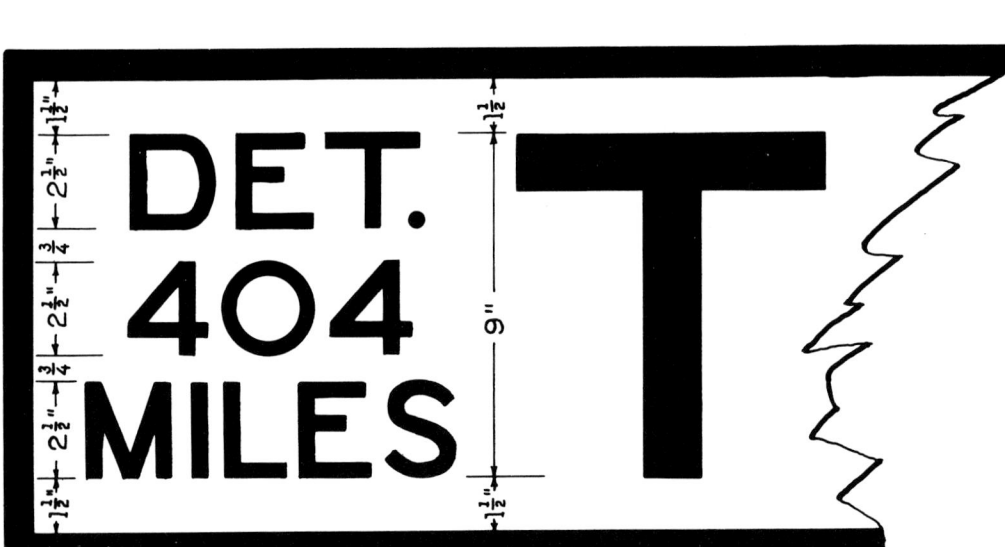

DET. 404 MILES TAYLORVILLE ST. L. 85 MILES

DET. 404 MILES

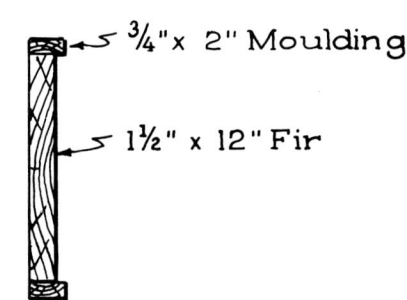

¾" x 2" Moulding

1½" x 12" Fir

Section of Board

FOR BRICK:-
 Letters - Gilt on black back-
                    ground.

 Moulding - Gilt

FOR FRAME:-
 Letters - Black on white back-
                    ground

 Moulding - Black.

STATION SIGN

Approved:- _____
Vice-Prest & Gen'l Man'gr

Approved:- _____
Chief Engineer

Redrawn Feb. 20, 1931 - J.C.W.
PLAN NO. 1665

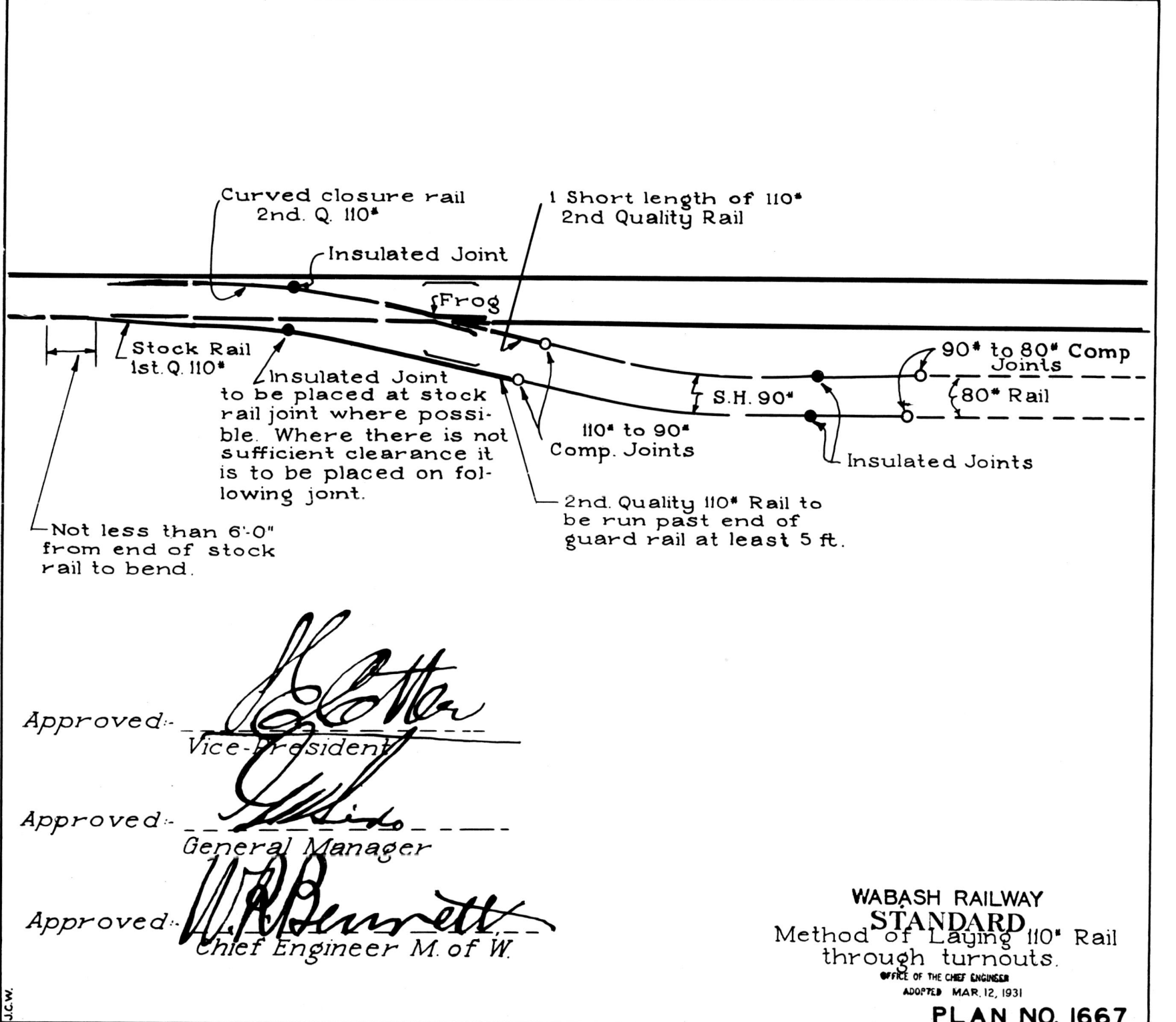

Curved closure rail 2nd. Q. 110#

1 Short length of 110# 2nd Quality Rail

Insulated Joint

Frog

Stock Rail 1st. Q. 110#

Insulated Joint to be placed at stock rail joint where possible. Where there is not sufficient clearance it is to be placed on following joint.

90# to 80# Comp Joints

80# Rail

S.H. 90#

110# to 90# Comp. Joints

Not less than 6'-0" from end of stock rail to bend.

2nd. Quality 110# Rail to be run past end of guard rail at least 5 ft.

Insulated Joints

Approved :- _____
Vice-President

Approved :- _____
General Manager

Approved :- _____
Chief Engineer M. of W.

WABASH RAILWAY
STANDARD
Method of Laying 110# Rail
through turnouts.
OFFICE OF THE CHIEF ENGINEER
ADOPTED MAR. 12, 1931

PLAN NO. 1667

J.C.W.

51

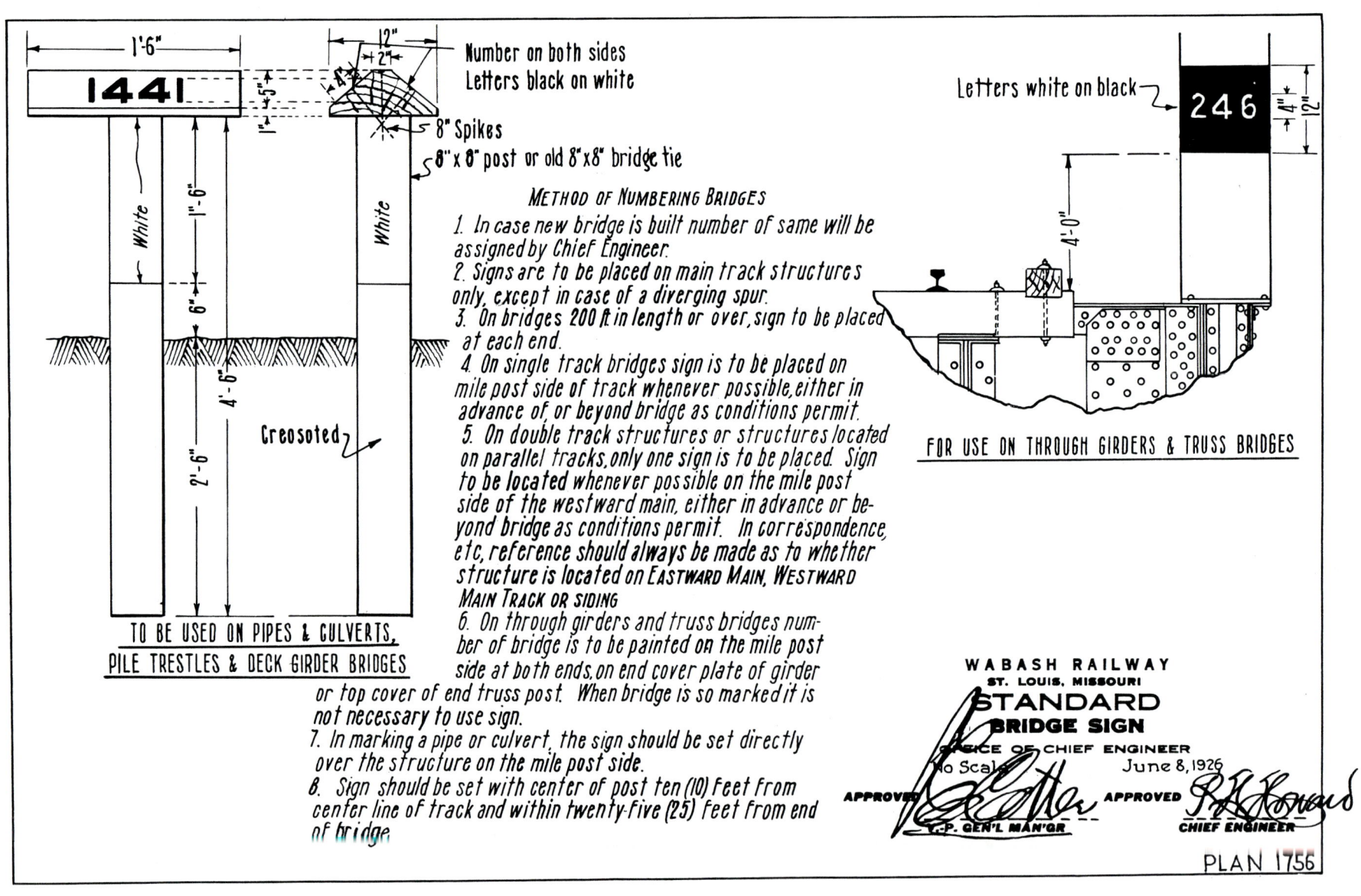

Number on both sides
Letters black on white

8" Spikes
8" x 8" post or old 8"x8" bridge tie

Letters white on black

1441

White

White

Creosoted

TO BE USED ON PIPES & CULVERTS,
PILE TRESTLES & DECK GIRDER BRIDGES

246

FOR USE ON THROUGH GIRDERS & TRUSS BRIDGES

METHOD OF NUMBERING BRIDGES

1. In case new bridge is built number of same will be assigned by Chief Engineer.
2. Signs are to be placed on main track structures only, except in case of a diverging spur.
3. On bridges 200 ft. in length or over, sign to be placed at each end.
4. On single track bridges sign is to be placed on mile post side of track whenever possible, either in advance of, or beyond bridge as conditions permit.
5. On double track structures or structures located on parallel tracks, only one sign is to be placed. Sign to be located whenever possible on the mile post side of the westward main, either in advance or beyond bridge as conditions permit. In correspondence, etc, reference should always be made as to whether structure is located on EASTWARD MAIN, WESTWARD MAIN TRACK OR SIDING
6. On through girders and truss bridges number of bridge is to be painted on the mile post side at both ends, on end cover plate of girder or top cover of end truss post. When bridge is so marked it is not necessary to use sign.
7. In marking a pipe or culvert, the sign should be set directly over the structure on the mile post side.
8. Sign should be set with center of post ten (10) feet from center line of track and within twenty-five (25) feet from end of bridge.

WABASH RAILWAY
ST. LOUIS, MISSOURI
STANDARD
BRIDGE SIGN
OFFICE OF CHIEF ENGINEER
No Scale   June 8, 1926
APPROVED   APPROVED
C.P. GEN'L MAN'GR   CHIEF ENGINEER

PLAN 1756

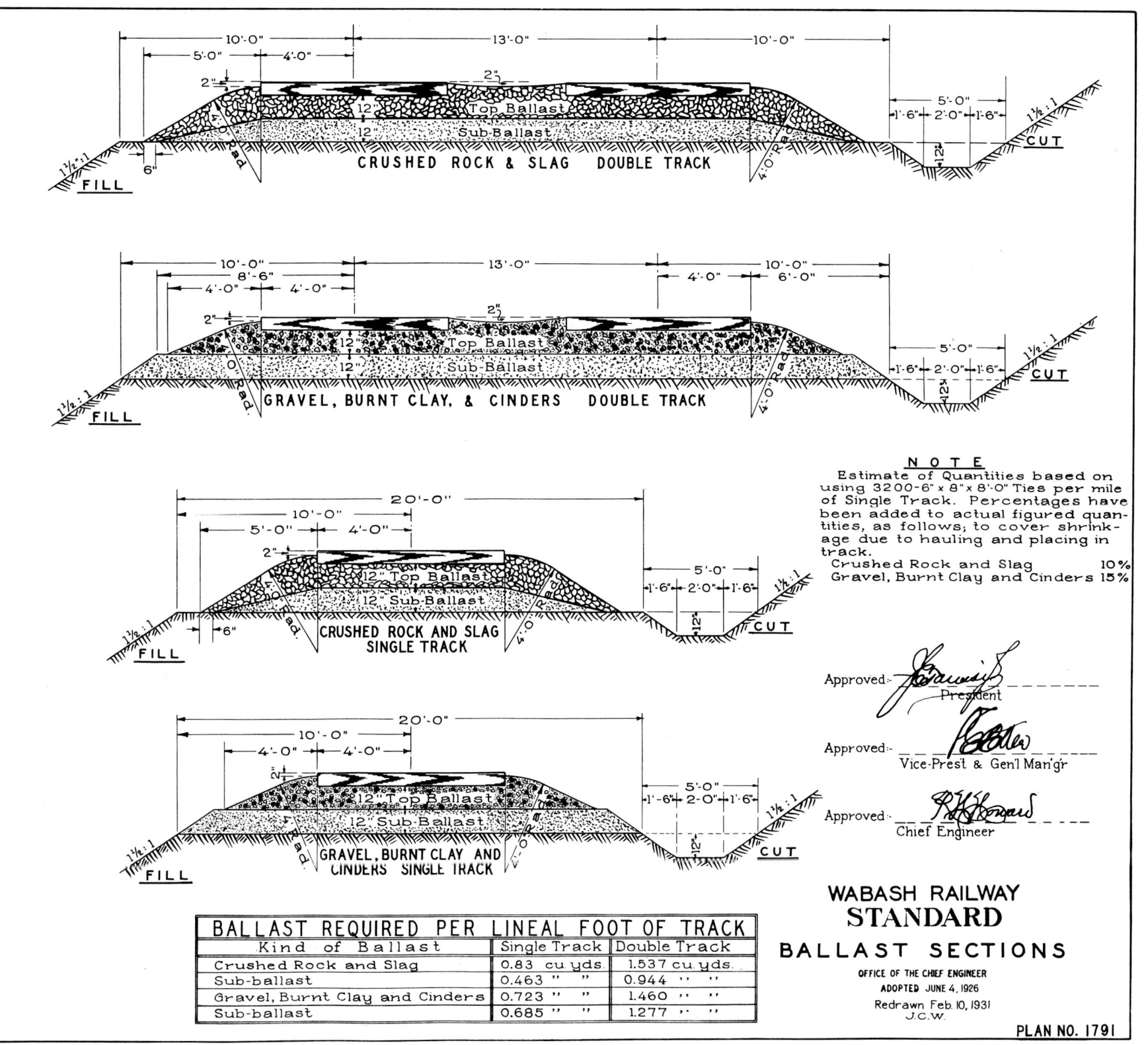

CRUSHED ROCK & SLAG DOUBLE TRACK

GRAVEL, BURNT CLAY, & CINDERS DOUBLE TRACK

CRUSHED ROCK AND SLAG SINGLE TRACK

GRAVEL, BURNT CLAY AND CINDERS SINGLE TRACK

N O T E

Estimate of Quantities based on using 3200-6" x 8" x 8'-0" Ties per mile of Single Track. Percentages have been added to actual figured quantities, as follows; to cover shrinkage due to hauling and placing in track.

Crushed Rock and Slag 10%
Gravel, Burnt Clay and Cinders 15%

Approved:- _____ President

Approved:- _____ Vice-Pres't & Gen'l Man'gr

Approved:- _____ Chief Engineer

WABASH RAILWAY
STANDARD
BALLAST SECTIONS

OFFICE OF THE CHIEF ENGINEER
ADOPTED JUNE 4, 1926
Redrawn Feb. 10, 1931
J.C.W.

BALLAST REQUIRED PER LINEAL FOOT OF TRACK		
Kind of Ballast	Single Track	Double Track
Crushed Rock and Slag	0.83 cu yds.	1.537 cu.yds.
Sub-ballast	0.463 " "	0.944 " "
Gravel, Burnt Clay and Cinders	0.723 " "	1.460 " "
Sub-ballast	0.685 " "	1.277 " "

PLAN NO. 1791

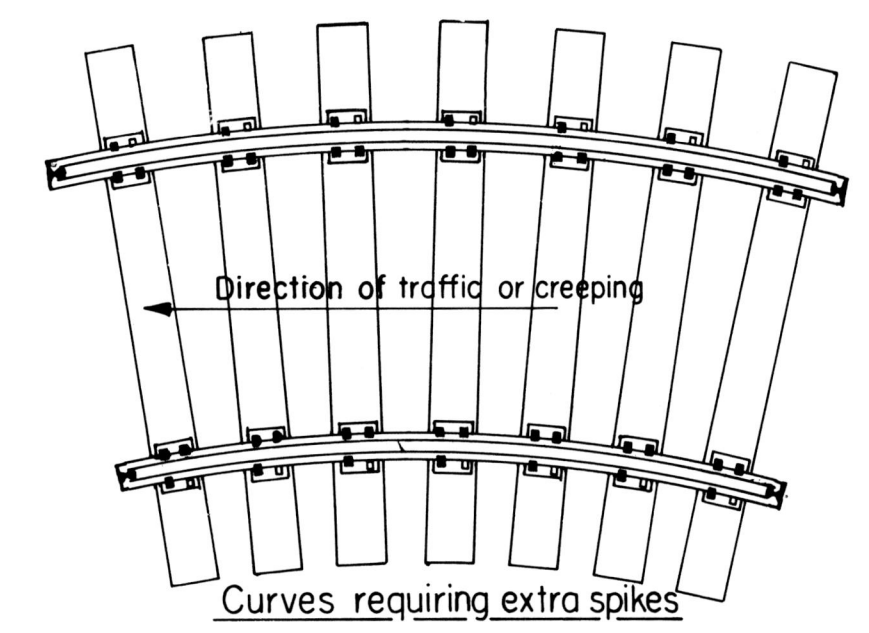

Direction of traffic or creeping

Curves requiring extra spikes

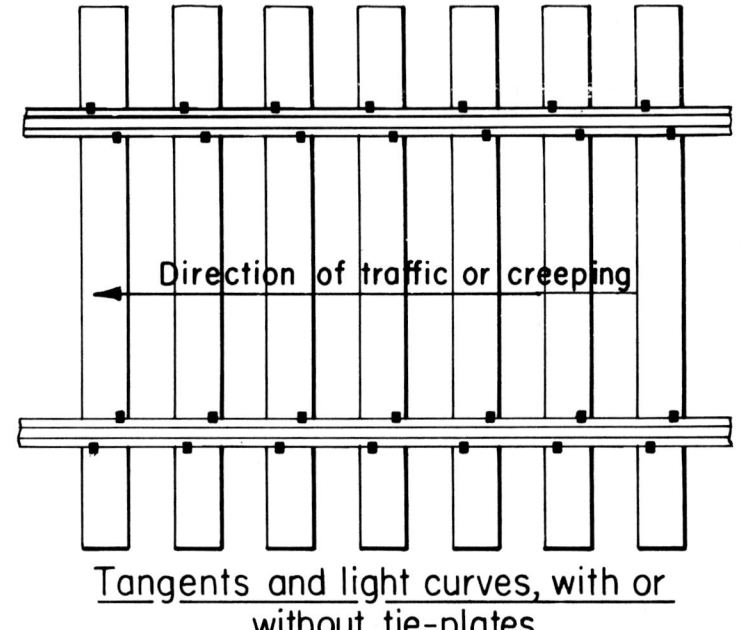

Direction of traffic or creeping

Tangents and light curves, with or without tie-plates

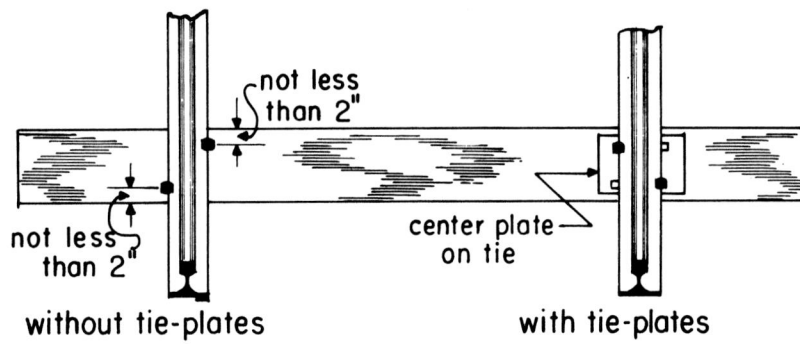

not less than 2"

not less than 2"

center plate on tie

without tie-plates   with tie-plates

Location of spikes in tie

Driving Spikes

All spikes must be driven vertically with the face in contact with the base of rail and must not be struck after they have come in contact with base of rail. The last few blows shall be given lightly to avoid damage to spike-head or rail.

Spikes should be driven into the plugs, unless the condition of the tie is such that they should be placed otherwise.

When tie-plates are not used, spikes shall be driven not less than 2 inches from nearest edge of tie.

On tangents and light curves, use two rail holding spikes, one inside and one outside, for holding each rail to each tie.

On curves of 2 degrees and over, on lines where maximum speed is 75 miles per hour or over, 3 spikes must be used to a rail in each tie not anchored with compression clips; the additional spike shall be used on the inside of each rail.

On curves of 3 degrees and over on other lines 3 spikes must be used to a rail in each tie not anchored with compression clips; the additional spike shall be used on the inside of each rail.

WABASH RAILROAD
Standard
RAIL SPIKING
Office of the Chief Engineer
April 8, 1942

J.C.W.

REVISED 4-6-'42

PLAN Nº 2191

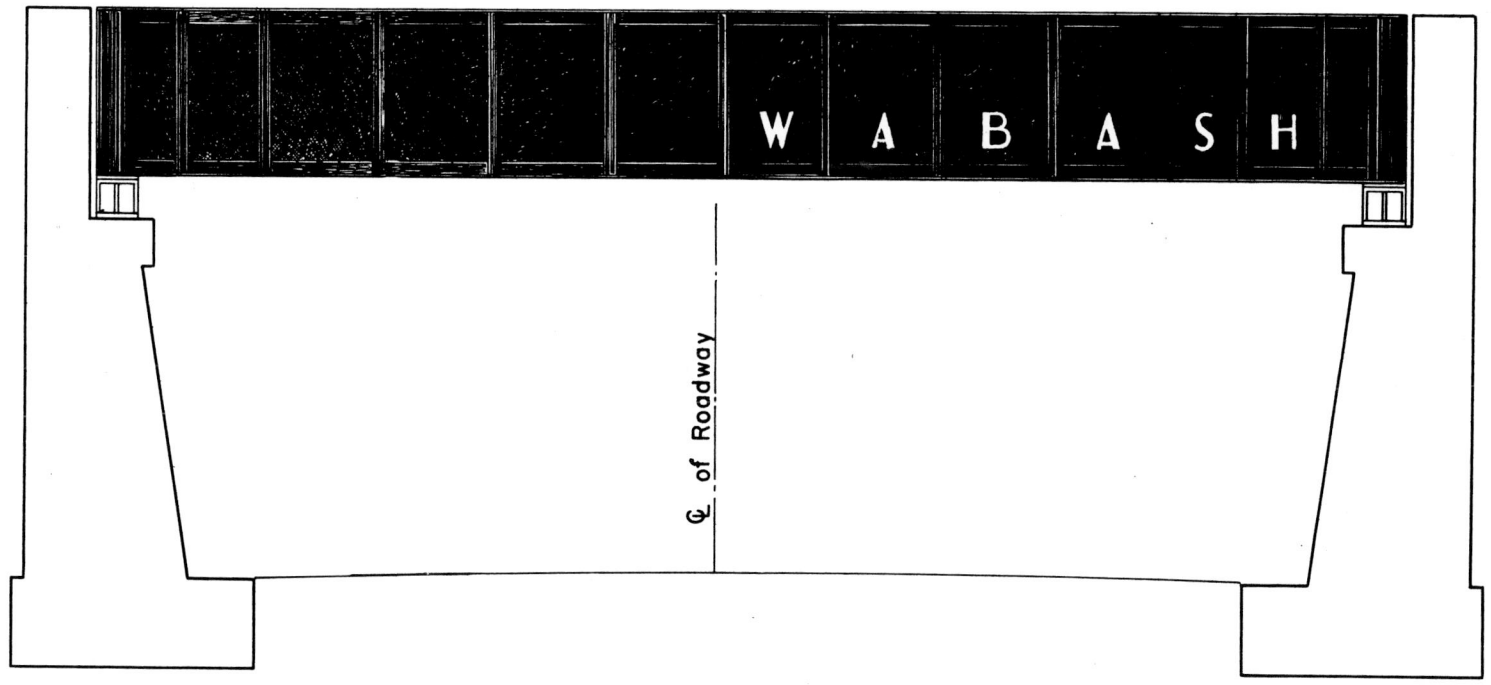

On steel girders, place letters not less
than 6 inches above bottom flange angle.

Space letters across right side of roadway. Do not crowd letters together.

Stencils to be cut from full-size template,
PLAN NO. 3366

WABASH RAILWAY
Standard
SIGN FOR BRIDGES
Office of the Chief Engineer
Aug. 8, 1939

SUPERSEDES PLAN NO. 1952

PLAN NO. 3365

J.C.W.

55

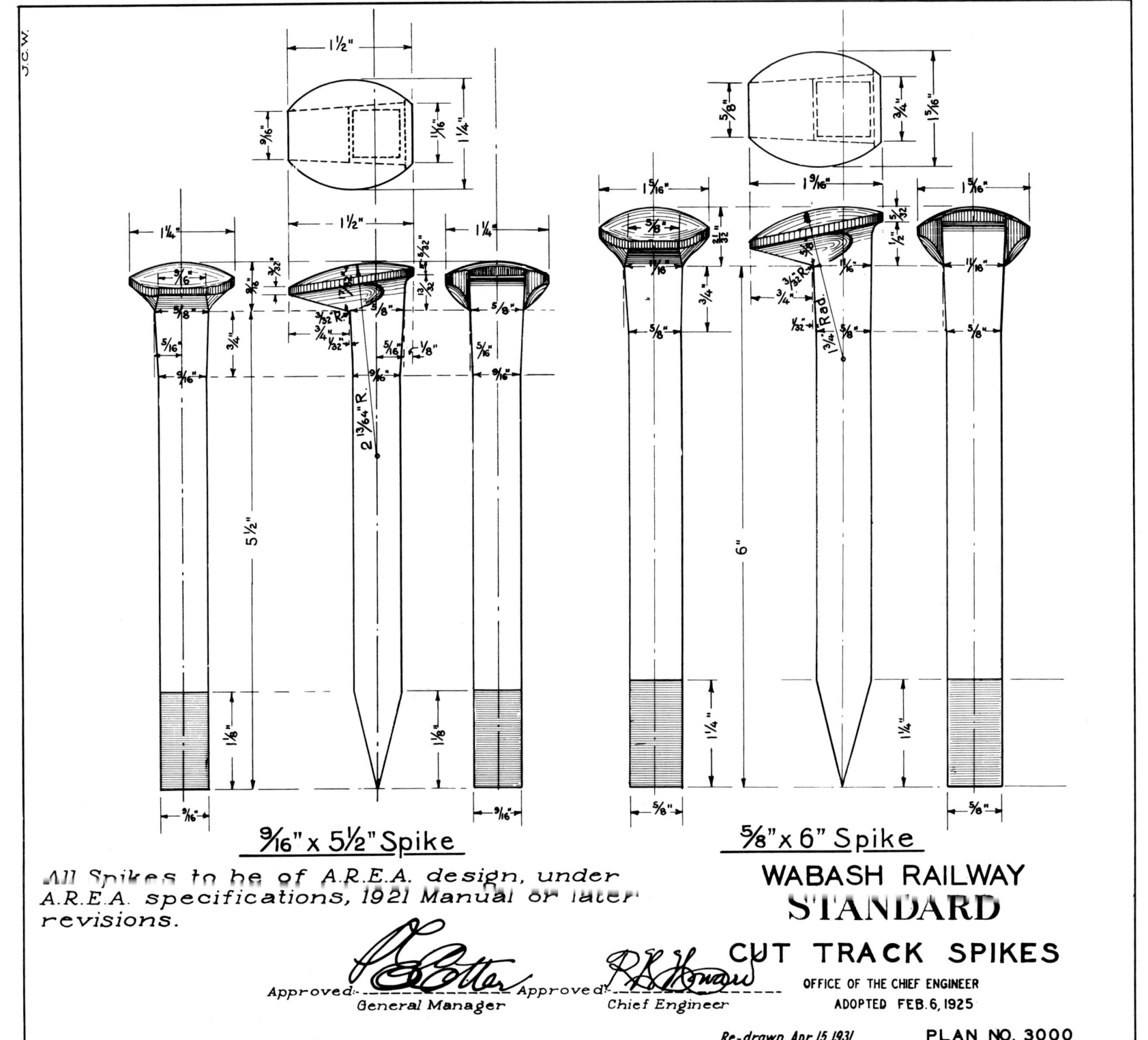

9/16" x 5½" Spike

5/8" x 6" Spike

All Spikes to be of A.R.E.A. design, under A.R.E.A. specifications, 1921 Manual or later revisions.

WABASH RAILWAY
STANDARD
CUT TRACK SPIKES

Approved: _____
General Manager

Approved: _____
Chief Engineer

OFFICE OF THE CHIEF ENGINEER
ADOPTED FEB. 6, 1925

Re-drawn Apr. 15, 1931

PLAN NO. 3000

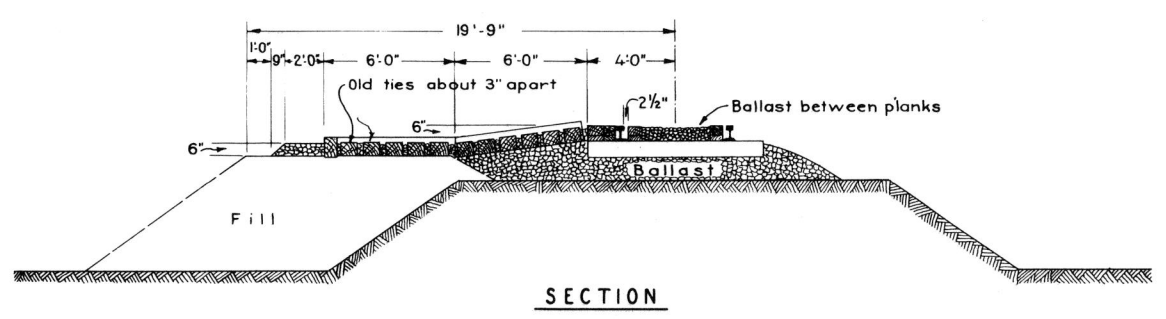

19'-9"

1'-0" | 9" 2'-0" | 6'-0" | 6'-0" | 4'-0"

Old ties about 3" apart

6" 6"

2½"

Ballast between planks

Ballast

Fill

SECTION

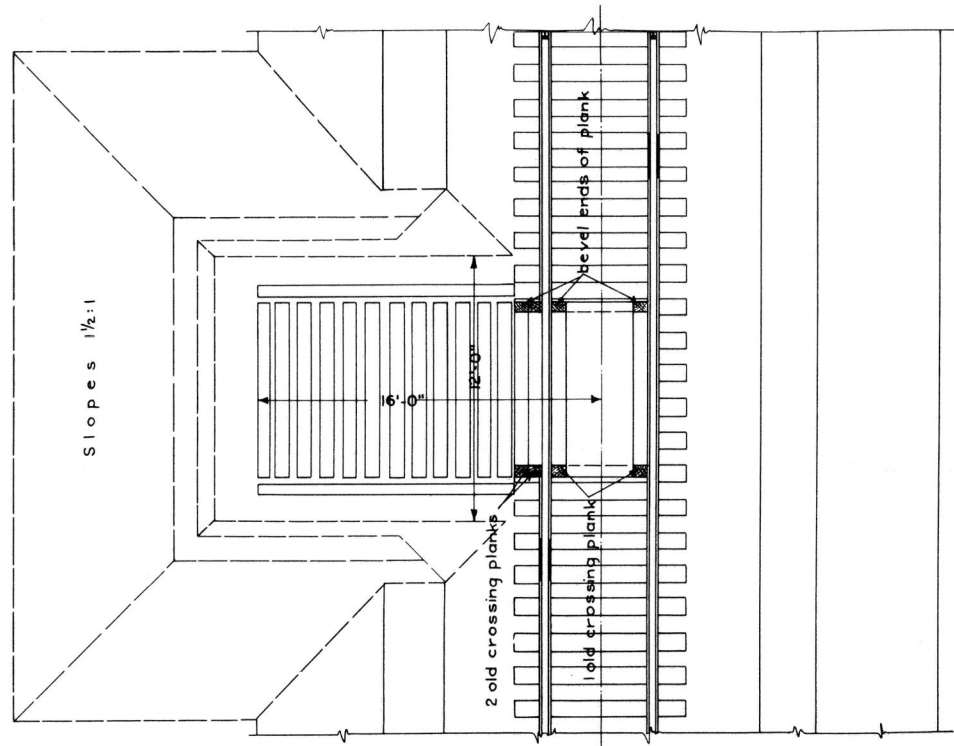

Slopes 1½:1

bevel ends of plank

16'-0"

12'-0"

2 old crossing planks

1 old crossing plank

PLAN

Turnouts to be placed ⅓ of a mile
apart. Every third turnout to be placed
at a mile post. Necessary variation from
this spacing, made to avoid obstacles, to
materially lessen cost, to increase use-
fulness, or to avoid construction in cut
or on extremely high fills, will be per-
mitted.

On double track, turnouts to be placed
opposite one another when practicable.
Whenever practicable in signal territory turnout should be placed near a
signal for convenience of signal main-
tainer.

In territory where fills are constructed of sandy material slopes are to be
covered with protective material.

Filling between planks in track and
for dressing around ties in turnout to
be of same material as ballast.

Turnouts must not be located opposite joints of either rail.

Approved _____ Approved _____ Approved _____
Vice-President   General Manager   Chief Engineer M. of W.

WABASH RAILWAY
STANDARD
TRACK CAR TURNOUT
OFFICE OF THE CHIEF ENGINEER M. OF W.
ADOPTED MAY 7, 1931

PLAN NO. 3003

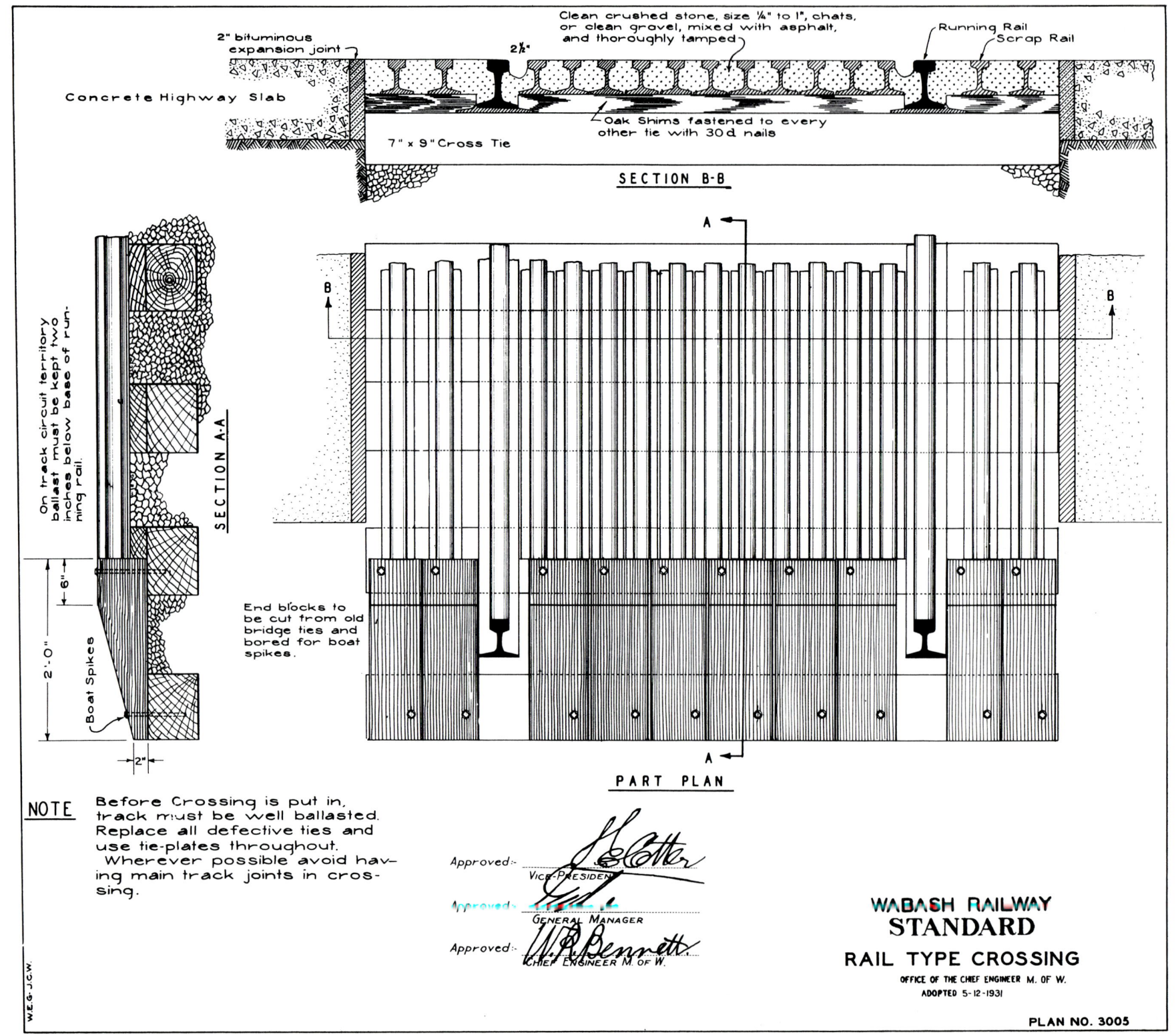

Clean crushed stone, size ¼" to 1", chats, or clean gravel, mixed with asphalt, and thoroughly tamped

2" bituminous expansion joint

Running Rail
Scrap Rail

2½"

Concrete Highway Slab

Oak Shims fastened to every other tie with 30 d nails

7" x 9" Cross Tie

SECTION B-B

A

B

B

On track circuit territory ballast must be kept two inches below base of running rail.

SECTION A-A

6"

2'-0"

Boat Spikes

2"

End blocks to be cut from old bridge ties and bored for boat spikes.

A

PART PLAN

NOTE   Before Crossing is put in, track must be well ballasted. Replace all defective ties and use tie-plates throughout.
  Wherever possible avoid having main track joints in crossing.

Approved:- J. C. Cotter
VICE-PRESIDENT

Approved:-
GENERAL MANAGER

Approved:- W. B. Bennett
CHIEF ENGINEER M. OF W.

WABASH RAILWAY
STANDARD

RAIL TYPE CROSSING

OFFICE OF THE CHIEF ENGINEER M. OF W.
ADOPTED 5-12-1931

PLAN NO. 3005

W.E.G. J.C.W.

58

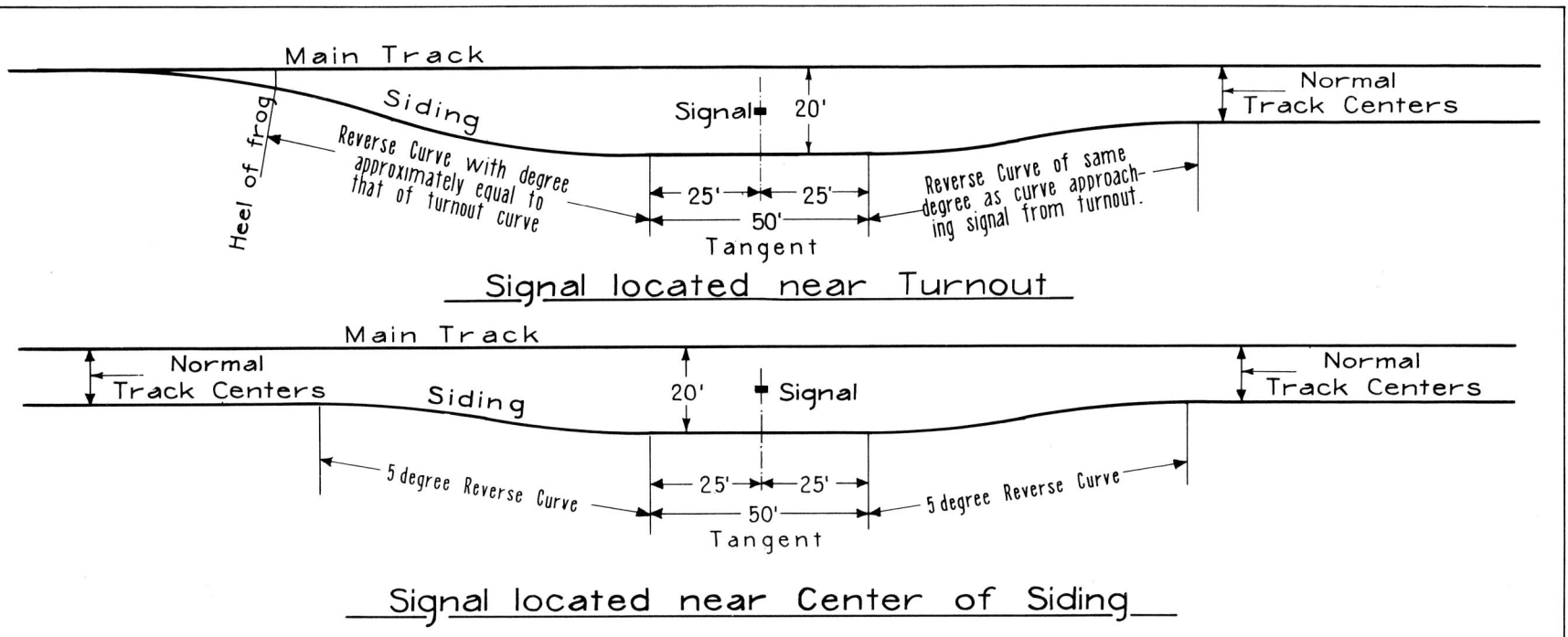

Signal located near Turnout

Main Track

Siding

Signal — 20'

Heel of frog

Reverse Curve with degree approximately equal to that of turnout curve

25' | 25'

50'

Tangent

Reverse Curve of same degree as curve approaching signal from turnout.

Normal Track Centers

Signal located near Center of Siding

Main Track

Normal Track Centers

Siding

20' | Signal

Normal Track Centers

5 degree Reverse Curve

25' | 25'

50'

Tangent

5 degree Reverse Curve

When Signal is located between Main Track and Siding, tracks must be maintained on 20 foot centers for a distance of 25 feet each side of Signal.

The curvature between heel of frog and the point of tangency shall be approximately that of turnout. If there is not enough room between heel of frog and point of tangency at the signal to maintain the turnout curvature, the lightest curvature possible shall be used and duplicated on the other side of signal where tracks go back to normal centers.

At locations where signal is near center of siding, use 5° reverse curves to provide 20 foot track centers.

Approved:- _____
Vice-President

Approved:- _____
General Manager

Approved:- _____
Chief Engineer M. of W.

WABASH RAILWAY
STANDARD
Siding Clearance at Signals

OFFICE OF THE CHIEF ENGINEER M. OF W.

ADOPTED 6-2-31

PLAN NO. 3013

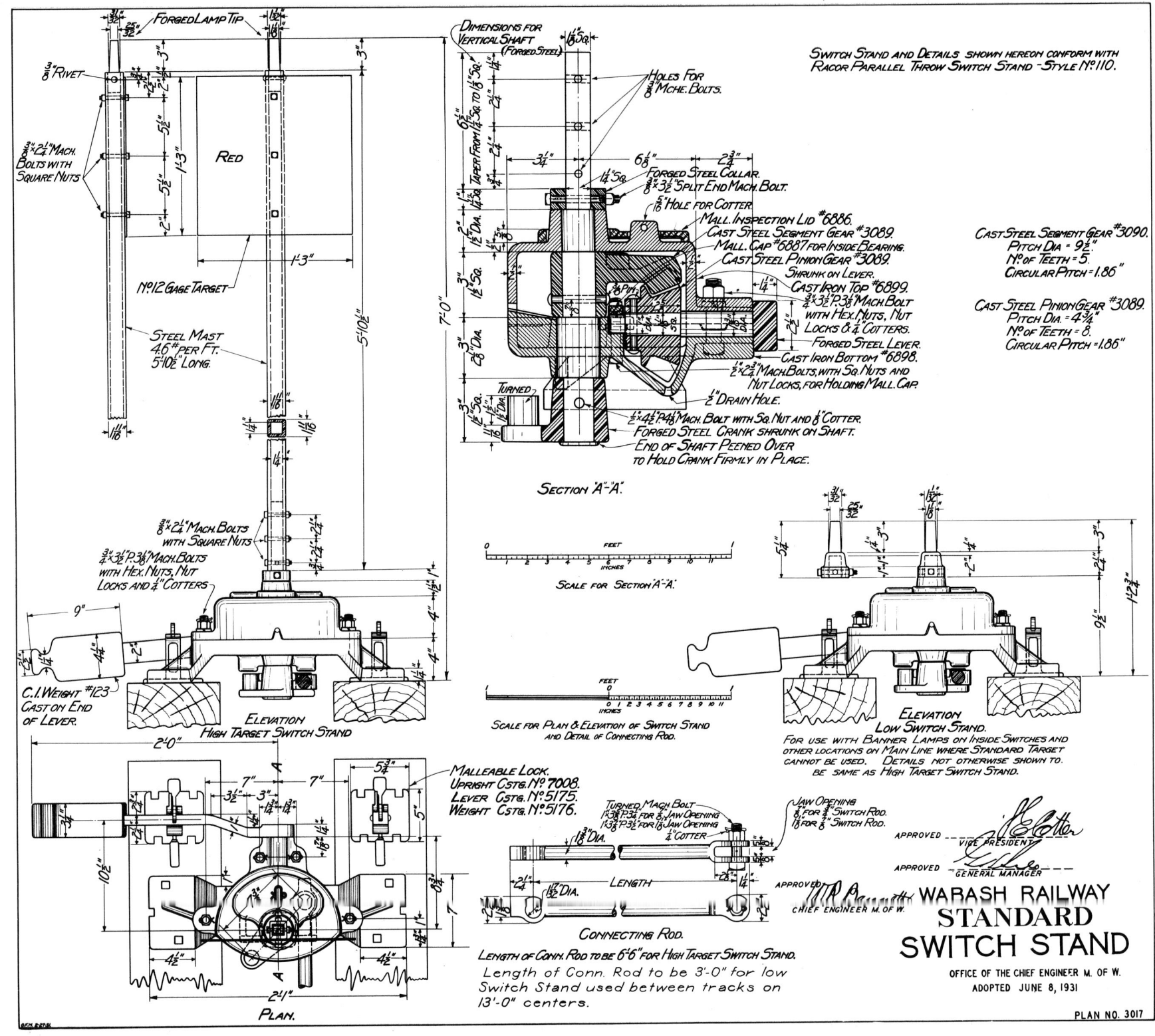

Switch Stand and Details shown hereon conform with
Racor Parallel Throw Switch Stand - Style No. 110.

Forged Lamp Tip

Rivet

Red

No. 12 Gage Target

Steel Mast
4.6# per Ft.
5'-10½" Long.

C.I. Weight #123
Cast on End
of Lever.

Elevation
High Target Switch Stand

Dimensions for
Vertical Shaft
(Forged Steel)

Holes for ⅜" Mche. Bolts.

Forged Steel Collar.
Split End Mach. Bolt.
Hole for Cotter
Mall. Inspection Lid #6886.
Cast Steel Segment Gear #3089.
Mall. Cap #6887 for Inside Bearing.
Cast Steel Pinion Gear #3089.
Shrunk on Lever.
Cast Iron Top #6899.
Mach. Bolt with Hex. Nuts, Nut Locks & ¼" Cotters.
Forged Steel Lever.
Cast Iron Bottom #6898.
Mach. Bolts, with Sq. Nuts and Nut Locks, for Holding Mall. Cap.
Drain Hole.
Mach. Bolt with Sq. Nut and ⅛" Cotter.
Forged Steel Crank shrunk on Shaft.
End of Shaft Peened Over
to Hold Crank Firmly in Place.

Turned

Section "A"-"A".

Cast Steel Segment Gear #3090.
Pitch Dia. = 9½".
No. of Teeth = 5.
Circular Pitch = 1.86".

Cast Steel Pinion Gear #3089.
Pitch Dia. = 4¾".
No. of Teeth = 8.
Circular Pitch = 1.86".

Scale for Section "A"-"A".

Scale for Plan & Elevation of Switch Stand
and Detail of Connecting Rod.

Elevation
Low Switch Stand.

For use with Banner Lamps on Inside Switches and
other locations on Main Line where Standard Target
cannot be used. Details not otherwise shown to
be same as High Target Switch Stand.

Plan.

Malleable Lock.
Upright Cstg. No. 7008.
Lever Cstg. No. 5175.
Weight Cstg. No. 5176.

Turned, Mach. Bolt
Jaw Opening
¼" Cotter.

Jaw Opening
for Switch Rod.
for Switch Rod.

Connecting Rod.

Length of Conn. Rod to be 6'-6" for High Target Switch Stand.
Length of Conn. Rod to be 3'-0" for low
Switch Stand used between tracks on
13'-0" centers.

Approved
Vice President
Approved
General Manager
Approved
Chief Engineer M. of W.

WABASH RAILWAY
STANDARD
SWITCH STAND

OFFICE OF THE CHIEF ENGINEER M. OF W.
ADOPTED JUNE 8, 1931

PLAN NO. 3017

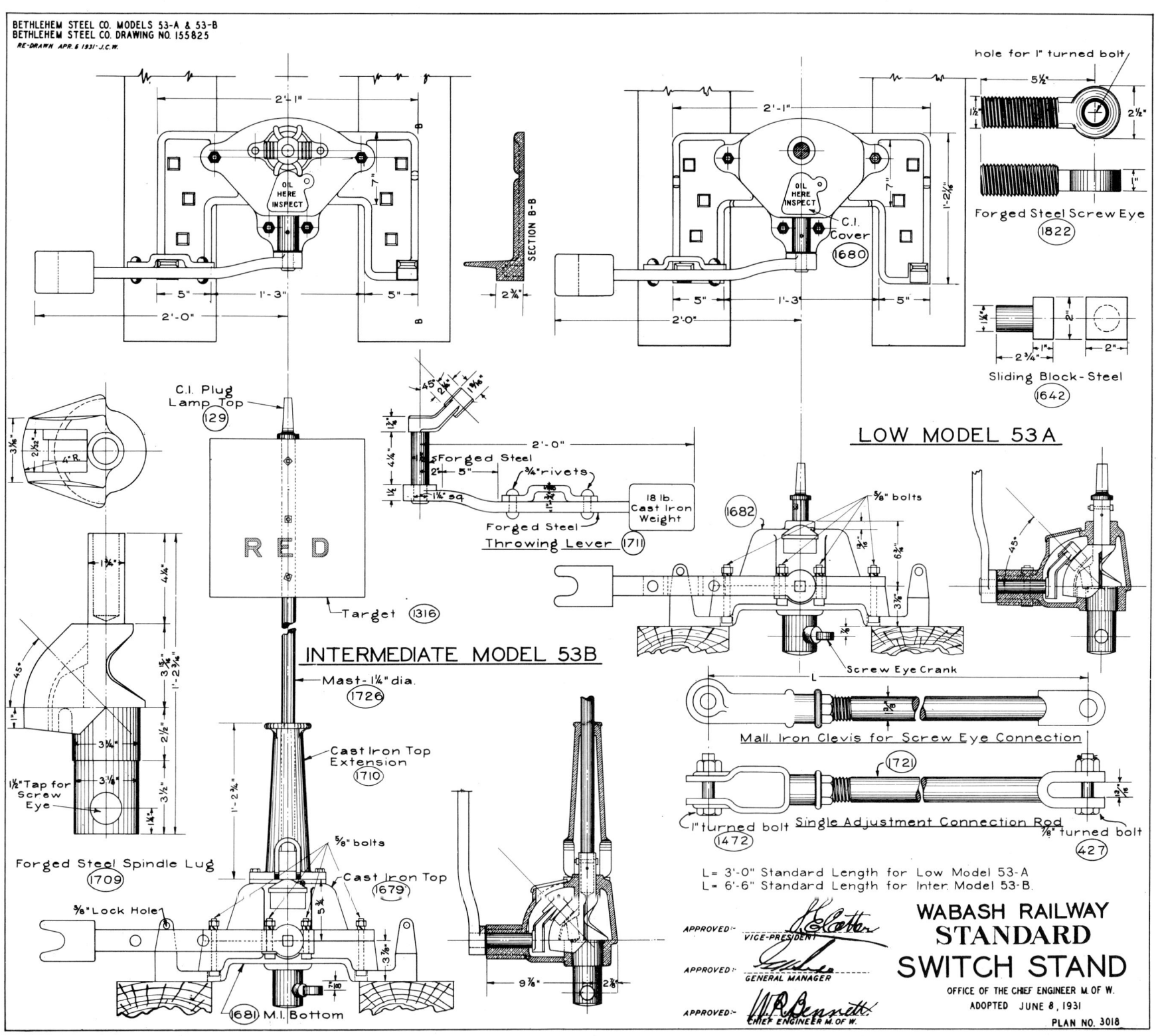

BETHLEHEM STEEL CO. MODELS 53-A & 53-B
BETHLEHEM STEEL CO. DRAWING NO. 155825
RE-DRAWN APR. 6 1931 J.C.W.

SECTION B-B

hole for 1" turned bolt

Forged Steel Screw Eye
(1822)

Sliding Block-Steel
(1642)

OIL HERE INSPECT

C.I. Cover
(1680)

C.I. Plug
Lamp Top
(129)

Forged Steel

45°

18 lb. Cast Iron Weight

Forged Steel
Throwing Lever (1711)

LOW MODEL 53A

(1682)

⅝" bolts

Screw Eye Crank

RED

Target (1316)

INTERMEDIATE MODEL 53B

Mast-1¼" dia.
(1726)

Cast Iron Top
Extension
(1710)

Mall. Iron Clevis for Screw Eye Connection
(1721)

1" turned bolt
(1472)

Single Adjustment Connection Rod

⅞" turned bolt
(427)

L= 3'-0" Standard Length for Low Model 53-A
L= 6'-6" Standard Length for Inter. Model 53-B.

45°

1½" Tap for Screw Eye

Forged Steel Spindle Lug
(1709)

⅝" Lock Hole

⅝" bolts

Cast Iron Top
(1679)

(1681) M.I. Bottom

APPROVED:-
VICE-PRESIDENT

APPROVED:-
GENERAL MANAGER

APPROVED:-
CHIEF ENGINEER M. OF W.

WABASH RAILWAY
STANDARD
SWITCH STAND

OFFICE OF THE CHIEF ENGINEER M. OF W.
ADOPTED JUNE 8, 1931

PLAN NO. 3018

Selections from the Wabash Annual Report of 1925

WABASH CLUB

WABASH RAILWAY COMPANY

TABLE OF MILEAGE

December 31, 1925

	First Main Track	Second Main Track	Third Main Track	Side Tracks	Total Miles All Tracks
OWNED AND OPERATED:					
Detroit to Delray, Mich.				15.22	15.22
Oakwood, Mich.				.65	.65
Delray, Mich. to Butler, Ind.	109.93	71.01		99.10	280.04
Montpelier, Ohio to Clarke Jct., Ind.	149.55	4.98		64.08	218.61
Toledo, Ohio to Alladin, Ill.	460.50	69.69		279.82	810.01
Maumee to Montpelier, Ohio	49.60			9.77	59.37
Butler to New Haven, Ind.	26.25			7.93	34.18
Attica to Covington, Ind.	14.80			2.97	17.77
C. & W. I. Jct. to Effingham, Ill.	204.72	28.36		89.93	323.01
Fairbury Junction to Streator, Ill.	30.90			6.76	37.66
Shumway to Altamont, Ill.	9.40			.51	9.91
Sidney to Champaign, Ill.	11.73			3.18	14.91
Decatur to Bridge Jct., Ill.	109.39	104.01		92.99	306.39
Bridge Jct. to East St. Louis Frt. House, Ill.	.61			3.66	4.27
Chicago to C. & W. I. Jct., Ill.				3.07	3.07
Edwardsville to Edwardsville Jct., Ill.	1.77			2.51	4.28
Bluffs to Camp Point, Ill.	39.54			5.07	44.61
Clayton to Elvaston, Ill.	34.51			1.78	36.29
Hamilton, Ill.				.15	.15
Maysville to Pittsfield, Ill.				1.07	1.07
Camp Point to Quincy, Ill.				.17	.17
Alladin, Ill. to Hannibal, Mo.				1.40	1.40
Quincy, Ill.	.90			6.35	7.25
Hannibal, Mo., North Street, to Union Depot				.45	.45
St. Louis, Mo., Tayon Ave. to 23rd St.	.43				.43
St. Louis, Mo., 23rd St. to Harlem, Mo.	274.36	55.66		140.06	470.08
St. Louis, Mo., Franklin Ave. to North Market St.				3.45	3.45
St. Louis, Mo., Carr St. to Ferguson, Mo.	10.67	5.10		32.96	48.73
Centralia to Columbia, Mo.	21.59			2.60	24.19
Moberly, Mo. to Ottumwa, Iowa	131.25			23.33	154.58
Moulton Jct. to Albia, Iowa	28.31			2.73	31.04
Albia to Chesterfield, Iowa	65.81			10.00	75.81
Tracy, Iowa, to Pershing Coal Co.				6.07	6.07
Salisbury to Glasgow, Mo.	15.37			1.41	16.78
Brunswick to Chillicothe, Mo.	38.35			4.38	42.73
Chillicothe to Pattonsburg, Mo.	41.38			3.97	45.35
Pattonsburg, Mo. to Council Bluffs, Iowa	143.67			29.09	172.76
Excelsior Springs Jct. to Excelsior Springs, Mo.	9.10			1.32	10.42
Harlem to Kansas City, Mo.				3.12	3.12
TOTAL	**2,034.39**	**338.81**		**963.08**	**3,336.28**
LEASED:					
Buffalo, N.Y.—Erie R.R.				1.03	1.03
Chicago to C. & W. I. Jct., Ill.—Chicago & Western Ind. R.R.				12.63	12.63
Quincy, Ill.—Quincy, Omaha & Kansas City R.R.				.45	.45
Alladin, Ill. to Hannibal, Mo.—Hannibal Bridge Co.	2.90			.23	3.13
Streator, Ill.—Chicago, Wilmington & Franklin Coal Co.				.18	.18
Lafayette, Ind.—Lafayette Union Ry.				5.45	5.45
Hannibal to Moberly, Mo.,—Missouri-Kansas-Texas R.R.	69.75			19.04	88.79
TOTAL	**72.65**			**39.01**	**111.66**
OPERATED UNDER TRACKAGE RIGHTS:					
Buffalo to Black Rock, N.Y.—Delaware, Lackawanna & Western R.R.	14.77	14.17			28.94
Black Rock, N.Y., to Detroit, Mich.—Canadian National Rys.	228.20	90.24		139.75	458.19
Welland Jct., Ont., to Suspension Bridge, N.Y.—Canadian National Rys.	18.00	6.50			24.50
Detroit Union Depot to Delray, Mich.—Detroit Union Railroad Depot & Station Company	4.45	4.45			8.90
Detroit Union Depot to Delray, Mich.—Pere Marquette Ry., Joint Ownership				14.38	14.38
CARRIED FORWARD	**265.42**	**115.36**		**154.13**	**534.91**

WABASH RAILWAY COMPANY

TABLE OF MILEAGE—Continued

December 31, 1925

	First Main Track	Second Main Track	Third Main Track	Side Tracks	Total Miles All Tracks
OPERATED UNDER TRACKAGE RIGHTS—Concluded					
BROUGHT FORWARD	265.42	115.36		154.13	534.91
Detroit, Mich.—West Belt, Pennsylvania R.R.				9.41	9.41
Detroit, Mich.—Oakman Branch, Pennsylvania R.R.	1.48			.58	2.06
Delray, Mich.—Pere Marquette Ry.	.13			.13	.26
Detroit, Mich.—Pere Marquette Ry.	12.86	2.16		6.35	21.37
Detroit, Mich.—Canadian National Rys.				5.00	5.00
Milan, Mich., to Hallett, O.—Ann Arbor R.R.	26.62			2.16	28.78
Hallett, O., to Gould, O.—Toledo Terminal R.R.	10.48			.17	10.65
Peru, Ind.—Peru Belt R.R.				2.52	2.52
Clarke Junction, Ind. to State Line, Ind.-Ill.—B. & O. Chicago Terminal R.R.	5.67	5.67		.25	11.59
State Line, Ind.-Ill., to C. & W. I. Junction, Ill.—Chicago & Western Indiana R.R.	11.85	11.85			23.70
Chicago to C. & W. I. Junction, Ill.—Chicago & Western Indiana R.R.	7.98	7.98		57.49	73.45
Chicago, Ill.—Chicago, Indianapolis & Louisville R.R.				.18	.18
Chicago, Ill.—Chicago Junction Ry.				1.52	1.52
Forrest to Fairbury Junction, Ill.—Toledo, Peoria & Western R.R.	6.12				6.12
Altamont, Ill.—Baltimore & Ohio Southwestern R.R.	.85			.97	1.82
Bridge Junction, Ill., to St. Louis Union Station, Mo.—Terminal R.R. Ass'n of St. Louis	3.85	3.85			7.70
Hamilton, Ill., to Keokuk, Iowa—Keokuk Bridge Company	1.28				1.28
Elvaston to Hamilton, Ill.—Toledo, Peoria & Western R.R.	6.53				6.53
Maysville to Pittsfield Ill.—Louisiana & Pike County R.R.	6.17				6.17
Camp Point to Quincy, Ill.—Chicago, Burlington & Quincy R.R.	22.89				22.89
Quincy to East Hannibal, Ill.—Chicago, Burlington & Quincy R.R.	16.22			2.13	18.35
Keokuk, Iowa—Chicago, Rock Island & Pacific R.R.				4.60	4.60
St. Louis, Mo., Union Station to Twenty-third St.—Terminal R.R. Ass'n of St. Louis	.66				.66
St. Louis, Mo. Washington Ave. to Carr St.—Missouri Pacific R.R.	.36			.36	.72
Albia to Albia Connection, Iowa—Minneapolis & St. Louis R.R.	.24			.60	.84
Chesterfield to Des Moines, Iowa—Des Moines Union Ry.	2.40			24.89	27.29
Carrollton Junction to Camden Junction, Mo.—Atchison, Topeka & Santa Fe R.R.		29.63	13.38	12.78	55.79
Birmingham to Harlem, Mo.—Chicago Burlington & Quincy R.R.		8.23			8.23
Harlem to Kansas City Old Union Depot, Mo.—Chicago, Burlington & Quincy R.R.	1.35	1.35		1.49	4.19
Kansas City, Mo. Old Union Depot to New Union Station—Kansas City Terminal R.R.	2.61	2.61			5.22
Kansas City, Mo., Santa Fe St.—St. Louis-San Francisco R.R.				.12	.12
Council Bluffs, Iowa to Omaha, Neb.—Union Pacific R.R.	2.80	2.80			5.60
Wabash Connection to Council Bluffs Union Depot, Iowa—Chicago, Milwaukee & St. Paul R.R.	.34				.34
TOTAL	**417.16**	**191.62**	**13.38**	**287.70**	**909.86**
TOTAL MILEAGE OPERATED DECEMBER 31, 1925	2,524.20	530.43	13.38	1,289.79	4,357.80
TOTAL MILEAGE OPERATED DECEMBER 31, 1924	2,524.20	513.95	13.38	1,243.32	4,294.85
INCREASE		16.48		46.47	62.95
OWNED, NOT OPERATED:					
Edwardsville Junction to Edwardsville Crossing, Ill.—Leased to Illinois Terminal R.R.	6.83			.36	7.19
Detroit, Mich.—Leased to Detroit & Western Ry.				2.41	2.41
TOTAL	**6.83**			**2.77**	**9.60**

SUMMARY

	First Main Track	Second Main Track	Third Main Track	Side Tracks	Total Miles All Tracks
Mileage Owned and Operated	2,034.39	338.81		963.08	3,336.28
Mileage Operated and Not Owned	489.81	191.62	13.38	326.71	1,021.52
Mileage Owned and Not Operated	6.83			2.77	9.60
TOTAL	**2,531.03**	**530.43**	**13.38**	**1,292.56**	**4,367.40**

WABASH RAILWAY COMPANY

TABLE OF MILEAGE—Concluded

December 31, 1925

MILEAGE OF SECOND AND THIRD MAIN TRACKS OWNED AND UNDER TRACKAGE RIGHTS

OWNED				UNDER TRACKAGE RIGHTS:		
DETROIT DIVISION:				BUFFALO DIVISION:		
Delray to Britton, Mich........	42.32			· Black Rock to Buffalo, N. Y......	14.17	
Lima Jct. to Montpelier, Ohio...	28.69			Windsor to Glencoe, Ont........	80.06	
Gary to Clarke Jct., Ind........	4.98	75.99		Bridgeburg to Welland Jct.Ont...	8.79	
PERU DIVISION:				Niagara Falls, N. Y. to Clifton		
New Haven to Hugo, Ind........	8.60			Junction, Ont........	1.39	
Peru, Ind................	2.77			Port Robinson to Welland Jct.,		
Lafayette, Ind........	1.68			Ont............	6.50	110.91
State Line, Ind.—Ill. to Tilton,Ill.	10.88	23.93		DETROIT DIVISION:		
DECATUR DIVISION:				Detroit to Delray, Mich........	6.74	
Tilton to Fairmount, Ill........	8.16			Clarke Jct., Ind. to C. & W. I.		
Tolono to Decatur, Ill........	37.60			Jct., Ill........	17.52	24.26
Decatur Jct. to Granite City,Ill.	104.01			DECATUR DIVISION:		
C. & W. I. Jct. to Orland, Ill...	15.31			Bridge Jct., Ill. to St. Louis		
Lodge to Bement, Ill.........	13.05	178.13		Union Station, Mo........	3.85	
MOBERLY DIVISION:				Chicago to C. & W. I. Jct., Ill....	7.98	11.83
St. Louis, Mo., 23rd. St. to Page				WESTERN DIVISION:		
Ave........	6.35			Birmingham to Harlem, Mo.....	8.23	
St. Louis, Mo. Carr St. to Luther	5.10			Bridge Jct. to Kansas City, Mo.		
Clark to Moberly, Mo..........	13.28	24.73		Old Union Depot........	1.35	
WESTERN DIVISION:				Kansas City, Mo. Old Union		
Moberly to Huntsville, Mo......	4.64			Depot to New Union Station..	2.61	
Salisbury to Brunswick, Mo.....	18.15			Council Bluffs, Iowa to Omaha,		
Excelsior Springs Jct. to Birm-				Neb........	2.80	
ingham, Mo............	13.24	36.03		Carrollton Jct. to Camden Jct.		
				Mo.:		
TOTAL........			338.81	Second Main Track.......	29.63	
				Third Main Track.......	13.38	43.01	58.00
				TOTAL................			205.00

MILEAGE BY STATES

	OWNED				LEASED LINES AND TRACKAGE RIGHTS					Total Miles All Tracks
	First Main Track	Second Main Track	Side Tracks	Total	First Main Track	Second Main Track	Third Main Track	Side Tracks	Total	
New York...					15.57	14.17		1.03	30.77	30.77
Canada......					245.40	96.74		139.75	481.89	481.89
*Michigan..	75.82	54.50	86.45	216.77	43.99	6.74		37.76	88.49	305.26
Ohio......	164.52	16.51	77.49	258.52	12.03			.29	12.32	270.84
Indiana.....	352.34	18.22	162.71	533.27	5.67	5.67		8.22	19.56	552.83
*Illinois.....	668.25	188.82	373.56	1,230.63	82.93	21.35		75.78	180.06	1,410.69
Missouri.....	576.98	60.76	223.96	861.70	78.06	44.15	13.38	33.79	169.38	1,031.08
Iowa.....	203.31		41.68	244.99	5.56	2.20		30.09	37.85	282.84
Nebraska....					.60	.60			1.20	1.20
TOTAL..	2,041.22	339.81	965.85	3,345.88	489.81	191.62	13.38	366.71	1,061.50	4,367.40

*Includes trackage leased to Illinois Terminal R. R.
#Includes sidetracks leased to Detroit & Western Ry.

WABASH RAILWAY COMPANY

TRANSPORTATION STATISTICS

Year Ended December 31, 1925, Compared with Previous Year

	1925	1924	AMOUNT		PER CENT	
			Increase	Decrease	Increase	Decrease
TRAIN MILES						
REVENUE SERVICE:						
Freight........	8,203,742	7,788,424	415,318		5.33	
Passenger........	6,014,576	6,002,587	11,989		.20	
Mixed........	185,094	71,675	113,419		158.24	
Special........	3,712	6,278		2,566		40.87
TOTAL........	14,407,124	13,868,964	538,160		3.88	
Non-Revenue........	227,760	196,893	30,867		15.68	
TOTAL TRAIN MILES........	14,634,884	14,065,857	569,027		4.05	
CAR MILES						
REVENUE SERVICE:						
Freight:						
Loaded........	258,385,794	236,102,291	22,283,503		9.44	
Empty........	118,560,823	101,341,209	17,219,614		16.99	
Caboose........	8,301,196	7,885,885	415,311		5.27	
TOTAL........	385,247,813	345,329,385	39,918,428		11.56	
Passenger:						
Coach and Chair........	13,837,427	13,548,680	288,747		2.13	
Parlor and Observation....	410,412	448,865		38,453		8.57
Sleeping........	9,139,547	8,441,115	698,432		8.27	
Baggage, Mail and Express..	10,408,494	10,382,101	26,393		.25	
Dining........	1,881,798	1,693,547	188,251		11.12	
Official........	153,602	149,670	3,932		2.63	
TOTAL........	35,831,280	34,663,978	1,167,302		3.37	
Special Freight:						
Loaded........	47,068	76,886		29,818		38.78
Empty........	8			8		
Caboose........	3,712	6,278		2,566		40.87
TOTAL........	50,788	83,164		32,376		38.93
Special Passenger:						
Coach and Chair........	18,880	29,371		10,491		35.72
TOTAL........	18,880	29,371		10,491		35.72
TOTAL REVENUE SERVICE CAR MILES....	421,148,761	380,105,898	41,042,863		10.80	
· Non-Revenue........	1,291,188	1,158,959	132,229		11.41	
Work Car Miles in Revenue Trains.......	801,136	501,043	300,093		59.89	
TOTAL TRAIN CAR MILES........	423,241,085	381,765,900	41,475,185		10.86	
MISCELLANEOUS FREIGHT						
Foreign Loaded Car Miles........	191,694,639	181,369,012	10,325,627		5.69	
Foreign Empty Car Miles........	82,887,830	73,301,279	9,586,551		13.08	
TOTAL........	274,582,469	254,670,291	19,912,178		7.82	
Wabash Loaded Car Miles........	66,738,223	54,810,165	11,928,058		21.76	
Wabash Empty Car Miles (including Cabooses).......	43,977,909	35,932,093	8,045,816		22.39	
TOTAL........	110,716,132	90,742,258	19,973,874		22.01	
Average number of Wabash Cars in Service (exclusive of Work Trains) per day........	23,461	22,612	849		3.75	
Average number of Wabash Cars on other Roads per day..	9,965	10,113		148		1.46
Miles per Car per day Wabash Cars on Wabash Road..	20.79	18.11	2.68		14.80	
Average number of Foreign Cars on Wabash Road per day	11,827	10,932	895		8.19	
Miles per Car per day Foreign Cars on Wabash Road..	63.60	63.63		.03		.05
Average Revenue Freight Train Miles per day........	22,834	21,417	1,417		6.62	
Average Loaded Cars per Train Mile........	31.00	30.12	.88		2.92	
Average Empty Cars (excluding Cabooses) per Train Mile	14.23	12.93	1.30		10.05	
Average Loaded and Empty Cars per Train Mile........	45.23	43.05	2.18		5.06	
Average Total Cars (including Cabooses) per Train Mile.	46.22	44.05	2.17		4.93	
Per Cent of Loaded Car Miles to total Car Miles........	67.07	68.37		1.30		1.90
PASSENGER						
Total Wabash Passenger Train Car Miles........	33,966,128	32,552,915	1,413,213		4.34	
Total Foreign Passenger Train Car Miles........	1,004,002	1,240,464		236,462		11.98
Average Revenue Passenger Train Miles per day........	16,627	16,459	168		1.02	
Average number of Cars per Passenger Train Mile........	5.90	5.75	.15		2.61	

Wabash Passenger Trains

Artist's rendering of Wabash streamliner *City of St. Louis* **with both Wabash and Union Pacific logos on the locomotive nose.**

WABASH *Blue Bird* NEW LUXURY IN RAILROAD TRAVEL

TODAY, Wabash continues in the tradition of progress with the new streamliner *"Blue Bird"—most modern train in America.* Get aboard the *"Blue Bird"* next time you are traveling between Chicago and St. Louis. Enjoy riding in the modern domes. Relish a meal in the pleasant diner or a snack in the Coffee Shop Club. Where else can you find such travel luxury with safety and economy?

Go Wabash anywhere *in The Heart of America*

Sixteen modern, diesel-powered Wabash trains serve travelers in The Heart of America. In addition to the *"Blue Bird,"* this Wabash fleet includes the completely new streamliners *"City of Kansas City"* and *"City of St. Louis."* The *"City of St. Louis"* offers through service, St. Louis to the West Coast.

WABASH RAILROAD

MODERN SERVICE IN THE HEART OF AMERICA

"Follow the Flag"
WABASH

WABASH *Blue Bird*

"BLUE BIRD" SCHEDULE

	Summer # Schedule	Winter * Schedule
SOUTHBOUND		
Lv. Chicago Dearborn Station	4:35 PM	4:45 PM
Lv. Chicago Englewood Station	4:49 PM	4:59 PM
Lv. Decatur	7:33 PM	7:43 PM
Ar. St. Louis Delmar Station	9:42 PM	9:52 PM
Ar. St. Louis Union Station	10:00 PM	10:10 PM

#—Last Sunday in April through last Saturday in September.
*—Last Sunday in September through last Saturday in April.

NORTHBOUND	
Lv. St. Louis Union Station	8:55 AM
Lv. St. Louis Delmar Station	9:08 AM
Lv. Decatur	11:10 AM
Ar. Chicago Englewood Station	1:50 PM
Ar. Chicago Dearborn Station	2:05 PM

(Central Standard Time)

A stately Wabash observation car on the end of the *Cannon Ball. Collection of Don Heimburger*

The inbound *Blue Bird* swings through trackage in Chicago at Western Avenue. *William Raia*

Early postcard showing *City of Kansas City.*

NOW! 2 Great WABASH Streamliners
Bring You Truly Luxurious Service

"CITY OF KANSAS CITY" — This completely new Wabash Streamliner offers you the ultimate in modern rail travel. Daily service between St. Louis and Kansas City. Diesel-powered, of course. *Extra* comfort . . . *but no extra fare.*

"CITY OF ST. LOUIS" — This sleek Wabash Streamliner, a companion train to the "City of Kansas City," is in daily service between St. Louis, Kansas City, Denver and the West Coast. Through sleeping cars and coaches to Los Angeles and Portland. Through sleeping car to San Francisco.

TOM M. HAYES, Passenger Traffic Manager
1495 Railway Exchange Building
St. Louis 1, Missouri

Work or Play . . . Go the WABASH WAY!

Relax in the superb "Coffee-Shop-Club" car on the "City of Kansas City." You'll also enjoy this Streamliner's cozy cocktail lounge . . . its finer diner . . . its reclining, revolving "Sleepy Hollow" seats . . . its magnificent Observation-Parlor-Lounge.

View the scenic West from a comfortable armchair in the Club Lounge Car of the Wabash Streamliner "City of St. Louis." You'll like the many Wabash "extras" . . . the smooth-riding roadbeds . . . the courteous Wabash service.

Dining is Delightful on the WABASH!

You'll really enjoy the good cooking . . . the superb service . . . the delicious food . . . on Wabash diners. Whether you select a light snack or a tender, juicy steak, you'll find that Wabash chefs are wonderfully skilled at preparing dishes sure to satisfy your discriminating taste.

Enjoy meals the Wabash Way . . . in the club-like atmosphere of a Wabash diner. Choose from a wide variety of tasty dishes . . . prepared by experts . . . served by courteous, well trained waiters. You'll say, "On the Wabash, dining is *delightful!*"

P. E. GRIFFITH
Superintendent Dining Cars
St. Louis 3, Mo.

For help in planning your trip . . . PHONE WABASH!

For your convenience, Wabash has experienced, efficient passenger agents in 44 offices throughout the United States and Canada. Any time you want expert help in planning a trip, just phone your Wabash agent.

You'll find a complete list of Traffic Representatives on the front inside cover of this timetable. For prompt service, phone or write the Wabash office nearest you.

WABASH RAILROAD

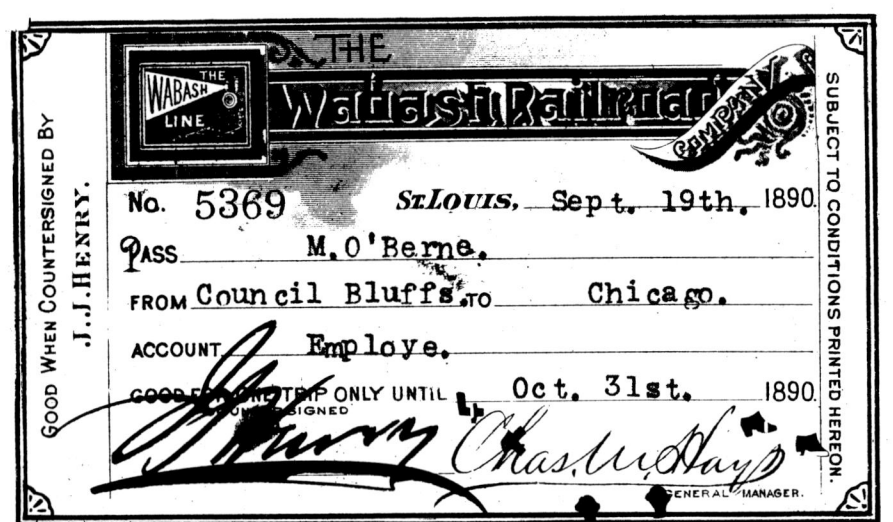

GOOD WHEN COUNTERSIGNED BY J.J.HENRY.

SUBJECT TO CONDITIONS PRINTED HEREON

THE Wabash Railroad COMPANY

WABASH LINE

No. 5369   St. Louis, Sept. 19th, 1890.

PASS   M. O'Berne.

FROM Council Bluffs, TO   Chicago.

ACCOUNT   Employe.

GOOD FOR ROUND TRIP ONLY UNTIL   Oct. 31st,   1890.
COUNTERSIGNED

Chas. M. Hays
GENERAL MANAGER.

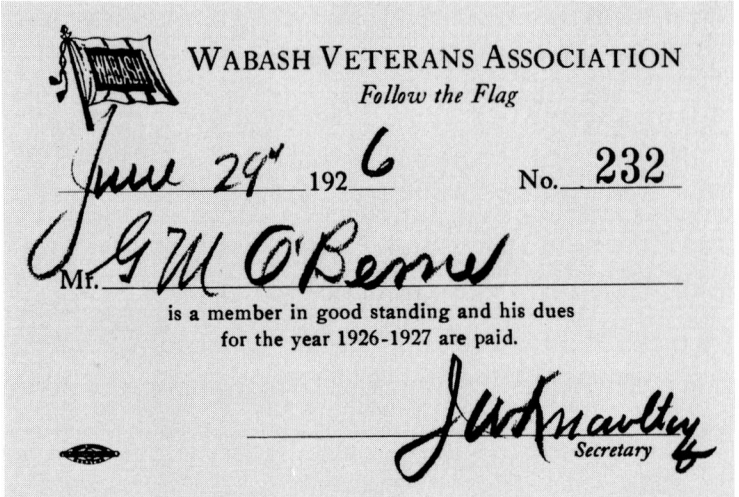

WABASH VETERANS ASSOCIATION

Follow the Flag

June 29th 1926   No. 232

Mr. G M O'Berne

is a member in good standing and his dues
for the year 1926-1927 are paid.

Secretary

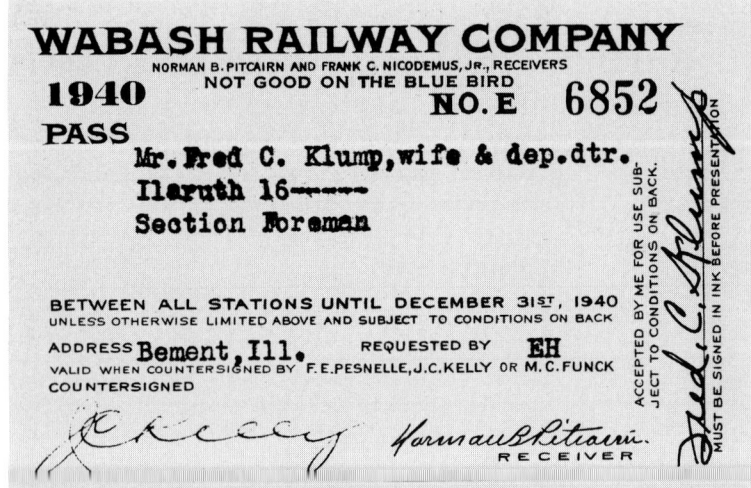

WABASH RAILWAY COMPANY

NORMAN B. PITCAIRN AND FRANK C. NICODEMUS, JR., RECEIVERS
NOT GOOD ON THE BLUE BIRD

1940   NO. E 6852

PASS

Mr. Fred C. Klump, wife & dep. dtr.
Maruth 16------
Section Foreman

BETWEEN ALL STATIONS UNTIL DECEMBER 31ST, 1940
UNLESS OTHERWISE LIMITED ABOVE AND SUBJECT TO CONDITIONS ON BACK

ADDRESS Bement, Ill.   REQUESTED BY EH
VALID WHEN COUNTERSIGNED BY F.E.PESNELLE, J.C.KELLY OR M.C.FUNCK
COUNTERSIGNED

Norman B. Pitcairn
RECEIVER

ACCEPTED BY ME FOR USE SUBJECT TO CONDITIONS ON BACK.
MUST BE SIGNED IN INK BEFORE PRESENTATION

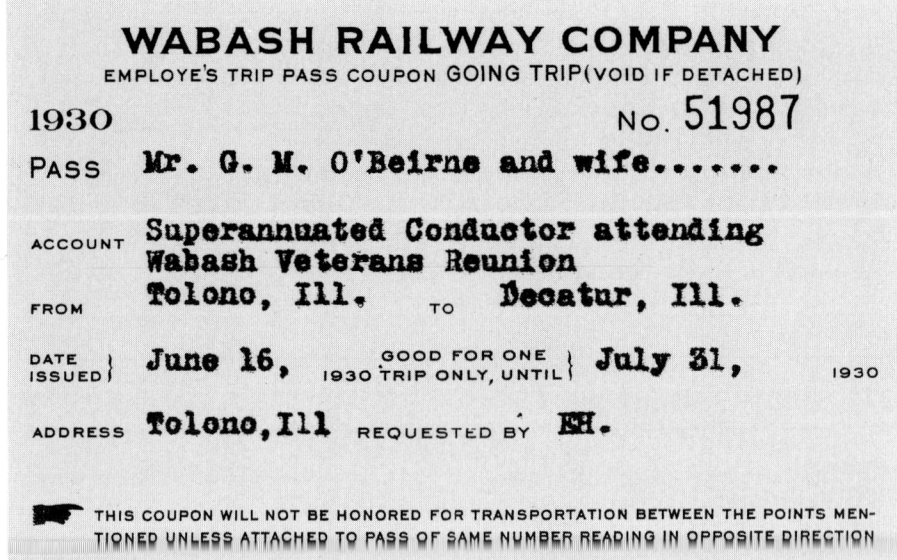

WABASH RAILWAY COMPANY

EMPLOYE'S TRIP PASS COUPON GOING TRIP (VOID IF DETACHED)

1930   No. 51987

PASS   Mr. G. M. O'Beirne and wife.......

ACCOUNT   Superannuated Conductor attending
Wabash Veterans Reunion

FROM   Tolono, Ill.   TO   Decatur, Ill.

DATE ISSUED } June 16,   GOOD FOR ONE 1930 TRIP ONLY, UNTIL } July 31,   1930

ADDRESS   Tolono, Ill   REQUESTED BY EH.

THIS COUPON WILL NOT BE HONORED FOR TRANSPORTATION BETWEEN THE POINTS MEN-
TIONED UNLESS ATTACHED TO PASS OF SAME NUMBER READING IN OPPOSITE DIRECTION

ABOVE. A very grimy E-7 #1017 delivers a six-car passenger train to Decatur on September 1, 1963. The diesel looks like it should be sent to the paint shop; it was originally built in 1946 and numbered 1000, then renumbered 1002A, and in 1961 it received #1017. Two years after this photo was taken the unit was retired. *William Raia*

LEFT. Wabash #667 J-1 leads Train #4, the *Detroit Special*, through Decatur on June 28, 1948. A connection was made at Ft. Wayne with this train for Toledo passengers. *Collection of M.D. McCarter*

With her domes painted and striped, #683 4-6-2 pounds through East St. Louis in April of 1942 with passenger varnish trailing. *Richard Ganger*

The Columbia, Missouri mixed train ran between Centralia and Columbia. In 1963 Wabash sponsored two mixed dailies and a passenger daily each way. The distance between the two towns was 21.7 miles, and four stops were made enroute including Hallsville, Browns, Stephens and Switzler. This photo was taken on May 30, 1964; the GP-7 has a baggage car and one lone coach in tow. *Louis Marre*

THE WABASH CLUB

Passenger diesel #1005 was a 2,250 hp E-8 shown here at 12th Street in Chicago. *Bruce Meyer*

Wabash Steam Locomotives

The Wabash, and its predecessor lines, owned a number of steam locomotives of various classes and wheel arrangements. The following listing highlights Wabash steam locomotives generally from the smaller to the larger wheel arrangements, and from smaller numbered locomotives to higher numbered locomotives.

A Lima product, No. 1552 0-8-0 was built in 1926 and scrapped in 1953. *M.D. McCarter*

Wabash No. 546, an 0-6-0 with slope back tender, was one of a number of such Class B-7 switchers purchased by the Wabash from both Rhode Island and Baldwin Locomotive Works. No. 546 is at Decatur, Illinois in February of 1951. *Collection of Don Gruber*

This 0-8-0 Class C-1 was rebuilt from an I-1 2-8-0. It was formerly numbered 2162; the locomotive was scrapped in 1947. *E. Lindquist, collection of C.T. Felstead*

Wabash Class F-5 No. 573, originally No. 754, was a Rhode Island Locomotive Works product built in 1899. Here it sits with sister locomotives.

American Locomotive Company's Richmond Shop turned out this beautiful 2-6-0 for the Wabash in 1899. The locomotive's driving wheels were 63 inches and the locomotive had a boiler pressure of 185 lbs.

The Prairie 2-6-2 Class G-1 was built for freight service on the Wabash by Baldwin in 1906.

No. 622, a high-stepping 4-4-2, is a Brooks Locomotive Company product of 1903. This locomotive served on the railroad until it was scrapped in November of 1944. *M.D. McCarter*

Baldwin-built No. 608, a high-stepping 4-4-2, with small Wabash flags stencilled under the engineer's window, was a beautiful locomotive. It featured 79 inch drivers and a working boiler pressure of 220 lbs.

No. 609, a member of the E-2 Class of Atlantics, was subsequently renumbered to 697 and then to 627. It was built in 1901 by Richmond and scrapped in December of 193▮

WABASH St. Louis, Kansas City and Des Moines.

This sleek 1904 Baldwin 4-6-0 was a member of the Class H-12s on the Wabash. It was scrapped in December of 1931.

Class J 4-6-2 No. 675 moves cars at Chicago in July of 1948. It was a Baldwin product.

Perhaps the classiest steam locomotive on the Wabash roster was the P-1 Class, the large 4-6-4 types. No. 705, ex-2744, was built by the Wabash Decatur Shops in 1946. Ten years later, it was scrapped. *P.H. Stringham, collection of C.T. Felstead*

EIGHT FAST TRAINS EVERY DAY

FOUR VIA VANDEVENTER, DELMAR, FLORISSANT AVENUES

St. Louis to Chicago		Chicago to St. Louis	
Lv. Union Station....	1 30PM 9 17PM	Lv. Dearborn Station	12 04PM 9 17PM
Lv. Vandeventer Ave.	1 36PM 9 23PM	Lv. Forty-seventh St.	12 14PM 9 27PM
Lv. Delmar Avenue..	1 45PM 9 32PM	Lv. Englewood (63d St.)	12 19PM 9 32PM
Lv. Florissant Ave...	2 00PM 9 47PM	Ar. Florissant Ave...	7 19PM 6 27AM
Ar. Englewood (63d St.)	9 14PM 6 44AM	Ar. Delmar Ave......	7 35PM 6 43AM
Ar. Forty-seventh St.	9 19PM 6 49AM	Ar. Vandeventer Ave.	7 42PM 6 50AM
Ar. Dearborn Station	9 30PM 7 00AM	Ar. Union Station....	7 57PM 7 05AM

FOUR VIA MERCHANTS BRIDGE AND ELEVATED

St. Louis to Chicago		Chicago to St. Louis	
Lv. St. Louis.........	8 30AM 11 32PM	Lv. Chicago	9 00AM 11 43PM
Lv. Washington Ave..		Lv. Forty-seventh St.	9 10AM 11 56PM
Lv. Granite City......	8 55AM 11 59PM	Lv. Englewood.......	9 15AM 12 01AM
Ar. Englewood.......	4 43PM 7 43AM	Ar. Granite City.....	5 12PM 7 22AM
Ar. Forty-seventh St.	4 48PM 7 48AM	Ar. Washington Ave.	5 30PM 7 42AM
Ar. Chicago..........	4 59PM 7 59AM	Ar. St. Louis.........	5 40PM 7 53AM

The last Wabash steam locomotive to be scrapped was No. 706 in September of 1956. Here it rests its final rest at Decatur on September 10, 1956.

Decatur-built 4-6-4 #700 (ex-2600) sits by awaiting assignment on October 21, 1950 in Decatur. The steamer featured 80″ drivers. *C.E. Prusia, collection of C.T. Felstead*

Class K-2 2-8-2 No. 2205 is at Des Moines, Iowa on November 8, 1947. Schenectady built it in 1918.

g 2-8-2 No. 2213 was an ex-Western Pacific No. 321 built by Baldwin in 1918. *R.J. Foster, collection of C.T. Felstead*

St. Louis and Omaha.

Schenectady-built 2-8-2 No. 2220 is at Des Moines, Iowa in 1947.

. 2507 was a Brooks product of 1917; it was scrapped in 1951. This photo was taken in 1939. *M. Anderson, collection of C.T. Felstead*

LEFT. Sitting behind the Decatur shops, No. 2515 looks heavy and powerful. It was built by Brooks in 1917 and sold in 1950, 12 years after this photo was taken, to the Chicago & Illinois Midland where it was renumbered 658. *Robert Morgan, collection of Louis A. Marre*

BELOW. Another 2-10-2 that was sold to the Chicago & Illinois Midland was No. 2523. *P. Eilenberger, collection of C.T. Felstead*

Schenectady-built No. 2739 is shown here, apparently after some shop work. The 2-8-2 locomotive was built in 1925 and was part of Class K-4.

A total of 20 K-4bs were built, all with boosters: note the counterbalance on the third driver. *M.D. McCarter collection*

The big M-1s of 4-8-2 wheel arrangement were built by Baldwin in early 1930. Engine #2806 was scrapped just 23 years later. *Collection of H.L. Broadbelt*

assive Baldwin-built No. 2817 of the M-1 Class plied the Wabash rails from 1930 to 1955. *C.E. Prusia, collection of C.T. Felstead*

WABASH

This retouched photograph of M-1 No. 2824 relates the ruggedness of the 4-8-2 types of Wabash power. This unit served the Wabash for 23 years.

The big Class O-1 Northern types were the heaviest class of power on the Wabash. They featured 70-inch drivers and developed 70,817 lbs. of tractive effort. *P. Eilenberger, collection of C.T. Felstead*

The huge Wabash 4-8-4 0-1s were a 1930 Baldwin product. This is a builder's photo, including 12-wheel tender. *Collection of H.L. Broadbelt*

This photo of 4-8-4 No. 2919 was taken just about 40 years from its scrapping date in 1953. *Collection of J.M. Gruber*

Wabash Diesel Locomotives

The Wabash owned a variety of diesel locomotives including SW-1s, NW-2s, Fairbanks H-12-44s, GP-7s, F-7s, FAs, GP-9s, Es, PAs, DL-640As, U-25Bs and GP-35s. This listing highlights various diesel classes from the smaller to the larger units, generally from smaller to larger numbers.

Venerable Wabash No. 51, a General Electric-built switcher locomotive of 1939, sits at St. Thomas, Ontario, Canada with its siderods down on June 2, 1950. *Richard Ganger*

Of the SW-1 EMD class of sleek diesel switchers, the Wabash owned four, including No. 102, a 600 hp diesel. *M.D. McCarter*

The Class D-6 600 hp locomotives of the Wabash included Nos. 100 and 150. The builder was American Locomotive Company, and the engine builder was McIntosh and Seymour. The D-6 had a maximum permissible speed of 40 miles an hour. *M.D. McCarter*

This very bold, rugged-looking locomotive, No. 202, was built in 1947 by Baldwin and had a rating of 660 hp. It was retired in 1964. The Wabash owned sisters 201 and 202. *M.D. McCarter*

The Fairbanks-Morse Wabash diesels were beautifully styled locomotives. The Wabash owned five of these Class D-10 models, rated at 1,000 hp.

A view of Fairbanks-Morse No. 382 H10-44 at Decatur, Illinois on September 1, 1963, slightly weather beaten. *Collection of Louis A. Marre*

Lima Locomotive Works built this D-12 1,200 hp diesel switcher in 1950. This is its birthday photograph taken by Lima. The unit was retired 15 years later in 1965. *Allen County Historical Society*

Lima D-12 profile view.

Wabash's beautiful white, blue and gray color scheme is amplified in this profile view of No. 451, a GP-7 shown here right after it was manufactured. *Collection of Don Heimburger*

LEFT. GP-7 1,500 hp road switcher No. 461 is on a Belt Railway of Chicago Clearing Yard-bound transfer of hoppers in 1963 at 79th Street in Chicago. *William Raia*

abash GP-7 D-15 No. 466 is at Des Moines, Iowa on December 8, 1962. The
it was built by EMD in February of 1952.

On a transfer run to the Santa Fe on a hot 101 degree day, Wabash No. 468 rambles through
Kansas City, Missouri in July of 1964. *Louis A. Marre*

No. 478 and No. 479 behind, rest
on Wabash tracks at North Kansas City, Missouri on July 24,
1964. *Louis A. Marre*

No. 506 was one of 15 locomotives in the series 500-514 built by General Electric, each with a rating of 2,500 hp. This unit is at Chicago in March of 1965. *Louis A. Marre*

The Wabash U-25Bs such as this No. 512 were built in 1962 by General Electric. No. 512 was wrecked in October of 1964 and subsequently scrapped. *Bruce Meyer*

A three-quarter view of blue and yellow Wabash No. 547 shows this 2,500 hp GP-35 at Decatur, Illinois in May of 1964. *Bruce Meyer*

me of the more husky-
ooking diesels the Wabash
wned were the Fairbanks-
orse model H-24-66s.
os. 550 and 551 were
iginally FM demonstrat-
s numbered TM-1 and
M-2. These were original-
2,400 hp locomotives
ilt in 1954. *J.M. Gruber*

GHT. A group of eight
350 hp Fairbanks-Morse
23 diesels were built be-
veen 1954 and 1956 for
e Wabash. Here, No. 597
s at Chicago in 1965. *L.G.*
aac

Originally numbered 1107A, this No. 624 EMD-built F-7 was constructed in 1949 and retired in 1964. *Collection of J.M. Gruber*

Renumbered in 1961, No. 633 is shown at Des Moines, Iowa in April of 1962. The unit was constructed in June of 1950.

The blue body paint scheme with silver roof No. 668 is at Windsor, Ontario on May 30, 1961. *Louis A. Marre*

Model F-7 No. 680 was built in 1951 and retired in 1966. These F-7 units saw a lot of road service on the Wabash.

F-7 D-15 No. 694 is seen at North Kansas City, Missouri in September 196

F-7 No. 695 is at North Kansas City, Missouri in July of 1964. *Louis A. Marre*

Here is ABA set of F-7s as they
were delivered from EMD in
1949. This set featured 4,500 hp
and a length over couplers of 151
ft. 4 in. The No. 1104 was retired
in 1964.

RIGHT. No. 1143A is at Detroit,
Michigan in July of 1951. *Elliott
Kahn, collection of Louis A. Marre*

Together these two F units pack 3,000 hp. They sit at Des Moines, Iowa in June of 1959, nine years after being delivered by EMD.

Nos. 1155 & 1155A were built by EMD in December of 1950. *M.D. McCarter*

It's New Year's Day, 1960, and three F-7 A units pull a freight train at Windsor, Ontario. *Bruce Meyer*

AA units 1164 and 1164A await their next assignment at Fort Erie, Ontario on the last day of July, 1955. *Richard Ganger*

F-7 No. 1175A leads a freight train at Albia, Iowa in 1953.

Wabash No. 1179 was leased to the Central of New Jersey Railroad. The unit was built in 1952 and later renumbered to 705. It sits in December of 1960 at North Kansas City, Missouri Louis A. Marre

No. 1180 F-7 shows how bottom plate spreads to expose front coupling area. *M.D. McCarter*

The FA-2s were Class D-16 1,600 hp models and included four units, Nos. 820-823, all coming originally from the Ann Arbor Railroad in 1963. This pair [at Moberly, Missouri in 1965. *J.M. Gruber*

No. 822 FA-2 was part of the acquisition from the Ann Arbor in 1963. The unit was originally built in 1950 and traded to Alco in 1965.

No. 823 is also ex-Ann Arbor No. 55. This unit was at Moberly, Missouri in 1965. *J.M. Gruber*

The B-900 series of Alco DL-640A locomotives were originally built for NdeM and were used as booster units on the Wabash. The set of seven 2,400 hp diesels were delivered in March of 1964. No. B905 is at Decatur in March of 1965. *Louis A. Marre*

Wabash No. 1001, Union Pacific No. 984C (middle unit), and Wabash No. 1001A pull the *City of St. Louis* at Denver, Colorado in May in 1949. No. 1001 is a 2,000 hp E-7A.

TOP, LEFT. No. 1002A was built in 1946 and retired in 1965. Here it is shown at St. Louis, Missouri in August of 1957. It was the first Wabash passenger unit, having been originally numbered 1000.

RIGHT. Part of the series E-8A models from EMD was No. 1006, a 2,250 hp Class D-22 model built by EMD in 1949 and retired in 1967. The unit is at Decatur, Illinois in May of 1957.

The Wabash owned several Alco PA 2,000 hp models, including No. 1021 built in 1949 and retired in March of 1965. The unit rests here at Decatur, Illinois in March of 1957. It was subsequently renumbered 1052.

Miscellaneous

This section includes a variety of items from timetables, and shows a reefer, cushion underframe car, diesel shops, cabooses, troop sleeper, freight stations, locomotive cranes and the Ann Arbor-owned *Wabash* Great Lakes ferry.

Inside cover of Wabash October 28, 1956 Timetable.

"Are the frontiers of railroading dead? Not on the Wabash!"

CROSS A TRAIN AND A TRUCK and you get "Piggy Back"—an all-weather, door-to-door service for shippers . . . a modern-day method of moving freight speedily and safely across Wabash's vast Heart of America route.

In the words of Wabash President A. K. Atkinson, "Never before in history have the drama and excitement of railroading—and the prospects for future developments—been greater than today.

"Here on the Wabash, we're in the midst of a revolution in railroading. Today, we're serving the Heart of America with a new and infinitely better kind of railroad—modern, efficient, built of new ideas and 'look-ahead' planning.

"For example, Wabash 'Piggy Back' service offers shippers advantages not available to them a few short years ago. Luxurious Domeliners make Wabash passenger travel more attractive, more fun. And these few examples can only begin to tell the full story of today's Wabash, alive and alert to your growing needs . . . and building toward greater things tomorrow.

"The romance of railroading gone? The frontiers dead? Not on the Wabash! We're always moving . . . ahead!"

Arthur K. Atkinson

WABASH ROAD OF THE MEN WHO MOVE THE GOODS

From the Wabash Yardman's Pay Schedule Book of May 1, 1912.

 125

THE WABASH RAILROAD CO.

F. A. Delano, W. K. Bixby, E. B. Pryor, Receivers
Office of General Superintendent

St. Louis, Mo., April 25, 1912.

Schedule for Yardmen

(Except Chicago Switching District)
Effective May 1, 1912

The following rates of pay, rules and regulations, apply to yardmen in the yard designated:

ARTICLE I.

(a) Rates of pay per hour:

	Day Foremen	Night Foremen	Day Helper	Night Helper
St. Louis	38c	40c	35c	37c
East St. Louis	38c	40c	35c	37c
Kansas City	38c	40c	35c	37c
Council Bluffs	38c	40c	35c	37c
Detroit	37c	39c	34c	36c
Toledo	37c	39c	34c	36c
Fort Wayne	37c	39c	34c	36c
Danville	37c	39c	34c	36c
Tilton	37c	39c	34c	36c
Decatur	37c	39c	34c	36c
Forrest	37c	39c	34c	36c
Springfield	37c	39c	34c	36c
Moberly	37c	39c	34c	36c
Stanberry	37c	39c	34c	36c
Peru	36c	38c	33c	35c
Montpelier	36c	38c	33c	35c
Lafayette	36c	38c	33c	35c
Quincy	36c	38c	33c	35c
Adrian	36c		33c	
Streator	36c		33c	

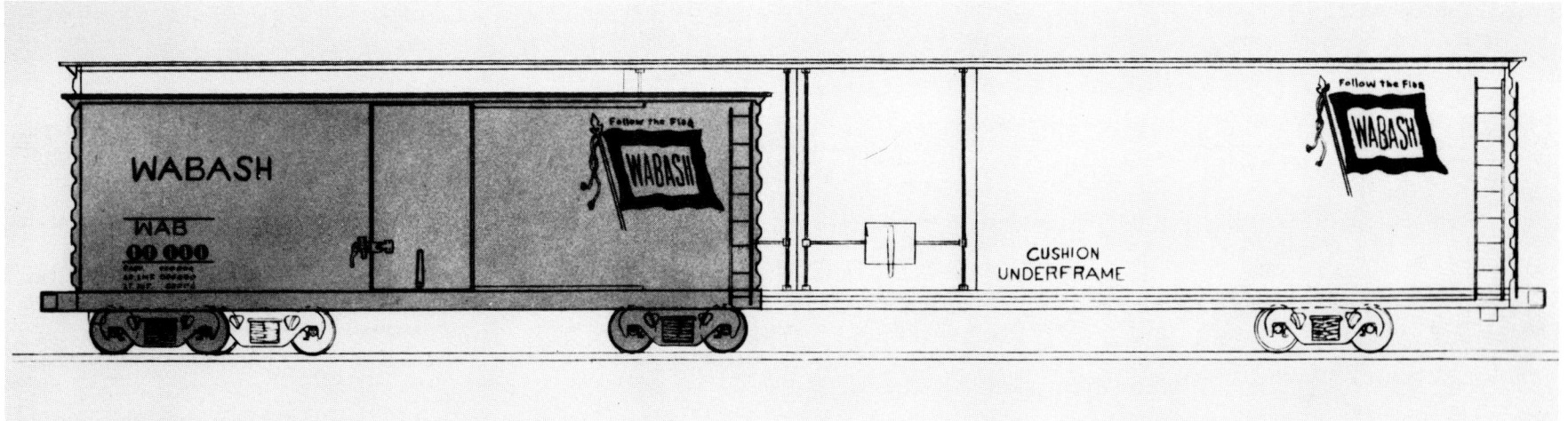

This sketch of Wabash freight cars shows the extreme difference between the elongated cushioned underframed cars and the typical 40 ft. Wabash box car.

American Refrigerator Transit Company (Wabash-Missouri Pacific owned) plug door refrigerator car No. 28545 when it was built new.

This is a view of the heavy locomotive repair shops at Decatur. A number of diesels are in the shop, including from front to back, an F-7, an FA, a switcher, a Jeep, a PA and at the far end, an F-7 as well as a small steam locomotive. *Collection of Don Heimburger*

The Wabash used ex-U.S. Army troop sleepers for their mainten-ance-of-way department. Here, No. 5709 sits at Ashtabula, Ohio on July 20, 1965. *Richard Ganger*

Wood caboose No. 2601 at South Bend, Indiana and not looking very roadable in October of 1963. *L.G. Isaac*

Cupolaless wood caboose No. 2657 at Chicago in June of 1948.

Red, white and blue steel-sided caboose No. 2767 pulls through Danville, Illinois on April 25, 1964. *L.G. Isaac*

WABASH R.R. STATION   SADORUS ILL

The Wabash freight/passenger station at Sadorus, Illinois, about four miles west of Tolono, has been gone for many years.

Wood sided wrecking crane No. 3183 and idler flat car sit at North Kansas City, Missouri in September of 1961, awaiting next assignment. The wrecker was built by the Industrial Works of Bay City, Michigan in 1908.

This 70-ton capacity two-bay covered hopper was built in July of 1959 by the Greenville Steel Car Co. of Greenville, Pennsylvania. Note both the "New 7-59" and "Built 7-59" stenciling on the side. *Collection of Kevin Kohls*

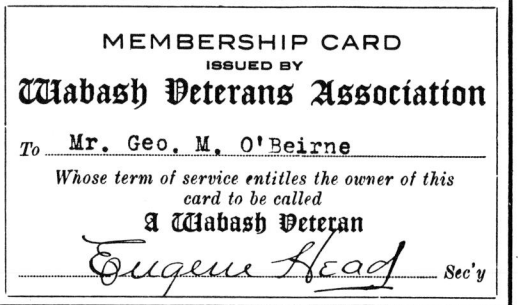

MEMBERSHIP CARD
ISSUED BY
Wabash Veterans Association

To Mr. Geo. M. O'Beirne

Whose term of service entitles the owner of this card to be called

A Wabash Veteran

Eugene Head Sec'y

Courtesy E. O'Beirne

The Ohio Locomotive Crane Company made this model C 15-ton eight-wheel crane shipped in April of 1913 to the Wabash at their Decatur, Illinois yards.
Collection of Kevin Kohls

Another Ohio Locomotive Wabash crane is this 15-ton four-wheel steam-driven unit with a 40-foot boom. It was shipped on February 24, 1912 to the Wabash's Toledo, Ohio facility. *Collection of Kevin Kohls*

Three more Ohio Locomotive cranes—the top one a Wabash unit at Decatur—plus, at left, a Bass Foundry & Machine Co. crane at Fort Wayne, Indiana, and a Hocking Valley unit at Columbus, Ohio. *Collection of Kevin Kohls*

WABASH

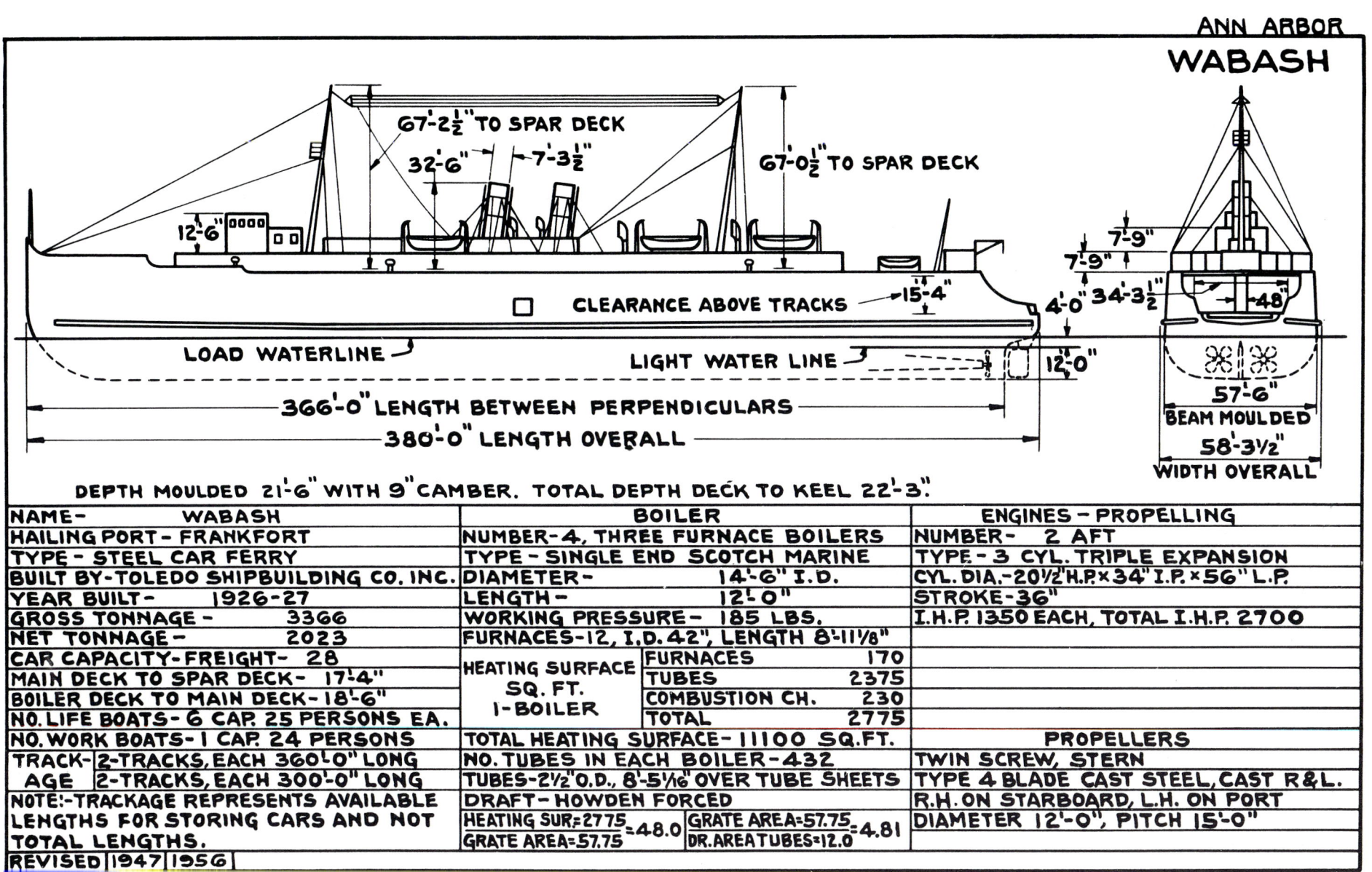

67'-2½" TO SPAR DECK

32'-6" 7'-3½"

67'-0½" TO SPAR DECK

12'-6"

7'-9"

7'-9"

4'-0" 34'-3½"

CLEARANCE ABOVE TRACKS 15'-4"

48

LOAD WATERLINE

LIGHT WATER LINE 12'-0"

57'-6"
BEAM MOULDED
58'-3½"
WIDTH OVERALL

366'-0" LENGTH BETWEEN PERPENDICULARS

380'-0" LENGTH OVERALL

DEPTH MOULDED 21'-6" WITH 9" CAMBER. TOTAL DEPTH DECK TO KEEL 22'-3".

NAME- WABASH	BOILER			ENGINES – PROPELLING
HAILING PORT- FRANKFORT	NUMBER-4, THREE FURNACE BOILERS			NUMBER- 2 AFT
TYPE - STEEL CAR FERRY	TYPE - SINGLE END SCOTCH MARINE			TYPE - 3 CYL. TRIPLE EXPANSION
BUILT BY- TOLEDO SHIPBUILDING CO. INC.	DIAMETER- 14'-6" I.D.			CYL. DIA.-20½"H.P.×34"I.P.×56"L.P.
YEAR BUILT- 1926-27	LENGTH – 12'-0"			STROKE-36"
GROSS TONNAGE - 3366	WORKING PRESSURE- 185 LBS.			I.H.P. 1350 EACH, TOTAL I.H.P. 2700
NET TONNAGE - 2023	FURNACES-12, I.D. 42", LENGTH 8'-11⅛"			
CAR CAPACITY-FREIGHT- 28	HEATING SURFACE SQ. FT. 1-BOILER	FURNACES	170	
MAIN DECK TO SPAR DECK- 17'-4"		TUBES	2375	
BOILER DECK TO MAIN DECK-18'-6"		COMBUSTION CH.	230	
NO. LIFE BOATS- 6 CAP. 25 PERSONS EA.		TOTAL	2775	
NO. WORK BOATS-1 CAP. 24 PERSONS	TOTAL HEATING SURFACE-11100 SQ. FT.			PROPELLERS
TRACK- 2-TRACKS, EACH 360'-0" LONG	NO. TUBES IN EACH BOILER-432			TWIN SCREW, STERN
AGE 2-TRACKS, EACH 300'-0" LONG	TUBES-2½"O.D., 8'-5 1/16" OVER TUBE SHEETS			TYPE 4 BLADE CAST STEEL, CAST R&L.
NOTE:-TRACKAGE REPRESENTS AVAILABLE LENGTHS FOR STORING CARS AND NOT TOTAL LENGTHS.	DRAFT- HOWDEN FORCED			R.H. ON STARBOARD, L.H. ON PORT
	HEATING SUR=2775 =48.0 GRATE AREA=57.75	GRATE AREA=57.75 =4.81 DR.AREA TUBES=12.0		DIAMETER 12'-0", PITCH 15'-0"
REVISED 1947 1956				

Wabash Painting Guide

Wabash No.	Manufacturer's No.	Color	Description	Where Used
27	#601	Aluminum	Duralum	Steam generator, room, and roofs of passenger diesels and roofs of road engines.
	88-762	Black	DuPont "Dulux"	Switch diesel locomotives, trucks, underframes, etc. of diesel locomotives and MofW equipment, stenciling MofW equipment.
37		Black	Prepared cement per Wabash specification C-14	Bottom of water service tanks.
	26	Black	"Ajax" motor insulating paint-Sherwin-Williams Co.	Electric motors.
	95-7469	Black	Prepared paint - DuPont Co.	Stenciling locomotive cranes.
	83-9709	Blue	DuPont	Body of diesel road locomotives (new).
	83-9709	Blue	DuPont	Body of diesel road locomotives (repairs).
	248	Blue	Spanish blue - P.D. George Co.	Safety track signs.
	681-8006	Buff	DuPont sealer	Crankcase of diesel engines.
	3273	Reflective Gold	Scotchlite	Letters and numbers - Diesel road locomotives. Striping (new and repairs).
	83-503	Gray-suede	DuPont "Dulux"	Engine room of diesel locomotives, shop machinery
	83-27200	Harbor Mist Gray	DuPont "Dulux"	Trucks of all passenger and road locomotives.
	68-24557	Postal Green	DuPont "Dulux"	Desks, cupboards, locks, etc. Shop work benches, vises, etc. Interior of diesel locomotives cabs.
		Gray	Non-slip flock covering.	Multi-level
	254-55883	Red	DuPont "Duco"	Flag on diesel road locomotives.
	1617	Red	Floor paint	Office floors, cab floors, switch diesels.
23	801	Red	Coroc Sunfast Enamel - Cook Paint & Varnish Co.	Fire hose reels, shop jacks, safety signs, etc.
	1201	Red	Insulating glyptol	Diesel traction motors and generators.
	289-1	White	DuPont lettering "Duco"	Flags on passenger diesels, letters and figures on switch diesel locomotives.
		White	Enamel quick-dry vitrolite	Interior of shower baths.
	83-27199	Armour Yellow	Dulux enamel	Striping on end sill plates, grabirons, etc. on diesel switch locomotives, signal hose coupling heads, locomotive cranes and MofW equipment.
53		Yellow	Prepared paint-quick drying	Marking traffic lanes and safety zones.
	3271	Yellow	Scotchlite	Striping on switch engines.

CAR DEPARTMENT PAINTS

Wabash No.	Manufacturer's No.	Color	Description	Where Used
	585	Aluminum	Duralum	Passenger car water coolers, overhead tanks in kitchens, air receivers.
		Aluminum	Powder-Sunbright-Buttler Sunbright Manufacturing Co.	Deluxe cars and streamline trains.
		Aluminum	Plasti-Kote #99 self spray in 12 oz. cans. Authorized Reference Parts Co.	Air conditioning cooling coils.
37		Black	A flexible paint cement with a "Gilsonite" base, mixed with a long fibre asbestos and sufficient semi-drying vegetable oils, preferably linseed and china wood oils.	Underframes of all freight car equipment, old roofs of passenger cars and to stop leaks in bottom of water service tanks, stenciling on trucks of passenger cars.

CAR DEPARTMENT
PAINTS

Wabash No.	Manufacturer's No.	Color	Description	Where Used
48		Black	Prepared quick dry paint with Gilsonite pitch base and with sufficient semi-drying vegetable oils, preferably linseed or china wood oil.	Store Dept. company service. Numbers and letters of covered hoppers, letters and numbers of MofW cars. All freight car trucks.
56		Black	Brushing lacquer, ready mixed, except for thinner.	For obliterating re-weigh, re-packs, air cylinder stencils on all freight cars, previously painted black color #48. Used only when cars are not held long enough for color #48 to dry. Patch painting on repair tracks when quick drying is required.
	4	Black	Cement - #4 Mortex. J.W. Mortell Co.	Inside of sides and ends, outside of roof on new box cars, caulking, etc. Hoods for hood cars, outside.
		Black	Black drop ivory in Japan	Blackboards, mix paint.
	26	Black	Black drop ivory in Japan	Blackboards, mix paint.
	26	Black	"Ajax" motor insulating paint - Sherwin-Williams Co.	Electric motors.
	Carbozite	Black	Battery coating	Batteries.
41	83-9709	Blue Banner	DuPont	Blue paint cars-body-outside, sash and inside of vestibule. Automotive racks.
	83-9709	Blue Banner	DuPont	Touch-up painting of passenger cars.
	248	Blue	Spanish - P.D. George Co.	Safety track signs, barrels.
	808	Dark Blue	Naz-Dar	Emblem and lettering on steel caboose.
	1237	Blue-gray	Insulating glyptol	Electric motors.
		Bronze	Patent antique bronze - W.H. Kemp Co.	Passenger car hardware.
		Gold Bronze	Mix at Decatur ready for brush	For touch-up, tinting and mixing.
		Reflective Gold	Scotchlite	Letters, figures and striping on all passenger equipment assigned to main line service, except truck letters and figures.
	83-27200	Gray	Prepared paint-Harbor Mist Gray-DuPont Co. Dulux	Passenger car trucks, underframes, platforms, steps, battery boxes, handrails, iron work, etc. Roof, skirt, diaphragms, trucks and ends - *City of St. Louis* cars.
60	1111	Gray	Floor enamel - Williams-Hayward Varnish Co.	Floors of mail and passenger cars.
	83-503	Gray-suede	DuPont "Duco"	Shop machinery. Interior side walls of baggage and express cars, caboose side walls and ceilings.
	#8	Gray	Detroit Graphite (Acid Resistant)	Covered hopper cars. (One coat, direct to metal)
	68-24557	Green	DuPont Dulux mail car green - semi-gloss interior enamel	Mail cars-interior walls.
	818-V-33	Orange	Orange-Persian-utility - Cook Paint & Varnish Co.	Store Department-mechanical equipment.
23	801	Red	Coroc-Sunfast enamel - Cook Paint & Varnish Co.	Outside of steel cabooses, fire department hose reels, boxes, houses, signal targets, jacks, etc.
55		Red	Brushing lacquer, ready mixed, except for thinner	For obliterating re-weigh, re-packs, air cylinder stencils on all freight cars previously painted red color #10. Used only when cars are not held long enough for color #10 paint to dry. Patch painting on repair tracks when quick drying is required.
	83-6491	Red	Bright red "Dulux" DuPont Co.	Stripes - *City of St. Louis* cars.
	1201	Red	Insulating glyptol	Electric motors.
	3282	Red	Scotchlite	Letters and figures-*City of St. Louis* cars.
10		Red	Prepared paint-Quick dry. Direct to metal.	Outside of wooden cabooses, box, auto, open top hopper and gondola freight cars.
	6486-2	Tan-light	Prepared paint-Sherwin-Williams Co.	End doors and inside of vestibule-*City of St. Louis* cars.

CAR DEPARTMENT
PAINTS

Wabash No.	Manufacturer's No.	Color	Description	Where Used
19		White	White lead prepared in oil.	Crossing signs and gates, whistle posts, phone boxes, etc.
58	801	White	Coroc-Gloss white enamel-Cook Paint & Varnish Co.	Ice boxes, interior of cars painted in gloss, lockers.
59	802	White	Coroc-dull satin-Cook Paint & Varnish Corp.	Walls, ceilings, etc. interior of deluxe passenger cars.
	3017	White	Gloss enamel-Williams-Hayward Varnish Co.	Postal car ceilings, hangers and braces, safety rods, light fixtures, overhead water tanks, baggage car ceilings, tops of passenger car step boxes. Interior of toilets, toilet seats, showers, etc. of business cars.
	81-60749	White	DuPont "Dulux" enamel	Upper part of steel cabooses.
	28-8103	White-stencil	DuPont "Dulux"	Spray stenciling of freight cars.
		White lead	Lead-paste-white in oil 25, 50 and 100 lb. kegs	Hand stenciling.
	83-27199	Armour Yellow	DuPont "Dulux" enamel	Exterior of car sides - *City of St. Louis* cars and MofW equipment. MofW cars.

MAINTENANCE OF WAY DEPARTMENT
PAINTS

Wabash No.	Manufacturer's No.	Color	Description	Where Used
27	601	Aluminum	Duralum	Bridges, signal cases and posts.
	88-762	Black	DuPont "Dulux"	Letters and figures on equipment painted yellow.
113	R-412-LO	Black	Flat black-Rust-Oleum Corp.	Signals and bulletin boards.
118		Black	Prepared paint	Exterior trim-wood and metal.
	88-762	Black	DuPont "Dulux"	Underframes of work cars, trucks, cranes, crawlers, etc. Window and door screens.
48		Black	Prepared paint-quick drying	Building roofs.
37		Black	Prepared cement per Wabash Spec. C-14	Underground cables.
	DMC	Black	Cable paint-Edward Smith Co.	Cables.
	248	Blue	Spanish - P.D. George Co.	Safety track signs.
	23812	Gray	"Cemgard" - Detroit Graphite Co.	Concrete relay houses.
	83-503	Gray-suede	DuPont "Duco"	Shop machinery, air compressors, engineers, etc.
106		Green-drab	Prepared paint	Lockers, desks, etc.
	35033	Green	Copper Verde-Pittsburgh Plate Glass Co.	Mechanical Dept.
22		Green	Enamel	Switch targets.
	986	Green-surf	Surf green - Detroit Graphite Co.	Interior of shops and offices.
	7529	Green	Dado enamel - Detroit Graphite Co.	Trim-interior of shops and offices.
23	801	Red	Coroc-Sunfast enamel - Cook Paint & Varnish Co.	Switch targets, etc.
10		Red	Prepared paint - quick drying.	Fire barrels.
	769	Red	Rust-Oleum - damp proof paint	Track scales and boats.
	1617	Red	Floor paint - Detroit Graphite Co.	Store room floors.
114	198	Red lead	Quick dry - Detroit Graphic Co.	Structural steel.
111		White	Mill white.	Inside work.
	3017	White	Gloss enamel-quick dry - Williams Hayward Co.	Material racks.
	7216	White	Coat	Signals
	83-27199	Yellow Armour	DuPont Dulux Enamel	Work cars, trucks, cranes, crawlers, blades, switch targets, etc.
53		Yellow	Prepared paint-quick drying	Safety zones, traffic lanes.
	801	Sun-fast Red	Cooks	Four gas tanks and gas caps, motor car engines.

Highlights....

	1963	1962	1961	1960	1959
Operating Revenues	$124,006,221	$120,416,285	$110,092,768	$112,628,471	$119,624,653
Operating Expenses	93,742,013	91,490,354	85,328,726	88,629,282	96,257,619
Ratio of Expenses to Revenues	75.59%	75.98%	77.51%	78.69%	80.47%
Taxes — Federal, State and Local	7,292,477	7,947,322	7,677,559	8,121,370	8,112,120
Equipment and Joint Facility Rents	13,393,254	12,375,362	10,385,190	9,872,040	9,468,491
Net Railway Operating Income	9,578,476	8,603,247	6,701,293	6,005,778	5,786,423
Rate of Return on Investment	3.86%	3.49%	2.72%	2.43%	2.35%
Other Income Less Deductions	2,835,050	2,863,639	2,429,466	2,157,379	1,754,413
Income Available for Fixed Charges	12,413,526	11,466,886	9,130,759	8,163,157	7,540,836
Fixed Charges	3,655,164	3,605,252	3,370,463	3,408,868	3,051,485
Times Fixed Charges Earned	3.40	3.18	2.71	2.40	2.47
Contingent Interest	695,864	695,864	695,864	700,431	707,864
NET INCOME	8,062,498	7,165,770	5,064,432	4,053,858	3,781,487
Preferred Stock Dividend Requirement	1,399,635	1,399,635	1,399,635	1,399,635	1,399,635
Net Income per Share of Common Stock	11.13	9.63	6.12	4.43	3.98
Dividends Declared per Share of Common Stock	7.50	8.50	5.50	8.50	3.50
Sinking Fund Requirements	318,866	318,866	318,866	320,366	320,366
Working Capital	6,829,893	5,038,322	7,936,406	10,391,369	5,414,311
Property Improvements	10,609,649	12,533,604	9,112,105	9,369,901	13,966,498
Equipment Obligations Incurred	8,090,956	7,128,910	4,621,420	9,034,508	6,930,360
Funded Debt and Equipment Obligations Retired	6,493,222	5,808,832	6,091,397	6,092,374	5,480,920
Funded Debt and Equipment Obligations at Year End	109,643,058	108,045,324	106,725,246	108,195,222	105,253,088
Average Number of Employes	7,700	7,901	7,810	8,480	9,570
Payroll Costs, Including Taxes and Fringe Benefits	$60,919,078	$60,548,149	$57,280,062	$60,220,137	$64,582,995
Average per Employe	$7,820	$7,663	$7,334	$7,101	$6,784
Percent of Operating Revenues	49.13	50.28	52.03	53.47	53.99

**Wabash 1963
Annual Report Pages**

Continued

Wabash Railroad Company

TO THE SHAREHOLDERS:

The upward trend in Wabash business through 1963 is evidenced by the "highlight" figures on the opposite page. The net income of $8,062,498 in 1963 was the best result since 1957 and was 12.5% higher than 1962. After providing for the annual $4.50 dividend on the preferred shares and before sinking fund requirements, the net earnings applicable to the common stock in 1963 were equivalent to $11.13 per share compared with $9.63 in 1962.

Operating revenues in 1963 totaled $124,006,221, also the highest since 1957. Carloads increased to 805,711. One of the brightest spots in our 1963 business was the continued increase in the movement of new automobiles and trucks on multi-level flat cars, which accounted for $10,608,118 in revenue and 33,384 carloads. The movement of other major commodities handled by the Wabash was in line with the high level of the national economy.

The proposed plan which would place Wabash operations under one management and control with the Norfolk and Western Railway Company and the New York, Chicago and St. Louis Railroad Company (Nickel Plate) is awaiting final approval of the Interstate Commerce Commission. The initial application was filed on March 17, 1961, hearings were completed in late 1962, and the Examiner's favorable recommended Report and Order were released April 17, 1963. The climate for final approval of several railroad merger or control proposals seems favorable, and we are hopeful that a decision in the Norfolk & Western-Nickel Plate-Wabash case will be forthcoming in the near future.

Last year we reported that the Interstate Commerce Commission on December 28, 1962, authorized the Detroit, Toledo and Ironton Railroad Company to acquire control of The Ann Arbor Railroad Company, and that the Railway Labor Executives' Association had filed objections which were delaying the consummation of the transaction. On August 31, 1963, the stock of The Ann Arbor Railroad Company was transferred to the DT&I, thereby effecting the transfer of control and ending an association which had existed for more than 37 years.

This is my first report to you since I came to the Wabash on October 1, 1963, when Mr. Pevler left to become President of the Norfolk and Western Railway. During the past several months, I have covered nearly every mile of the Wabash line and have found the property in excellent condition. More important, however, I have found a dedicated team of officers and employees, determined to keep Wabash service the best in its territory. I am confident that this fine spirit cannot fail to produce the kind of railroad service our patrons appreciate and the kind of successful business operation our investors and shareholders desire.

St. Louis, Missouri
March 27, 1964

President

COMMODITY STATISTICS—REVENUE FREIGHT

	TONS				GROSS REVENUE			
	1963	Percent of Total	1962	Percent of Total	1963	Percent of Total	1962	Percent of Total
PRODUCTS OF AGRICULTURE:								
Wheat	506,181	2.00	477,802	1.98	$2,086,794	1.68	$2,168,398	1.80
Corn	1,744,688	6.90	1,925,310	7.99	5,922,748	4.77	6,054,626	5.03
Other Grain	142,582	.56	104,591	.43	539,105	.43	413,472	.34
Flour, Meal and Other Mill Products	1,025,032	4.06	980,449	4.07	3,953,620	3.18	3,503,769	2.91
Soybeans, Oil Cake and Meal	1,573,720	6.23	1,376,435	5.71	3,617,730	2.92	3,548,025	2.95
Fruits, Fresh	338,013	1.34	305,188	1.27	2,480,445	2.00	2,356,761	1.96
Vegetables, Fresh	804,331	3.18	744,095	3.09	5,158,590	4.16	4,787,218	3.98
Other	324,666	1.29	302,863	1.26	1,542,421	1.24	1,485,878	1.23
TOTAL	6,459,213	25.56	6,216,733	25.80	25,301,453	20.38	24,318,147	20.20
ANIMALS AND PRODUCTS:								
Live Stock	53,932	.21	52,488	.22	566,513	.46	577,477	.48
Meats and Packing House Products	86,098	.34	88,504	.37	731,706	.59	653,340	.54
Other	158,784	.63	147,279	.61	1,121,981	.90	1,103,652	.92
TOTAL	298,814	1.18	288,271	1.20	2,420,200	1.95	2,334,469	1.94
PRODUCTS OF MINES:								
Anthracite Coal	91,514	.36	61,283	.25	186,293	.15	138,854	.12
Bituminous Coal	2,763,640	10.94	2,657,473	11.03	3,531,623	2.84	3,701,395	3.08
Coke	335,918	1.33	329,444	1.38	778,179	.63	783,843	.65
Ores and Concentrates	348,749	1.38	313,998	1.30	752,771	.60	729,964	.61
Clay and Bentonite	336,749	1.33	325,543	1.35	840,603	.68	727,566	.60
Sand, Gravel, Stone and Rock	1,062,327	4.20	860,964	3.57	1,464,575	1.18	1,068,119	.97
Salt	192,704	.77	251,849	1.04	690,212	.56	1,056,271	.88
Other	333,432	1.32	322,889	1.34	971,203	.78	927,313	.77
TOTAL	5,465,033	21.63	5,123,443	21.26	9,215,459	7.42	9,233,325	7.68
PRODUCTS OF FORESTS:								
Lumber, Shingles and Lath	908,615	3.60	809,556	3.36	3,621,258	2.91	3,281,592	2.73
Veneer and Plywood	282,985	1.12	263,343	1.09	1,362,045	1.10	1,281,536	1.06
Other	71,077	.28	76,062	.31	348,198	.28	374,774	.31
TOTAL	1,262,677	5.00	1,148,961	4.76	5,331,501	4.29	4,937,902	4.10
MANUFACTURES AND MISCELLANEOUS:								
Petroleum Products	290,230	1.15	343,235	1.42	1,305,520	1.05	1,614,887	1.34
Vegetable Oils	303,628	1.20	334,528	1.39	1,516,136	1.22	1,730,417	1.44
Chemicals	512,646	2.03	427,792	1.78	2,801,279	2.26	2,439,806	2.03
Fertilizer	520,016	2.06	536,335	2.23	1,319,374	1.06	1,293,981	1.08
Iron and Steel, including Scrap	1,349,780	5.34	1,254,408	5.20	7,266,411	5.85	6,974,588	5.79
Non-Ferrous Metals	416,673	1.65	428,694	1.78	2,415,843	1.95	2,464,611	2.05
Machinery, Tools and Parts	164,403	.65	143,540	.60	1,687,849	1.36	1,524,388	1.27
Automotive Vehicles and Parts	2,289,385	9.06	2,091,642	8.68	29,109,244	23.45	27,254,647	22.64
Cement and Masonry Products	721,671	2.86	713,495	2.96	2,393,574	1.93	2,352,348	1.95
Paper and Products	424,361	1.68	397,327	1.65	2,164,993	1.74	2,139,859	1.78
Wall Board	261,371	1.03	257,793	1.07	1,148,007	.92	1,175,294	.98
Food Products and Beverages	1,198,482	4.74	1,095,141	4.54	6,261,372	5.04	5,783,291	4.80
Feed, Animal and Poultry	434,938	1.72	445,941	1.85	1,458,045	1.18	1,591,915	1.32
Other	2,276,194	9.01	2,118,952	8.79	14,956,831	12.05	13,997,185	11.63
TOTAL	11,163,778	44.18	10,588,823	43.94	75,804,478	61.06	72,337,217	60.10
FORWARDER TRAFFIC	584,742	2.32	689,799	2.86	5,340,794	4.31	6,213,130	5.16
TOTAL CARLOAD TRAFFIC	25,234,257	99.87	24,056,030	99.82	123,413,885	99.41	119,374,190	99.18
ALL LESS CARLOAD FREIGHT	32,815	.13	44,418	.18	729,759	.59	992,928	.82
GRAND TOTAL	25,267,072	100.00	24,100,448	100.00	124,143,644	100.00	120,367,118	100.00

INVENTORY OF EQUIPMENT

	On Hand December 31, 1962	Year 1963 — Changed, Built or Purchased	Year 1963 — Destroyed, Sold or Changed	On Hand December 31, 1963
DIESEL-ELECTRIC LOCOMOTIVE UNITS:				
Freight	141		4	137
Passenger	20			20
Road Switching	53		8	45
Switching	105			105
TOTAL	319		12	307
Average Tractive Power (Lbs.)	69,782			68,464
FREIGHT TRAIN CARS:				
Box	9,589	1,100	407	10,282
Box (Leased)	50	4		54
Stock	387	16	34	369
Gondola	1,714	80	191	1,603
Hopper	845	359	120	1,084
Hopper—Covered	1,058		15	1,043
Hopper—Covered (Leased)	168			168
Flat	452			452
Flat (Leased)	—	10		10
Caboose Standard	195			195
TOTAL	14,458	1,569	767	15,260
Average Capacity of Revenue Freight Cars (Lbs.)	105,499			108,797
PASSENGER TRAIN CARS:				
Dining—Tap—Cocktail	3			3
Postal	4			4
Baggage	36	3		39
Baggage and Mail	9	2	4	7
Baggage and Mail (Leased)	—	2		2
Combination	1			1
Combination (Leased)	2			2
Combination—Deluxe	1		1	—
Coaches	1		1	—
Coaches (Leased)	8			8
Baggage—Buffet—Lounge	1			1
Chair—Deluxe (4 Dome Type)	38		4	34
Chair—Buffet—Deluxe	1			1
Parlor	2			2
Parlor Observation (1 Dome Type)	4		1	3
Parlor Car—Dome Type	1			1
Sleepers	16		4	12
Cafe—Lounge	7		3	4
Lounge	1			1
TOTAL	136	7	18	125
WORK EQUIPMENT:				
Business Cars	4			4
Instruction Cars (1 Lecture)	2			2
Pile Drivers	2			2
Locomotive Cranes	9		1	8
Wrecking Cranes	5			5
Jordan Spreaders	3			3
Scale Test Cars	1			1
Caboose Box	29		3	26
Other Company Service	598	17	22	593
TOTAL	653	17	26	644
TOTAL CARS	15,247	1,593	811	16,029
FLOATING EQUIPMENT:				
Ferry Boats	3			3
MISCELLANEOUS EQUIPMENT:				
Automobile Trucks	164	8	8	164
Automobile Trailers	3			3
Automobile Passenger	108	44	29	123
Trailers For "Piggy-Back" Service	265			265
TOTAL	540	52	37	555